MEMORY
AND
CENTRAL
NERVOUS
ORGANIZATION

CONTENTS

Published in the United States by
Paragon House Publishers
90 Fifth Avenue
New York, New York 10011
Copyright © 1988 by Paragon House Publishers
An International Conference on the Unity of the Sciences book
Manufactured in the United States of America

Library of Congress Cataloging-in-Publication Data

Fair, Charles M.
  Memory & central nervous organization.
  An ICUS book
  Bibliography: p.
  Includes Index.
  1. Memory—Physiological aspects.   2. Brain.
  3. Neurophysiology.   4. Neural circuitry.   I. Title.
  II. Title: Memory and central nervous organization.
  [DNLM: 1. Brain—physiology.   2. Memory—physiology.
  3. Sleep, Rem.   WL 102 F163m]
  QP406.F35   1988   153.1′2   87-22217
  ISBN 0-89226-060-2

MEMORY
AND
CENTRAL
NERVOUS
ORGANIZATION

Charles M. Fair

An ICUS Book

Paragon House Publishers
New York

ACKNOWLEDGMENTS

Without implicating them in the results, I should like to thank the following for immediate or distant help in completing this work:

Dr. D. B. Lindsley, for inviting me to spend my Guggenheim year at the Brain Research Institute, at the University of California in Los Angeles.

Dr. T. H. Bullock, for putting up with me in the lab, and suggesting my appointment to a residency with M.I.T.'s Neurosciences Research Program.

Dr. F. O. Schmitt, for acting on Dr. Bullock's suggestion.

Dr. W. H. Sweet, for seeing that I got lab space.

Doctors Larry Stensaas, Jim Skinner, Jay Angevine, Ross Adey and many others, for useful or corrective ideas.

The late Dr. Warren McCulloch, for his sponsorship and great intellectual verve.

Special thanks are due Karl Pribram, for his help and patience over an acquaintance of many years.

I am also grateful to my wife, Dr. Louise Kiessling, for her sympathy and forbearance.

Finally, I am indebted to Patty Hatch who supplied most of the graphics in the text.

ACRONYMS

ACh	Acetylcholine
AD	Alzheimer's disease
CAT	Choline acetyltransferase
COMT	Catecholamine-O-methyltransferase
CNS	Central nervous system
CR	Conditioned response
CS	Conditioned stimulus
CSF	Cerebrospinal fluid
DA	Dopamine
DOPAC	3,4-dihydroxyphenylacetic acid (DA metabolite)
DM	Thalamic dorsomedial nucleus
E	Epinephrine (adrenaline)
FD	Fascia dentata (Dentate gyrus)
GP	Globus pallidus
GAD	Glutamic acid decarboxylase
HD	Huntington's disease
5-HIAA	5-Hydroxy-indoleacetic acid (5-HT metabolite)
5-HT	Serotonin (5-hydroxytryptamine)
HVA	Homovanillic acid (dopamine metabolite)
IPN	Interpeduncular nucleus
LC	Locus coeruleus
LP	Thalamic lateralis posterior (association) nucleus
LTP	Long-term potentiation
MAO	Monoamine oxidase(s)
MFB	Medial forebrain bundle
MHPG	3-Methoxy-4-hydroxy-phenylethylene glycol (central NE metabolite)
NE	Norepinephrine (noradrenaline)

6-OH-DA	6-hydroxydopamine
PCPA	Para-chlorophenylalanine (5-HT synthesis inhibitor)
PNMT	Phenylethanolamine N-methyltransferase (Converts NE to E)
POMC	Pro-opiomelanocortin
RAS	Reticular activating system
REM	Rapid eye-movement sleep
RF	Reticular formation
SD	Sensory deprivation
SWS	Slow-wave sleep
Ss	Subjects
TBH	Tyrosine beta-hydroxylase
VL-VA	Thalamic ventralis lateralis and ventralis anterior (motor) nuclei

PREFACE

It is now over thirty years since the historic Henry Ford Hospital Symposium on the Reticular Formation of the Brain (held in Detroit, March, 1957). At that meeting, Nauta and Kuypers (1958) presented a landmark paper defining the principal structures of what is today known as the mesolimbic system.

Other papers—by the Scheibels on reticular fine structure; by Ward, on the beautifully organized motor patterns elicitable by stimulation of the reticulospinal projection system in the cat; by Eldred and Fujimori, on reticular facilitation of the gamma motor system; by Lindsley, on the reduction of response–time by precurrent alerting or central arousal; by Papez, updating his earlier (1937) fundamental work on motivational-affective functions of the limbic system; by Adey, on the behavioral effects of bilateral entorhinal ablation; by Mason, on the apparently inverse relation between hippocampal peak activity and diurnal maxima in 17-OH-corticosteroid levels—all marked that symposium as epochal.

(All of the foregoing were published in the same bound volume. See the reference to Nauta and Kuypers above.)

In the last paper presented, Sir Geoffrey Jefferson reported evidence of an "anterior critical point" evidently necessary to the maintenance of consciousness in man. It lay outside the mainstream of ascending reticular projections, in forebrain areas supplied by the anterior cerebral and anterior communicating arteries. He described this finding as "particularly disturbing," and indeed, its significance has only recently become clearer in light of the neuropathology of Alzheimer's disease.

This book has to do with questions relating to some of those raised at that Symposium. Specifically, it concerns the vertical organization of the central nervous system, and the way in which the reticular, limbic, and mesolimbic systems may act jointly to "steer" attentional processes, or to regulate the conditions making for memory formation in the neocortex.

The most speculative sections concern the possible organization of memory-functions in small cortical assemblies, or vertical columns, and the distributed organization of these functions on a larger (interareal) scale in neocortex.

Certain of the other ideas presented are, I believe, new, if not in principle, in the way they are developed. For example, the periodic alternance of slow-wave and REM (rapid-eye-movement) stages of sleep is not ordinarily considered homeostatic, except in the crude sense that sleep corrects for fatigue.

The fact that selective deprivation of REM sleep can have extremely disturbing effects on human subjects, or on animals such as the cat, argues that this form of sleep has some unique stabilizing or corrective function. The transition from slow-wave (SWS) to REM sleep may indeed involve a "change in information processing mode" (Hobson, 1987); but why it occurs in higher vertebrates and what adaptive purpose it serves are still not understood.

What I have attempted to show is that slow-wave and REM sleep are, in a quite specific sense, functional complements. Each acts to reduce central nervous entropy, SWS at the intracellular level, by promoting metabolic recovery of neurons and glia, REM sleep at the intercellular level, by intervals of activation whose effect is to conserve acquired structure in the network. REM sleep has thus appeared relatively late in vertebrate evolution, *pari passu* as the CNS has come to include areas which are "open" (minimally preprogrammed; capable of memory-formation). These ideas and their implications are developed in detail, in chapter 5.

A second novelty, or novel shift in emphasis, has to do with the two types of learning which may be sequentially involved in the acquisition of conditioned responses. In many studies, the implication is that a transient sensitization, accompanying initial arousal or "orienting" responses, is responsible for subsequent primacy effects in serial recall. This initial sensitization may (as in lower organisms) have both short- and long-term forms, and in either case may figure in "contextually-cued recall" (Sara 1985). In mammals, it may coexist with learning of the more focal type, essentially because, under conditions in which focal learning is difficult or impossible, it provides an outlet into action. To the same extent, it may, under certain conditions, compete with learning of the more focal type.

As suggested in chapters 6 and 12, the distinction between sensitization and learning in the more usual sense may come down to the distinction between presynaptic learning, as modeled by Kandel and Schwartz (1985), and postsynaptic learning, as modeled by Lynch and Baudry (1985). More distantly, it may come down to the distinction currently made between "procedural" and "declarative" knowledge. (Squire 1986. Chapters 13 and 14, below.)

In the field of receptor types and their central nervous distribution, or of neuropeptide modulators, the current pace of discovery and the functional complexity suggested by some of the findings make interpretation difficult. However, in the reported properties of S1 and S2 serotonin receptors (Peroutka, Lebovitz and Snyder 1981), of alpha 1 and alpha 2 adrenergic receptors (Aghajanian and Rogawski 1984), of D1 and D2 dopamine receptors (Leff and Creese 1984), or of A and B GABA receptors (Snyder 1985), we are perhaps starting to see paired and, in some respects, "opposite" functions, paralleling some of those known electrophysiologically.

Thus S1 serotonin receptors reportedly mediate inhibition and are regulated by guanine nucleotides, while S2 receptors are "less affected" by guanine nucleotides, and are excitatory. (Snyder 1985.) D1 and D2 dopaminergic receptors respectively enhance or decrease adenylate cyclase activity, are found in the parathyroid (D1) or in the anterior pituitary (D2), and differ markedly in their binding-characteristics. (Snyder 1985) See also Creese (1985) on guanine-nucleotide-binding protein as a membrane component with which receptors such as D-1 may "link up," resulting in transduction into adenylate cyclase activity. The involvement of S2 receptor systems in the animal "serotonin syndrome," and of D2 receptor systems in cocaine self-administration in animals (Goeders and Smith 1983), is discussed in the text.

Alpha 2 adrenoceptors, besides reacting more selectively than alpha 1 receptors to one of a pair of optical isomers (Ruffolo 1984), may have an inhibitory, mainly presynaptic mode of action, whereas the alpha 1 type is chiefly postsynaptic and excitatory. (Aghajanian and Rogawski 1984). However see Bousquet, Rouot and Schwartz (1984), who conclude that alpha 2 receptors may be mainly postsynaptic; and U'Pritchard (1984) who states that "thus far, presynaptic and postsynaptic alpha 2 receptors are pharmacologically indistinguishable," making it difficult to quantitate these populations.

Alpha 1 receptors reportedly mediate fast (phasic), and alpha 2, slow (tonic) pressor responses (McGrath 1984). Still other workers cite data suggesting that central alpha 2 receptors may mediate arterial hypotension, whereas "there is a population of a1 receptors which have the opposite function." (Bousquet, Rouot, and Schwartz 1984.)

Morley, Farley, and Javel (1984) report that "there is indirect evidence that there may be two ACh binding-sites in the brain," one of which is blocked by bungarotoxin. Kilbinger (1984) presents evidence that muscarinic agonists and antagonists respectively decrease or increase ACh output of cat cortical neurons, suggesting presynaptic inhibitory reuptake. He notes that this mechanism "bears a marked resemblance" to the modulation of the output of aminergic neurons "by release-inhibitory autoreceptors." (See also Birdsall and Hulme 1984, concerning M1 and M2 muscarinic receptors in the forebrain.)

GABA and 5-HT receptors, having the same function (inhibition), but distinguishable in that one (the 5-HT) is blocked by spiperone and the other not, may nevertheless modulate the same potassium channel. This was inferred from the fact that the increase in K^+ conductance did not appear to summate when generated by both. The result, in both cases, appears to have depended upon a pertussis toxin-sensitive GTP-binding

(G) protein acting as a second messenger system. (Andrade, Malenka, and Nicoll 1986. The units were pyramids in rat hippocampus.)

Finally, Bowery (1984) reviews evidence indicating that GABA B receptors are "confined to" the molecular layer in the cerebellum, the stratum containing the parallel fibers, apical Purkinje cell dendrites, and the (inhibitory) stellate cells. GABA A receptors, by contrast, "predominate" in the granule cell layer, internal to the Purkinje cells.

GABA A receptors are reported to be bicuculline-sensitive, postsynaptic to GABA neurons, and Ca^{2+} inhibited. GABA B receptors are bicuculline-resistant, found on GABA or other neuron terminals, and Ca^{2+} activated (Snyder 1985). That these receptor types should have such clearly differential distribution, in what is perhaps the most cytoarchitectonically stereotyped major subdivision of the central nervous system, is surely an interesting finding. The experiments cited in chapter 3 suggest a similar distribution for GABA A and B receptors in neocortex.

The biochemical relations disclosed by neuropharmacology, increasingly since the early or mid 1970's, have greatly complicated the models we use to conceptualize brain functions. In effect, they add further dimensions to problems still fundamentally unsolved—the modus operandi of the cerebellum being one of them. Not unexpectedly, however, some of the relations established by the older methods appear to be corroborated by the new.

An example, taken at random, might be the relation of neurotensin to feeding behavior in rats. It has been known for some years that stimulation of the far-lateral hypothalamus can initiate feeding, while stimulation of the medial hypothalamus (e.g. the ventromedial nucleus) can arrest it. (Anand et al. 1961. Morgane 1961. Krasne 1962.)

Stanley, Eppel, and Hoebel (1982) report that neurotensin is released into the bloodstream after a meal. They also find that feeding behavior, elicitable by intrahypothalamic injection of norepinephrine (into the paraventricular nucleus), is "significantly attenuated by neurotensin pretreatment." Neurotensin may thus be an important biochemical link in the circuitry of the hypothalamic "satiety" system described in the earlier literature. (Its relations to the limbic and mesolimbic dopaminergic systems are discussed in chapter 11.)

I should add, in conclusion, that the use of thermodynamic concepts in chapter 5, as a way of accounting for the basic properties of slow-wave and REM sleep, is not without precedent in pharmacology. Creese (1985) reports that "in studies of the turkey erythrocyte membrane beta-adrenergic/adenylate cyclase system, it was shown that agonist, but not antagonist, affinities for beta-adrenergic receptors increase at lower temperatures . . . The binding of agonists is enthalpy-driven, with marked net decreases in entropy, whereas the binding of antagonists seems to be almost completely entropy-driven." (Creese 1985, p. 227.)

It may well be at the level of receptor kinetics rather than at that of conventional circuitry, that the questions I have raised here, concerning the differential entropy-reducing functions of slow-wave and REM sleep, may finally be settled.

ORGANIZATIONAL NOTE

The book is divided essentially into two sections. Chapters 1–7 deal with neocortical organization, sleep functions and memory.

Chapters 8–14 and the Appendix have to do with the organization of the limbic, mesolimbic and reticular systems, and the relations of these to higher-level central nervous activity.

MEMORY
AND
CENTRAL
NERVOUS
ORGANIZATION

CHAPTER 1

How Stable are Stable Networks?;
Implications for Memory Theory;
General Plan of Cortical Organization;
Implications of the Plan

HOW STABLE ARE STABLE NETWORKS?

The work of Mountcastle (from 1957) and of Hubel and Wiesel (early 1960s) led many to the conclusion that prime receiving cortex was "hard-wired," except in early developmental stages (e.g. in kittens before 4–8 weeks). In other words these divisions of prime receiving cortex set early in life and were thenceforth, in effect, nonmemory forming.

Subsequent work has shown that neither visual nor somesthetic cortex is as functionally rigid as had been thought. Kaas et al. (1981) reported that in adult monkeys, after section of the median nerve, the deafferented cortex in parietal areas 3b and 1 was silent. Over a period "of a few weeks" units that had fallen silent then became active again, responding to stimulation of other, still-innervated hand areas. These authors suggest that "cortical maps, even in adults, are probably subject to constant modifications based on the use or activity of the peripheral sensory pathways." (Kaas et al., 1981, p. 257.)

In the visual system, Creutzfeldt and Heggelund (1975) obtained a different but related result. They reported striking increases in the ratio of "uncommitted" to "committed" cells in the striate cortex of mature cats, following visual deprivation for 308 out of 336 hours. (This experiment is reviewed in detail in chapter 4.)

Blakemore (1974) said: "Perhaps it is the mere probability of experience that determines the final preference of a cell. Perhaps each neuron selects, as its preferred stimulus, the feature that it has seen most often." The Creutzfeldt-Heggelund experiment appears to support him. Neurons responding as he has suggested I will describe as working on Blakemore's

1

Principle. In short, supposedly stable networks such as striate cortex may not be truly that.

IMPLICATIONS FOR MEMORY THEORY

Neurons that work on Blakemore's Principle are by definition memory forming. In prime receiving cortex, however, their tendency to develop probabilistically determined response preferences may be masked under normal conditions by the fact that the range of inputs available to them is limited. The experiments reported by Kaas et al. (1981) imply that there is *some* choice perhaps available to such units, appearing in the form of alternate response preferences when originally preferred inputs have been shut off.

Such units may represent a population distinct from those, e.g., of temporal association cortex, some of whose response preferences may be selectively made more enduring by the mechanism of long-term potentiation (LTP) and associated Ca^{2+} mediated membrane changes. Reference is to the model of long-term memory (LTM) formation proposed by Lynch and Baudry (1985) discussed in chapter 6.

The processes underlying LTM formation, in systems lying closer to the effector side of the central nervous system (CNS), are as yet unknown. The fact that Milner's (bilateral hippocampal) patient Henry was unable to form "new" memories lasting more than 10 to 15 minutes, but still showed a normal learning curve for a mirror-writing task (Milner, 1964) appears to differentiate "procedural" from "declarative" learning. That is, it tells us that the two can function independently in the human nervous system, but beyond that, very little.

That neurons in specific projection areas show an unexpected plasticity suggests the conclusion that virtually all cortical neurons, which are not subject to special "fixing" mechanisms, may have short-term memory (STM) functions. The duration of the probabilistically established response preferences postulated to underlie STM may then vary according to the cortical areas in which they are established.

In areas such as striate 17, which are tightly linked via the thalamus to the periphery, and in which diversity of traffic is constrained accordingly, STM functions may ordinarily not be apparent. However, if input to such cortex is sufficiently reduced for a sufficient period, the results suggest both some memory-loss and some loss of functional organization, the two perhaps being the same.

In the experiments of Kaas et al. (1981), as the authors suggested, deafferentation by median nerve section may have left the parietal units still with "competitive" inputs to which they responded by default. In the Creutzfeldt-Heggelund (1975) experiment, the sufficient conditions for functional disorganization may more nearly have been met. It is discussed in chapter 4. Its relation to the findings in human sensory deprivation experiments is discussed in chapter 5.

GENERAL PLAN OF CORTICAL ORGANIZATION

Graybiel (1974) divides association cortex into proximal and distal sectors. The essential features of that division are that:

1. In both pre- and post-cruciate areas, proximal association cortex lies synaptically closer to the phylogenetically newer sectors of cortex—the specific thalamocortical, and the frontal supplementary and premotor systems.
2. Posterior distal association cortex receives less direct input than does proximal, from the specific receiving system, and more direct input from the limbic system (in particular the hippocampus). (See figure 1–1, from Graybiel 1974.)
3. The frontal distal division comprises the prefrontal association areas, making it further than frontal proximal cortex from the pyramidal outflow pathways, and more closely connected with the limbic system (in particular the amygdala).
4. The foregoing relations are systematically reflected in the posterior-anterior connections of the two divisions, such that each posterior division forms a loop with its frontal equivalent (see figure 1–1), the distal loop being the longer, and having the larger subcortical component.
5. Studies in the monkey (Pandya and Kuypers 1969; Jones and Powell 1970) have shown these relations to be maintained in the return projection-routes from frontal cortex. "Posterior association cortex receives a massive afferent system from the frontal lobe that is divisible into a *premotor* component directed preferentially toward areas most closely linked to the major sensory fields, and a *prefrontal* component distributed to the parietotemporal regions that represent distal association cortex." (Graybiel 1974, italics original.)

The projections just described are not shown in figure 1–1. They presumably include fronto-temporal connections via the arcuate and uncinate fasciculi, the latter arising in orbital cortex; and, of course, the bi-directional perforant path connecting temporal association cortex, via entorhinalis, with the dentate gyrus and hippocampus.)

The older idea that sense data are "elaborated" in stages, e.g., from area 17 to 18–19, has been replaced by a more thalamically based model, in which "families" of receiving systems (Graybiel and Berson 1981) are reached, in part serially, partly in parallel, by the same incoming data,

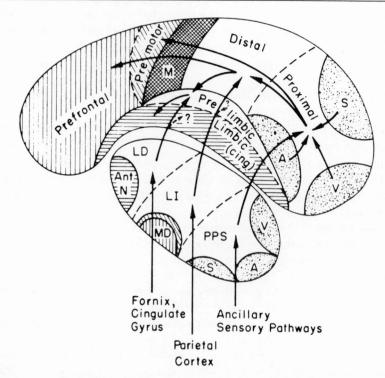

Figure 1–1.   Simplified schema showing thalamocortical and interareal input into proximal and distal association cortex, and projections of the latter to frontal, pre-limbic and limbic cortex.

Abbreviations: S, V, A = somatosensory, visual and auditory receiving areas, in thalamus and neocortex. Ant. N = anterior nuclei; LD = n. lateralis dorsalis; LI = n. lateralis intermedius; M = motor cortex; MD = n. dorsomedialis; PPS = posterior pulvinar system. (*From Graybiel 1974,* reprinted with permission.)

which are then processed somewhat differently. (See chapter 2.) Some of these relays are by way of LP and the pulvinar, and the data processed are cross modal. For instance, there are somesthetic neurons in area 7b of the macaque which are responsive to visual stimuli (Mountcastle 1986).

IMPLICATIONS OF THE PLAN

This plan of organization suggests two sets of pathways or loops, connecting frontal and posterior association areas.

The first, involving proximal association cortex, is the shorter and perhaps faster-acting. It presumably favors prompt behavior in situations in which sensory cues are unambiguous or thoroughly learned.

The second pathway or loop, involving distal association cortex, is synaptically longer and perhaps therefore slower-acting; and because of inclusion of the hippocampus, has important LTM functions. It is not yet clear what processes may underlie memory formation in frontal association cortex—for instance, in areas which, when lesioned, produce what Goldman-Rakić describes as "mnemonic scotomas" in the contralateral visual field. (Goldman-Rakić 1986.)

In general, distal association cortex, because of its extensive limbic-mesolimbic connections (chapters 8 and 9) appears to play a major role in lasting, selective memory formation, and thus in learned adaptive behavior. However, its participation in such behavior may become minimal at criterion (Pribram 1984) or during overtraining (Gabriel et al., 1980). This apparent principle of economy, according to which thoroughly learned responses cease to involve "declarative" knowledge and come largely to depend upon "procedural", is discussed in chapter 14.

Chapters 2–4 essentially have to do with cortical organization; the later chapters (8–13) with the vertical (caudo-rostral) organization of the NS, beginning approximately at the level of the medullary n. gigantocellularis.

CHAPTER 2

Thalamocortical Organization: Proximal and Distal Association Cortex; Cortical Structure; Differential Metabolic Rates in Vertical Columns

THALAMOCORTICAL ORGANIZATION: PROXIMAL AND DISTAL ASSOCIATION CORTEX

The thalamocortical visual system in mammals, having been among the most exhaustively studied, most clearly shows certain apparent discrepancies between the circuitry known to neuroanatomists or physiologists, and the behavioral effects that follow when some of those circuits are interrupted. The circuit diagram, and some of the findings of Hubel and Wiesel (1962; 1963) might suggest that conditioned responses involving visual pattern-discrimination depend upon areas 17–18 as primary data-sources.

Lesion studies in the cat indicate, however, that retention of visual patterns as conditioned stimuli is not dependent on these areas. Berlucchi and Sprague (1981) found that retention of the patterns shown in figure 2–1 was unaffected by bilateral subpial aspiration of 17–18. Nor was response time affected; the animals "behaved as if they immediately recognized the discriminative stimuli."

If area 19 was also removed, retention of both pattern and brightness discrimination was "markedly deficient." If the lesions were in suprasylvian cortex, sparing 17–18 and most of 19, the animals showed some savings on the brightness discrimination; however the number of trials needed to perform "a significant" run involving pattern discrimination suggested in fact that they were relearning the response. Finally, animals in which suprasylvian lesions included undercutting of 17, 18, and 19, performed at chance on both brightness and pattern discrimination, i.e. there was no evidence either of retention or new learning.

7

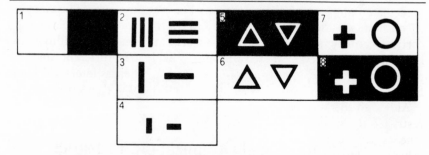

Figure 2–1.   Pairs of stimuli used in discrimination training, successively from pairs numbered 1–8. (*From Berlucchi and Sprague 1981,* reprinted with permission.)

Inferotemporal cortex in the macaque appears to be a cortical endstation in the processing of visual information, and one important in "categorization" (Wilson and DeBauche, 1981)—a point whose significance I will take up presently.

Ungerleider and Pribram (1977), following Chow's attempt to deafferent inferotemporal cortex (Chow 1961), compared the effects of two-stage bilateral lesioning—first to the pulvinar, then to prestriate cortex (four animals)—with the effects of bilateral inferotemporal lesions (eight animals; four unoperated controls.) Operant conditioning for a food reward was made dependent upon 1) a two-choice color discrimination, and 2) a two-choice discrimination between patterns formed of string, of graded difficulty. The animals were tested, both for their retention of discriminations learned preoperatively, and for their ability to learn further discriminations postoperatively.

The conclusion from this rather complex experiment appeared to be that even when extensive prestriate resections were combined with "massive destruction of the pulvinar," the resulting effects on the animals' performance were significantly less than those produced by bilateral inferotemporal lesions.

The authors note that limited resections of the latter type ("whether called 'prestriate' or 'foveal prestriate' or 'posterior inferotemporal' ") have different effects from those made more anteriorly. Deficits following the posterior lesions correlate with the physical dimensions of the cues; those made more anteriorly do not. (Cowey and Gross 1970; Gross et al. 1971).

The posterior sectors (in part perhaps transcortically) may be those more directly accessible to striate and peristriate outflows. Hence this cortex may be more dependent on literal (1:1) matching, or less capable of recognition of inputs under transform. The relevance of this point will become clearer in the discussion of the built-in generalizing functions of memory (chapter 14).

Graybiel and Berson (1981), give a detailed analysis of the "extended geniculate family" as it exists in the cat. These authors point out that area 17 outflows via the LP-Pulvinar complex overlap and extend beyond the cortical territory reached by corticocortical fibers from 17. In addition, the information conveyed by these two routes is likely to be different, since the projections from area 17 to LP arise in layer V, whereas interareal fibers from 17 originate chiefly in layers II–III.

Although in the monkey, geniculocortical projections are much more restricted than those found in the cat, Graybiel and Berson point out that "the visual system in cats and primates has a similar organization in many other respects, as though reflecting a common mammalian plan."

Two important features of that plan are: (1) the systematic inclusion, via the thalamus, of data concurrently reaching the brainstem (here the tectal and pretectal areas), and (2) the pattern of shifted overlap of thalamocortical and corticocortical fiber systems, such that the farthest ends of the cortical territory reached by them (e.g. areas 17 on the "near" end and 20 on the "far") are the least connected with each other.

The input-output relations of area 19 reported by Graybiel and Berson appear consistent with the finding of Berlucchi and Sprague (1981) that lesions to areas 17–18 alone did not impair learned visual discriminations in the cat, whereas lesions to 19 (only) produced "markedly deficient" responses.

This shifted-overlap system of input-reception is one, I believe, subserving generalization. In more distant cortical areas (vide the Ungerleider-Pribram study), it may permit the accumulation of generalized or multiple-purpose *components,* it being from these that the more lasting memories, e.g. in posterior distal association cortex, may be formed (chapter 7). An example of a single unit in macaque inferotemporal cortex showing this sort of multiple-purpose response (preferentially to the outline of a monkey's paw, but to other shapes as well) is cited by Cowey (1981. See Gross et al. 1971).

It is perhaps because processes equivalent to a several-stage smoothing or "integration" of primary inputs have been carried furthest in distal association cortex that a special apparatus has evolved in that cortex for the "fixation" of certain data in long-term memory. Current evidence suggests that such fixation depends upon circular interaction, via the perforant path, involving the fascia dentata, the CA3-CA1 fields of the hippocampus, and return projections to ipsi- or contralateral posterior association cortex.

The hippocampal-septal and other limbic pathways (e.g. inferotemporal-amygdaloid; see chapter 8) entrained in this process presumably add a motivational or affective weighting which may be decisive in determining what data are lastingly recalled. And because the ultimate components of such memories may be highly smoothed or generalized residues of experience, the memories themselves may derive their specificity from combinatorial re-use of the same components in a variety of different patterns. The specificity lies in the pattern (chapter 7).

In Chapter 1 above, I suggested, on the evidence presented by Graybiel (1974), that the cortex might be viewed as containing two major loops from the receptor to the effector side and back. The shorter loop, involving posterior proximal association cortex and frontal supplementary and pre-motor areas, I supposed might depend chiefly upon STM. Similarly, that faster-acting system may tap thalamocortical input at a stage in the latter's overlapping input corresponding roughly to areas 18 and 19 in the visual system.

By contrast, the longer loop, comprising frontal and posterior distal association cortex (and their relatively more extensive limbic and striatal connections) may tap the same thalamocortical input in areas such as 19, but not 17 and 18.

Looked at simply as retrieval systems, the first of these loops, subserving prompt motor outflows, is perhaps chiefly concerned with data of the immediate present, as modified by the recent past. It is therefore highly *input* specific.

The second, or longer-loop system is concerned with data which are primarily *experience* specific, the experience or group of them representing events which may be indefinitely distant in the organism's past. For memory in this system to be adaptively efficient, it must be such as to permit recognition of inputs under a certain range of transforms. Because day-to-day experience cannot be counted upon to repeat itself, a CS may need to be read as such, even when it and the context in which it occurs have greatly changed.

How the organization of memory functions in distal association cortex leads to this result—for instance to "categorization" in the monkey (Wilson and DeBauche 1981)—and to certain other features of cognition, is discussed in chapters 7 and 14.

CORTICAL STRUCTURE

An important feature of the "common mammalian plan" of cortical organization (Graybiel and Berson, 1981) is the laminar distribution of afferents and efferents, and the distribution of cell types in the several layers.

The figures from Jones (1981) and Gilbert and Wiesel (1981; figures 2–2 and 2–3, here) suggest the importance of the distinction between the external (I–IV) and internal laminae (V–VI) made by Lorente de Nó (1951). The scheme in figure 2–2 represents one which Jones (1981) considers "may be representative of all areas, at least in the primate."

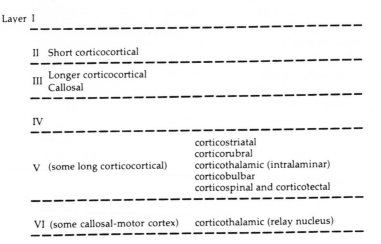

Layer I

II Short corticocortical

III Longer corticocortical
     Callosal

IV

V (some long corticocortical)   corticostriatal
                                   corticorubral
                                   corticothalamic (intralaminar)
                                   corticobulbar
                                   corticospinal and corticotectal

VI (some callosal-motor cortex)   corticothalamic (relay nucleus)

Figure 2–2. Laminar distribution of cortical efferent (pyramidal) cells, as determined by retrograde labelling studies. (*From Jones 1981*, reprinted with permission.)

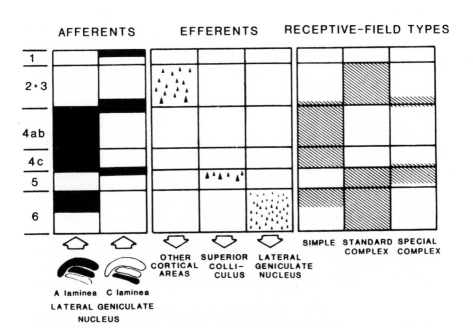

Figure 2–3. Laminar distribution of thalamic afferents to visual cortex, including receptive-field types, interareal and collicular efferents, and return projections to LG. (*From Gilbert and Wiesel 1981*, reprinted with permission.)

Jones mentions several points of particular importance. The first is that thalamic afferents, besides terminating on layer IV granule cells, "extend well upward among the large deeply situated pyramidal cells of layer III." He adds that "in areas outside the primary sensory areas (constituting some 80% of the primate cortex) they avoid layer IV and terminate mainly in the deep part of layer III," i.e., on the larger pyramids of that layer.

In association cortex, this structural revision would shift the plexus of thalamic afferents upward, into lower III—a feature whose functional significance I believe may be crucial to our understanding of the way information is processed, in particular in the association areas, and more particularly, perhaps, in the distal divisions of that cortex.

Jones also notes that in prime receiving areas, apical dendrites of (layer V–VI) pyramids, and basilar dendrites of pyramids in lower III, "as well as dendrites of nonpyramidal cells in adjacent layers traverse layer IV." He adds that it would be "rather surprising if thalamic inputs were to end solely on one class of cell, given the several varieties of interneuron present."

On this point, we might review Lorente de Nó's analysis (1951) of vertical cortical chains. These, he said are of two types.

> Some of the chains include short links with cells of a single layer. . . . Other links are long, and include cells of different layers. . . . The long links vary but little in different mammals, but the short links increase progressively in number from the mouse to man. . . . In human cortex there is an increase in the number of cells with ascending axons, but the increase in cells having short axons is much more pronounced, so much so that in some cortical regions they outnumber the cells with descending axons.

He notes this last to be particularly true of striate layer IV, and of V (the Betz cell layer) in motor cortex, repeating Cajal's suggestion that the increase in numbers of short-axon cells is probably a measure of the increase in "delicacy of function." (Lorente de Nó 1951 p. 308.)

There is evidence that various neuropeptides have differential distribution in six-layered cortex. Emson and Hunt (1981) report that vasoactive intestinal peptide (VIP) immunoreactivity has been shown in layers II–IV in the rat, the largest number of positive neurons being in II–III. VIP cells are chiefly fusiform bipolar neurons, apparently corresponding to the "nonspiny or sparsely spiny" bipolar cells found by others. (Feldman and Peters 1978.)

The Feldman and Peters study indicates that the axons of these bipolar cells arise on apical or basilar dendrites and are radially organized, though an occasional axon runs horizontally. Emson and Hunt (1981, p. 331) consider this finding "in good agreement with the histochemical observations that VIP terminals are concentrated in layers I–IV and are directed radially towards the pial surface." These units, though partially smooth, make asymmetric contacts and are presumed to be Gray Type I. VIP is strongly excitatory.

These authors note that "the ability of VIP to enhance local blood-flow in the cortical area influenced by the radial processes of the VIP neurons could produce the marked regional differences in metabolic activity in the cortex revealed by the deoxyglucose technique." (Lassen et al. 1978.) Paulson and Newman (1987) suggest what might be a next link in the process—a K^+ current, originating neuronally and relayed, via the end-feet of astrocytes, to arterioles, causing local dilation.

As indicated, both by ^3H studies and immunohistochemical localization of GAD (glutamic acid decarboxylase), GABA-accumulating neurons are found in all layers of rat cortex. These are for the most part multipolar smooth (non-spiny) stellate cells. They make symmetrical synapses involving flattened vesicles, morphological features considered typical of cortical Gray Type II (inhibitory) cells (Lund 1981). And their terminals are characteristically basket-like, enveloping the somata of cortical pyramids.

Colonnier (1981) gives a similar description, adding that the cells with these basket-like endings "are probably the 'large' stellate cells of electron microscopy. These cells are probably linked together by gap junctions, suggesting that they would be electrotonically coupled. A focal excitation of a group of these cells might thus result in lateral recruitment of other, similar inhibitory cells . . . yielding a field of inhibition wider than the excitatory zone of input. This could be one of the mechanisms of the inhibitory surrounds of cortical columns."

In the dentate gyrus and Ammon's Horn, GABA is reported to be found exclusively in interneurons. Emson and Hunt (1981, p. 326) consider that the presence of terminals of GABA-containing neurons on the "cell bodies of the output neurons seems to be a constant feature of cortical organization, as a similar localization of GAD-positive terminals has been seen in the monkey cortex."

Glutamate (or aspartate) is reportedly an excitatory transmitter in the hippocampal-FD system (Baudry and Lynch 1982); evidence from the undercutting of fronto-parietal cortex in the rat indicates it may be the neurotransmitter involved in layer V projections to the striatum. It also reportedly figures in corticothalamic transmission. Other data show that layer IV excitation, mediated via pyramidal-tract recurrent collaterals, can be blocked by glutamate antagonists (Emson and Hunt 1981; Stone 1976).

The laminar distribution of cholecystokinin octapeptide (CCK-8) appears similar to that of VIP, and their rates of synthesis and turnover are reportedly high. CCK neurons have the same morphology as VIP but may include nonspiny multipolar stellate cells (like those containing GAD). They "substantially" outnumber VIP units, their terminals are concentrated in II–V, and unlike VIP cells, have few endings in layer I.

Though CCK cells seem mostly to have asymmetric endings, and thus are Gray Type I, their laminar distribution, both in cortex and in the hippocampal CA3 area, differs from that of VIP. In cortex it is shifted downward, roughly by one layer (II–V, vs I–IV). In the hippocampus, CCK terminals are found in the stratum radiatum and are axosomatic. VIP terminals in the same area are found in the stratum radiatum and stratum oriens, and are axodendritic (Emson and Hunt 1981).

These authors note that whereas CCK terminals in older cortex (hippocampus, dentate gyrus, pyriform cortex) are on "principal" neurons, CCK units in neocortex affect chiefly apical dendrites. One might interpret this shift as one of a class of morphological changes which, in neocortex, have reduced the direct excitatory driving of cortical cells, in favor of indirect, and as it were, algebraic driving. The latter would be equivalent to an increase in inhibitory patterning of local inputs, with a corresponding increase in differentiation of outputs.

A direct demonstration of this relationship, showing the effects of a GABA antagonist on receptive field properties of cells in a Hubel and Wiesel column, is given in chapter 3. Figure 2-4, from Krieger (1985), indicates the relative concentrations of various neuropeptides, including VIP and CCK-8, in structures from neocortex to the medulla. It might be noted that whereas that figure shows negligible cortical concentrations for substance P, Emson and Hunt (1981, p. 338) state that "frontal cortex is unique in receiving a radially organized substance P input to laminae 2–4 (Ljungdahl, Hökfelt, and Nilsson 1978)."

The "classical" transmitters acetylcholine (ACh) and norepinephrine have quite wide cortical distribution, ACh "with relative sparsity in layer III and enrichment in layer IV" (Emson and Hunt 1981, p. 338). Noradrenergic fibers from the pontine locus coeruleus distribute widely to neocortex, "with some predominance in the outer molecular layers." (Taylor and Stone 1981). These authors add that dopaminergic fibers, originating in the substantia nigra, project chiefly to frontal association cortex, and there chiefly to the lower layers.

In rat neocortex, serotonergic fibers are "finer" than noradrenergic (as has been reported of frontal dopaminergic fibers), but their numbers appear to be greater, in parallel with the greater cortical concentration of 5-HT, relative to norepinephrine (Emson and Hunt 1981). Except that they may be part of the serotonergic system of the raphé, mediating slow-wave sleep, the functional role of cortical serotonergic fibers is uncertain. In rat posterior cingulate cortex, serotonergic fibers are concentrated in layers I and III, an arrangement these authors call "atypical." In neocortex, the distribution is to I and IV (Aghajanian 1987). Evidence cited elsewhere here suggests that in neocortex in the rat, some 5-HT is also atypically released, perhaps nonsynaptically, into the extracellular space. (Nauta and Feirtag 1986.)

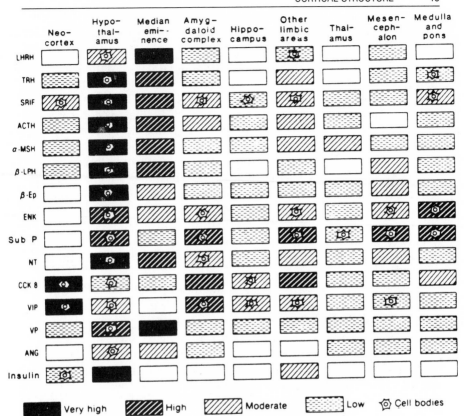

Figure 2–4. Central nervous distributions of certain neuropeptides.
  Abbreviations (from top down): LHRH = luteinizing hormone releasing hormone; TRH = thyrotropin releasing hormones; SRIF = somatostatin; ACTH = adrenocorticotropic hormone; alpha-MSH = alpha-melanocyte-stimulating hormone; beta-LPH = lipotropin; beta-Ep = beta-endorphin; ENK = enkephalin; Sub P = substance P; NT = neurotensin; CCK-8 = cholecystokinin octapeptide; VIP = vasoactive intestinal polypeptide; VP = vasopressin; ANG = angiotensin. (*From Krieger 1985,* reprinted with permission.)

Hökfelt et al., (1985) report that "extensive 5-HT networks" have been found "in virtually all parts of the brain." In the rat, 5-HT neurons are concentrated in the median raphé. Those in the medulla project to the cord and lower brainstem, whereas 5-HT units of the pontine dorsal raphé have "extensive projections to the entire forebrain." (Hökfelt et al. 1985, p. 205.) This transmitter is discussed briefly in chapter 6, apropos of its apparent role in sensitization in Aplysia.

DIFFERENTIAL METABOLIC RATES IN VERTICAL COLUMNS

It should first be noted that Emson and Hunt (1981) consider the neuro-peptides and GABA as relatively fast-acting, for instance in comparison to the noradrenergic or dopaminergic systems. CCK-, VIP- and GABA-containing cells "may be among the first activated" by thalamocortical input. They cite work showing that CCK and VIP undergo rapid biosynthesis. Krieger (1985) points out that neuropeptide synthesis "occurs in ribosomes within the perikarya . . . This is in contrast to the local synthesis, uptake and recycling mechanisms at the axon terminal, which occur in the case of the enzymatically synthesized neurotransmitters such as acetylcholine and the biogenic amines."

The concentration of CCK and VIP in cortical layers I–IV, and the relatively large cell populations, e.g. in parvocellular II and IV (Hess 1961) suggest that metabolic rates at these levels may be higher than they are in the internal lamina, or layers V–VI.

Vladimirov et al., (1961), made assays of ATP and phosphocreatine in the motor, auditory, visual and somatosensory cortex of the rat. In all cases, they found maximal concentrations in layers I–IV.

At the same symposium, Friede (1961) presented data as to the distribution of succinic dehydrogenase in cortical and subcortical systems in the guinea pig and cat. He defined a population of "effector" units at the base of the neocortex (layers V–VI; guinea pig) in which the enzyme was concentrated in perikaryal membrane, and a population of "receptor" units in layers I–IV, in which distribution of the enzyme was more dendritic than somatic.

In the brainstem reticular formation, Friede distinguished a medial magnocellular "effector" population, having a primarily somatic distribution, and a laterally-lying small-celled "receptor" population, having a primarily dendritic distribution, of succinic dehydrogenase. The conclusion of the paper reads, in part: "Two types of nerve cells were distinguished by different intracellular enzyme distribution which is likely to reflect their metabolic organization. The types probably represented receptor or integrative cells (dendritic type) and effector or relay cells (somatic type) . . . These cell types may differ also in their properties of vulnerability or regeneration. Investigations now in progress indicate that the accumulation of lipofuscin in the aging brain is a specific feature of the somatic cell type." (Friede 1961, p. 158.) Scheibel (1987) mentions the differential liability of cortical pyramids to age-related atrophy of the basilar dendrites.

Figure 2–5, from Lewin and Hess (1964) shows the laminar distribution of total ATPase (top trace), and the Mg^{2+} and Na^+ K^+ increments separately. These authors relate Mg-ATPase concentrations to cytochrome

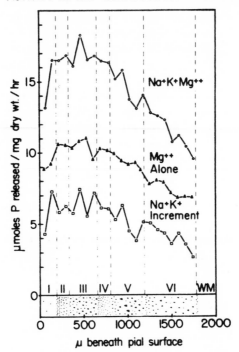

CYTOARCHITECTONIC DISTRIBUTION OF ATPase
ACTIVITY IN RAT SOMATOSENSORY CORTEX

Figure 2–5. Laminar distributions of total ATPase (top), MgTPase (middle), and Na-K ATPase (bottom curve). Mean values obtained at regularly spaced subpial depths, from 7 cylinders of cortex, from 5 animals (rat). Lamina numbers and Nissl cytoarchitecture shown below. (*From Lewin and Hess 1964*, reprinted with permission.)

oxidase and mitochondria, some of the latter being glial. They also mention that axosomatic terminals in general show a higher mitochondrial count than do axodendritic terminals, adding that "the density of synapses on, and hence of mitochondria in and around, dendrites decreases from the proximal to the most distal . . . The high activities of cytochrome oxidase and Mg-ATPase in layers II, III and IV can readily be ascribed to these distribution trends . . ."

Pope (1987) reports a similar laminar distribution for cytochrome oxidase and RNA, high concentrations of these being found in I–IV, "especially in sublayers IIIb–IIIc." He adds that this pattern "correlates well with the relative summed masses of neuronal perikarya and their large proximal dendrites which . . . are the principal loci of ribosomes (and) mitochondria." He concludes that high metabolic rates and associated protein turnover "are especially augmented in the cortical midzone, and in this respect correspond well with the density of the capillary bed."

Friede's suggestion, as to the differential vulnerability of cells of the "somatic" or "relay" type, finds support in a recent study by Sapolski and Pulsinelli (1985). These authors report that in the rat, ischemic cell losses induced by graded arterial occlusion, and aggravated by subsequent glucocorticoid administration, particularly involved neurons of the subiculum, CA3 and CA4 cells in the hippocampus, and units of layers III and V–VI in neocortex. They cite other work indicating that transient ischemia has a similarly selective effect on cerebellar Purkinje cells. The latter, and the magnocellular bands in cortical layers V and lower III, qualify as assemblies of the "relay" or "effector" type.

There are difficulties with Friede's "dendritic" and "somatic" scheme of cell classification, one being that the dendritic trees of some layer V or lower-III pyramids would be likely to figure in assays of enzymes made in tissue from overlying layers. Nevertheless, the distinction he makes may be a most fundamental one.

It perhaps reflects the fact that effector functions are the prime business of the CNS. Hence in phylogeny, through-put or simple effector systems appear first. To these are then added "processing" or receptor systems which act essentially as fine-meshed screens or active filters. This evolutionary sequence appears to be conserved in ontogeny, in the embryological order in which the neocortex is laid down—from "inside out," the basal layers first, the cells comprising the outer layers migrating through them. (Angevine 1965. Jones 1987.) In the sensory systems, the developmental order is also significant. Turkewitz and Kenny (1986) point out that in neonates, "the sequence of functional onset—vestibular, cutaneous, olfactory, auditory and visual, is invariant across all species of birds and mammals thus far studied."

Of all sensory systems, the vestibular is perhaps the most directly motor-related, since it underlies computation and adjustment of the body's position in space. It thus provides the necessary basis for many other motor functions; hence its priority of onset. As can be seen from its comparative anatomy (Herrick 1948, pp. 20 and 174–175), the vestibular system is phylogenetically very old.

In the rat (Hockfield, 1987), Purkinje cells of the flocculus and vermis project directly to the vestibular nuclei, bypassing the deep cerebellar nuclei. And in man, some fibers of the vestibular nerve bypass the vestibular nuclei, projecting directly to the cerebellum. "No other instance is known in which the cerebellum gets primary sensory input." (Nauta and Feirtag 1986, pp. 101–102.)

This order of priorities—motor or effector first—may be reflected in the organization of memory-functions as well (chapters 7 and 13). In parts of the CNS which are capable of learning, what is learnt may be outputs.

That is, memory-formation may particularly involve units which are among the last engaged in a given processing assembly, and which provide its relays to others elsewhere (ultimately to the autonomic and skeletal motor systems).

Even on the far-sensory side—in the hippocampal system or in cortical columns of posterior distal association cortex—this may be the case. What the hippocampus "remembers" may chiefly involve, not the granule cells of the fascia dentata, but the pyramids of CA3 and CA1 (vide Squire's patient, R.B.; Squire 1986, chapter 7.) What association cortex "remembers" may principally involve magnocellular arrays of lower–III and V, the columnar output neurons. The distinction Friede makes between "dendritic" or "processing," and "somatic" or "relay" cell types may have a parallel in this one, just as the tendency of lipofuscin granules to accumulate in cells of the latter type may relate to the gradual impairment of memory which often occurs with age.

Information Flow in a Vertical Column; Memory and Column Structure; the Bicuculline Experiment

INFORMATION FLOW IN A VERTICAL COLUMN

In a typical Hubel and Wiesel area 17 column (Hubel and Wiesel 1962; Gilbert and Wiesel 1981), simple field cells respond preferentially to slits of light of specific orientation. These cells have "distinct excitatory and inhibitory subdivisions. Illumination of part or all of an excitatory region increased the maintained firing of the cell, whereas a light shone in the inhibitory region suppressed the firing and evoked a discharge at 'off'" (Hubel and Wiesel 1962).

Increase in illumination to either subfield augmented responses by summation. Illumination overlapping both types of subfield resulted in algebraic summation, indicating "antagonism between excitatory and inhibitory regions." Enlargement of a slit beyond the optimal length caused a reduction in the response of the corresponding simple field cells. This is referred to as "end inhibition."

Figure 3–1, from Hubel and Wiesel, contrasts the center-surround arrangement of lateral geniculate receptive fields with those found in area 17 of the cat. "Complex" cells retain their orientation specificity (for slits of light) "but in comparison to simple cells, have gained some freedom in the precise position of the stimulus along the movement axis . . . Complex cells in each layer have unique properties . . ." (Gilbert and Wiesel 1981, p. 165.) Complex cells showing end inhibition correspond to those originally termed hypercomplex. Some complex cells show summation as the length of the slit illuminating their receptive fields is increased. They call these standard complex cells and report they are found in all layers but "rarely" in IV.

A second type—special complex cells—respond as well to illumination of a slit $\frac{1}{8}°$ as to one the length of a receptive field ($\sim 3°$). These cells are

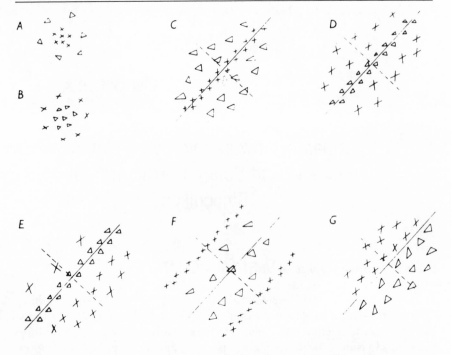

Figure 3–1.   Arrangement of "on" and "off" receptive fields in the lateral geniculate (A and B) and in visual cortex (C-G) of the cat. (*From Hubel and Wiesel 1962*, reprinted with permission.)

found at the bottom of layer III and in V, and may be described as having a generalizing or categorizing function, in that they respond to slits of various lengths, having orientation as a common property. (Invariance-sorting functions of the cortex are discussed in chapter 14.)

Superficial layer complex cells reportedly have smaller receptive fields than do complex cells of the deeper layers. And in layer VI "many cells show summation for increasing slit length up to very large values, some reaching 16 degrees in length." (Gilbert and Wiesel 1981, p. 166. This would seem to be an example of what these authors call "concatenation.")

Figure 3–2 shows a simple cell from layer IVab, whose axon collaterals distribute in the same layer and then have "a rich terminal arborization" in layers II–III. Collaterals are sparser in descending portions of the axon, which then enters the white matter. The authors state that "this general projection pattern was seen for all (HRP-) injected IVab spiny cells, and has also been observed with Golgi stains ... The horizontal extent of the axonal arborization was much larger than that of the dendritic arborization. This divergence could produce further mixing in the input from the two eyes onto layer II + III cells, and could account for the higher propor-

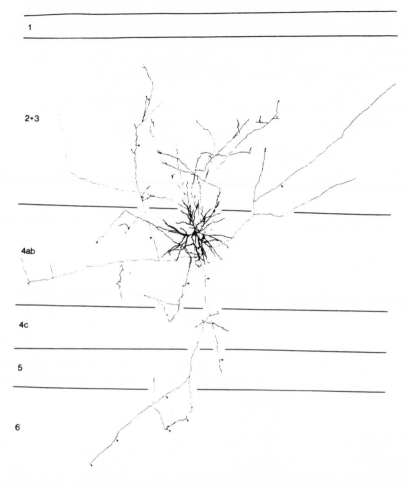

Figure 3–2.   Spiny stellate cell in layer IVAB having a simple receptive field with an on center and off flanks. The authors describe its axon as having multiple branches, with collaterals innervating the same layer, and a "rich terminal arborization" in layers II-III. Arrows indicate nodes of Ranvier. (*From Gilbert and Wiesel 1981,* reprinted with permission.)

tion of binocularly driven cells in that layer than in layer IV,"—a form of second-stage processing. By way of contrast, the authors show a smooth stellate cell of IVc whose axon ramifies chiefly in layer IV, which might be expected if the cell is inhibitory, and figures in first-stage processing of the input.

They conclude: "The predominant intracortical projection from layer IV appears to be to layer II + III, which would then represent the second level of cortical processing. Layer II + III contains complex cells almost exclusively." And finally: "The layer V complex cells may form their fields from the concatenation of the fields of the superficial complex cells, as suggested by the extensive projection from the layer II + III cells into layer V."

MEMORY AND COLUMN STRUCTURE

Figure 3–3 (modified from Figure 7 in chapter 2 and originally from Gilbert and Wiesel 1981) has been enlarged to include the approximate laminar distributions reported for GABA, CCK and VIP.

With allowance for the structural differences, e.g. between prime receiving areas, generalized eulaminate (association) cortex, and motor area 4, columnar organization is basically similar throughout the neocortex. The same is true of the partly parallel, partly serial relay of sensory data to the various cortical areas. (Pons et al. 1987, conclude from a study of the cortical somatosensory system that the areal distribution of input in the different modalities in fact follows a common plan.)

In the preceding chapter, I suggested that in the course of evolution, memory functions may have remained more prominent in effector (output) than in receptor (processing) assemblies. The distinction, though not

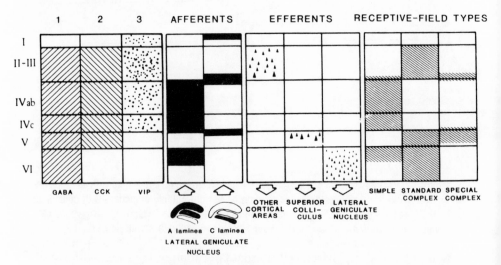

Col 1, left: laminar distribution of GABA
    2, left: laminar distribution of CCK
    3, left: laminar distribution of VIP

Darker stippling in 3, II-III indicates greater concentration of VIP at this level. (*After Emson and Hunt 1981*, reprinted with permission.)

Figure 3–3. Diagram combining data shown above (in Fig. 2-3) with data concerning the laminar distribution of GABA, CCK-8 and VIP. (*See text*, reprinted with permission.)

absolute, reflects the adaptive importance of actions and the priority there-fore given to the learning of outflows. It is perhaps only recently in phylogeny that "procedural" has come to be supplemented by "declara-tive" knowledge, and that by way of special adaptations, e.g. involving the temporal-entorhinal and hippocampal systems.

An early experiment by Murphy and Dusser de Barenne (1941) report-edly showed that bilateral thermocoagulation of area 4 in the macaque permitted recovery of fine finger movements if layer V was spared. If layer V was included, the loss was permanent. The implication was that in layer V there were motor memories which could somehow be re-accessed (possi-bly via the nonspecific projection-system) after the overlying input layers had been destroyed.

Morrell (1963) reported that acquisition of a visual CR in the rabbit was accelerated by bilateral anodal polarization of the visual cortex (depth negativity), and retarded by cathodal polarization (depth positivity). How-ever, with this animal Proctor et al. (1964) obtained decrements in perfor-mance of an avoidance CR with cathodal polarization, and "no consistent effects" with anodal.

More recently, Gabriel et al. (1980) found that in rabbits, during acquisi-tion of two types of CR, the initial focus of unit activity appeared to be in layers V–VI of posterior cingulate cortex. After the animals had reached criterion, the focus shifted to the overlying layers and to the AV nucleus in the thalamus. (The significance of these findings is discussed further in chapter 14.)

The input-output arrangements in cortical columns (as in many other parts of the CNS, including the ventral horn) imply that sense-data, after processing, are relayed in condensed or generalized form to assemblies elsewhere. Repeated many times en route to the final effector pathways, the net effect of these operations is to reduce the message to certain essentials, thereby shrinking down what we perceive and think into what we can actually do.

From the data of Gilbert and Wiesel it is apparent that some generalizing and some lumping or "concatenation" of primary input data occur in columns of primary visual cortex—in particular perhaps, in magnocellu-lar lower III; and then, as described above, in V–VI. It is significant, in this context, that layer II is reportedly a source of short corticocortical fibers, whereas III gives rise to longer corticocortical projections, and also to callosal fibers which distribute homotopically.

Layer V, besides giving rise to some long interareal fibers, is a major source of subcortical afferents—to LP, the intralaminar nuclei, striatum and red nucleus, to name several. (See chapter 2, Figure 2–2, and Jones 1981.) Layer VI, in addition to the connections shown in that figure, has reciprocal connections with the principal thalamic nucleus innervating the same area, and sends projections to areas which are "linked functionally" to its own (Jones 1987). Singer (1977) has suggested that layer VI projections to LGd may mediate "antagonistic" inhibition, favoring registration of new features in the input. It was in layer VI that Gilbert and Wiesel found many cells which showed summation for slit length "up to very large values."

To summarize: layers V–VI may be in receipt of data on which the primary work of analysis, and some of the work of generalization (e.g. in magnocellular lower III) has already been done. The foregoing would argue that layers I–IV, which receive the bulk of specific thalamic input and which have a relatively large small-celled population (in II, upper III and IV, in prime receiving areas), should show higher transaction rates and therefore greater metabolic turnover than V–VI. This conclusion is in apparent agreement with the reported laminar distributions of VIP and CCK, and with the other histochemical data reviewed in chapter 2.

The key question is then whether there is any warrant for the idea that there may be more hysteresis, or retention of pre-established patterns of responding, in units on the output side of a given cortical column than in those on its input side. If we assume that, in the absence of special (long-term) "fixing" mechanisms, neurons may in general tend to act on Blakemore's Principle (i.e. to respond preferentially to inputs they have "seen" most often) the question then becomes: are units in large-celled assemblies slower than those in parvocellular arrays to change their response-preferences? In other words, may units in larger-celled assemblies show greater hysteresis or "functional inertia" (Fair 1965) and therefore be definable as relatively memory forming?

There is, in fact, some evidence that that may be the case. Before examining it, I should first review pertinent data concerning the distribution of inhibitory units in neocortex.

Although GABA-containing cells are reported to be found in all cortical layers, Lund concludes on morphological grounds that "the proportion of smooth (Gray type 2) dendritic neurons may be slightly higher in laminae II and III." She adds that this fact, and the relative scarcity, in all layers, of cells having both type 1 and type 2 contacts, suggests that "one inhibitory neuron, or perhaps a small cluster, controls a much larger pool of excitatory neurons" (Lund 1981).

The evidently larger numbers of interneurons, including those of the basket type, in layers I–IV, would imply a higher proportion of inhibitory activity at that level. Much of that activity appears to be focused upon larger units (e.g. pyramids of lower III), and to be mediated by terminals on their somata and proximal dendrites. Morphological data suggest that, as has been shown for spinal motoneurons (Henneman 1987), the concentrations of inhibitory terminals on cortical units may be a direct function of cell size. The location of these synapses, in relation to those mediating excitation, is strategic. (Note also the intracellular distribution of cyto-chrome oxidase, Mg-ATP-ases and ribosomes described in chapter 2.)

Colonnier (1981) gives it as a rule that Gray type 1 synapses "are found on spines and dendritic shafts, never on somata. Type 2 synapses are found on somata and dendritic shafts, never on dendritic spines" (Colonnier 1981). He reports that a similar distribution of type 1 and type 2 synapses has been found in the hippocampus;[1] and that a type 3 neuron, a smooth stellate cell which is excitatory and contains VIP has been found chiefly in II and upper III of rat neocortex. According to Jones (1987), the majority of nonspiny nonpyramidal cells—amounting in aggregate to about 30% of all cortical neurons—are GABAergic.

Current theories of memory have proposed that, in vertebrates, changes in unitary response-preferences may result from differential changes in postsynaptic membrane, in particular involving dendritic spines (Routten-berg 1977; Lynch 1985; Lynch and Baudry 1985). Though subject to continual revision, particularly in regard to the intracellular mechanisms by which these membrane changes may be brought about, models of this type have some support in evidence.

The common feature of the Lynch-Baudry and Kandel-Schwartz models (chapter 6) is that, although the former is postsynaptic and the latter presynaptic, both depend upon excitation[2] as the critical factor. (See also Alkon 1982, 1983.) The question is whether the same applies, for instance to neurons in magnocellular arrays in prime receiving cortex—units I have supposed to act on Blakemore's Principle, but to differ from smaller-celled assemblies in being relatively retentive of their more proba-ble (most often repeated) inputs. By analogy with the Lynch-Baudry model, retentiveness in these units might depend upon excitatory inputs and result from internally mediated changes equivalent to a lowering of thresholds (increases in receptor numbers) at certain sites on dendritic membrane.

Presumably, such preferred responses in a given neuron will depend, *ab initio*, on the inhibitory "processing" of information in assemblies pre-synaptic to it, since that processing helps to determine the range of inputs the neuron "sees." Once, however, the internal changes equivalent to a preference for certain of those inputs had gone to completion, the inhibi-tory "gating" which initially helped to bring it about would have served its purpose. The cell's preferred response to a given excitatory input would be built into sites in its postsynaptic membrane, perhaps requiring a similar outlay of intracellular work to be built out again. (The evidence from conditioning studies suggests that in mammals thoroughly learned responses may not truly extinguish.)

Although highly speculative, these ideas lead to a testable conclusion, namely that learned responses in single units may become partially independent of the inhibitory processes which helped to establish them. Hence drugs which selectively impair inhibition, for instance by blockade of postsynaptic receptor sites, should have maximal effect on assemblies of the "non-learning" or receptor type, and minimal effect on assemblies of the "learning" or effector type.

THE BICUCULLINE EXPERIMENT

Bicuculline, known in the older pharmacological literature as a convulsant (Henry 1938), is a GABA A antagonist (Snyder 1985). In a set of experiments reviewed by Bloom (1981), bicuculline was iontophoretically administered to units of area 17 (cat), whose (Hubel and Wiesel) response-properties had first been determined in the conventional way. After iontophoresis, response-properties were again tested for effects of the drug.

"All simple cells tested lost their directional sensitivity . . . suggesting that . . . directional sensitivity for these cells arises within the cortex, as a result of a GABA-mediated inhibition."

More remarkably: "The type 1 complex cell behaved to bicuculline like the simple cells . . . directional selectivity was eliminated; *all such cells were encountered above layer IV.* The type 2 complex cell was unaffected by iontophoresis of bicuculline, even when it could be shown that sufficient antagonist was administered to antagonize simultaneous iontophoretic administration of GABA. *These cells were concentrated largely in layer V* but some more superficial neurons of this type were also seen." (In lower III?)

Finally: *"The type 3 complex cells also showed directional sensitivity which was unaffected by bicuculline, and were also concentrated in layer V."* (Bloom 1981, p. 361. See also Curtis and Johnston 1974; Krnjević 1974. Italics added.)

One might interpret these results as meaning that, in primary visual cortex, in assemblies of layers I–IV—possibly excluding magnocellular arrays of lower III—the direction-specificity of unit responses depends minimally upon lasting postsynaptic membrane-changes of the type discussed above. At these levels, when the patterning effects of inhibition were minimized by bicuculline blockade of postsynaptic GABA A receptor sites, the discriminatory responses of the system were disrupted. The result was a reversion to unitary visual responses characteristic of an early developmental stage, of the type described in other studies as "aspecific" or "immature." (Cooper 1981; Imbert and Buisseret 1975).

Such a reversion did not occur in neurons of layer V (and possibly of lower III) following iontophoretic administration of bicuculline. The implication is that in these arrays there were "savings." Units responsive, on Blakemore's principle, to most frequently "seen" inputs retained that capacity under conditions in which "processing" activity in assemblies presynaptic to them had been radically disorganized.

It is tempting to suppose that these bicuculline experiments mean what they seem to—that in effect they dissected out the "processing" functions and left the "remembering" functions, in columns of primary visual cortex. However, as Bloom points out, some of the results were puzzling. For example, the "distinguishing property" of the type 3 cells in layer V was that they were "generally spontaneously active cells, and this spontaneous activity was powerfully suppressed when the cells were stimulated with a slit object moved in the nonpreferred direction. This strong inhibition was also not affected by bicuculline, which at least indicates the existence of another potent intracortical transmission system" (Bloom 1981, pp. 361–362.)

At the time these experiments were done, GABA A and B receptors had not yet been characterized (by Bowery and his colleagues. See Bowery 1984, for a listing of this literature). Nor were we fully aware of the complex pharmacology of GABA, as illustrated by the fact that benzodiazepines, which enhance GABA A-mediated activity, can be displaced from their binding sites by ethyl β-carboline-3-carboxylate, a substance which opposes the anticonvulsant effects of diazepam and facilitates the convulsant effects of bicuculline (Martin 1984).

GABA A and B receptors, as already noted, have differential distribution in the cerebellum (Bowery 1984) and may also have in the hippocampus. The A type are muscimol activated, postsynaptic to GABA neurons, Ca^{2+} inhibited, and may increase membrane conductance for chloride ion. The GABA B type are baclofen-sensitive, presynaptic to GABA and other neuron terminals, Ca^{2+} activated, and may act by increasing membrane conductance for potassium (Snyder 1985; Bowery 1984; Andrade, Malenka and Nicoll 1987). The functional significance of these facts is not immediately clear.

Similarly, it is not clear why the type 3 complex cells in layer V which were spontaneously active should have continued to show sharp "off" responses to slits "moved in the non-preferred direction" (Bloom 1981). The fact that these layer V units retained their orientation specificity implies that they had other sources of visual input—perhaps by way of the LG projections to layer VI mentioned earlier.

It seems unlikely that this input, relayed to V, could have taken effect via postsynaptic GABA A receptors, since these were evidently blocked elsewhere in the same column. However, if these spontaneously active units were of the GABA B type, they might be auto-inhibited, giving frequency-dependent "off" responses to excitatory input which were mediated by presynaptic reuptake and unaffected by bicuculline.[3] One would still have to ask why these layer V units were also apparently unaffected by the functional disorganization of assemblies presynaptic to them in the same cortical column.

Given the foregoing uncertainties, the most that can be said of these bicuculline experiments is that in a rough way they support the hypothesis of memory functions outlined here. Bicuculline blockade of postsynaptic GABA A receptors results in an apparent loss of response specificity on the input side of visual cortical columns, and an apparent persistence of such selective responses on the output side. This result suggests that on the input side, such responses depend for their specificity on dynamic maintenance by GABA A inhibitory activity, whereas on the output side they have become independent of it.

CHAPTER 4

The Creutzfeldt-Heggelund Experiment; Analysis of the Results; Conclusion

In chapter 1, I quoted Blakemore, "Perhaps it is merely the *probability* of experience that determines the final preference of a cell. Perhaps each neuron selects as its preferred stimulus the feature that it has seen most often." He adds that this arrangement would have "adaptive value because it would ensure that the animal builds for itself a visual system optimally matched to its particular visual world." (Blakemore 1974)

The concept of developmental learning that seemed to follow from the early work of Hubel and Wiesel was that, in the visual system, structured inputs from the peripheral receptors set up corresponding structures in the thalamus and neocortex. Acquired as the organism matured, such structures, in the visual or other (auditory, somesthetic) cortex, presumably became fixed at maturity. They consequently did not constitute memories in the usual sense of the term.

The experiment of Creutzfeldt and Heggelund (1975) cast doubt on that conclusion, since it appeared to demonstrate that in mature cats the response characteristics of neurons in primary visual cortex were in fact not fixed. For brevity, I quote the abstract of their paper:

> Over a period of 2 weeks, [7] adult cats were twice a day exposed for 1 hour to a visual environment consisting only of vertical stripes, and for the rest of the time were kept in darkness. Subsequent investigations of the striate cortex showed a *decrease* in the number of neurons sensitive to orientations around the vertical, relative to those sensitive to horizontal orientations. This indicates that plasticity of functional properties of the cortical neuronal network still exists in adult animals. (Italics added.)

The authors point out that this is the reverse of the pattern found, for instance, by Blakemore and Cooper (1970) in kittens. Exposed to an environment of vertical stripes, at 4 weeks of age, defined by Blakemore (1974) as a developmental period of "extraordinary sensitivity," the visual cortical neurons of these animals, tested at 6 weeks, showed marked preferential responses to bars at or near the vertical.

Similarly, Spinelli et al. (1972) showed the remarkable persistence (up to one and a half years) of preferential monocular responses to horizontal and vertical lines, in kittens that had subsequently grown to maturity in a visually normal environment. (In the experimental condition, one eye had been exposed to vertical, the other to horizontal lines.)

THE CREUTZFELDT-HEGGELUND EXPERIMENT

Table 4–1 and figure 4–1 summarize the Creutzfeldt-Heggelund findings. The authors state that:

> The first cells recorded in a penetration were mostly sensitive to the same or a similar orientation, owing to the fact that the penetration started at a direction normal or nearly normal to the surface. In contrast to what is known from normal animals, the different orientations were not evenly distributed in the trained animals. Cells sensitive to vertical or next to vertical orientations ... were must *less* frequently found than cells sensitive to horizontal or near horizontal orientations. This was a consistent finding ...

They analyzed their data in another way. Using the first three cells encountered in any given penetration, they counted those showing one or the other type of orientation. In eight penetrations, the mean optimal orientation was horizontal ($\pm 15°$); in two it was vertical ($\pm 15°$), making the ratio 4:1. (Compare this with the ratios shown in figure 4–1.) By this method, they are likely in most cases to have been looking at units in the more superficial layers (I–IV). The bicuculline experiment suggests they might have gotten quite different results had response properties been systematically recorded at a full range cortical depths, with these penetrations being marked so as to permit histological follow-up.

Table 4–1. "Undefined" cells were those found unresponsive to the visual stimuli given.

Animal No.	Cells tested	Defined	Undefined	% Undefined
1	35	21	14	40
2	51	42	9	17.6
3	43	21	22	51
4	46	31	15	32.6
5	47	40	7	14.9
6	35	27	8	22.9
7	38	25	13	34.2
(Control)	31	30	1	3.22

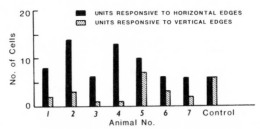

Figure 4–1. Neurons in cat visual cortex responsive to horizontal and vertical edges, following 14 days in which the animals were exposed to an environment of vertical stripes for 2 one-hour periods per day, and kept in darkness the remaining 22 hours. (*Redrawn from Creutzfeldt and Heggelund 1975,* reprinted with permission.)

Two other points are of interest. The tuning widths—defined as the total angular range over which the response could be elicited—were "about the same" for cells responding to either orientation, although a few cells with very narrow tuning widths were found, all of them "in the optimal orientation classes ±45° around the horizontal."

The second point, as stated by the authors, is:

> The number of cells which were unresponsive ... to visual stimuli was higher (about one third of the whole population) than we usually found in normal cats. In some penetrations, such unresponsive units were found in clusters, but this was not the rule.

Table 4–1 shows these data, including the percentage of "uncommitted" (visually unresponsive) units in the experimentals versus the controls. By "visually unresponsive" I take these authors to mean spontaneously firing neurons whose firing rate was unaffected by the presented stimuli.

ANALYSIS OF THE RESULTS

As the authors point out, their experiment appears to show that in the visual system, even early developmental learning is modifiable in mature animals. The critical variable in this experiment may, however, have been an unintended one—visual sensory deprivation. The animals were kept in the dark for 308 out of a total of 336 hours. As a result of that restriction of patterned visual input, changes equivalent to some loss of connectivity— some disorganization of normally tightly-knit assemblies, including those responsive to vertical bars—may have occurred. (See chapter 5 below, on the effects of sensory deprivation.)

The animals may, in other words, have shown some "forgetting" even of visual stimuli in the vertical orientation to which, during the experiment, they had been intermittently exposed. (See figure 4–1.)

The result of visual deprivation was greatly to increase the number of "uncommitted" cells. It may also have set up a condition in which mismatch signals were triggered maximally by "most forgotten" inputs—those having orientations farthest from the vertical. As suggested by Sokolov (1960), a basic feature of mismatch processes is that they appear to trigger some degree of reticulocortical activation. The latter may then raise the inhibitory-to-excitatory ratio, causing subsequent responses to the "forgotten" input to become more focal. A shorter pathway mediating such effects might be the one from layer VI to LGd mentioned earlier.

(As discussed in chapters 11 and 12, "orienting" or novelty responses appear to involve sequences of this kind. Hence primacy effects in serial learning, or the rapid memory formation that can occur under some forms of stress.)

In the present case, it is as though mismatch resulted in "overshoot," with the paradoxical result that the number of cells responsive to horizontally oriented edges not only exceeded those of cells responsive to vertical edges, but also, in some animals, substantially exceeded the number of cells found responsive to horizontal edges in the control (figure 4–1).

In other words, the immediate outcome was that the number of cells responsive to "most forgotten" inputs was relatively increased, while the number of those responsive to presumably "least forgotten" inputs remained relatively low. It is perhaps significant that some of the first group of neurons showed exceptionally narrow tuning-widths, since it suggests an increase in resolution of the kind often associated with increases in inhibition.

In contrast, the number of units responsive to vertical orientations, although reduced relative to those in the control, may still have been sufficiently large to preclude some or much of the mismatch effect. Hence new learning (reincorporation of uncommitted units into assemblies responsive to vertical edges) here proceeded more slowly, resulting in the imbalance in unitary responses shown in figure 4–1.

In time, then—if the system works in the probabilistic way suggested by Blakemore—the numbers of neurons responsive to horizontal and vertical edges should again have become approximately equal, as they were in the control. And parallelling this change, the numbers of uncommitted cells also should have dropped back into the low percentage range found in the control. If either conclusion is of interest, it could be tested by repetition of this experiment with longer-term follow-up.

CONCLUSION

The great increase of "uncommitted" cells in the experimental animals is perhaps a key finding in this study. I have supposed that it indicates some "destructuring" or loss of functional organization in striate cortex, and that this change was primarily due to an incidental variable—visual deprivation. The implication is that this cortex requires some minimum rate of miscellaneously patterned input if it is to maintain normal efficiency.

In chapter 5, I will try to show how these ideas relate to our need for REM sleep, and to some of the effects, on human subjects, of prolonged sensory deprivation.

Sleep Theories: A Brief Review; Entropy Levels in the Central Nervous System; Nature and Function of REM Sleep; Added Comment; A Model of Sensory Deprivation; Data from Sensory Deprivation Studies; Hallucinations of Other (Non-Organic) Origin

SLEEP THEORIES: A BRIEF REVIEW

Various explanations have been proposed for the fact that we seem to need REM sleep, and that we or other vertebrates suffer mild to grave behavioral disorders if deprived of it. Noting that human subjects seemed disturbed if selectively deprived of REM sleep, Dement (1960) concluded that we need a certain amount of dream-time per night. By selectively depriving cats of REM sleep, Jouvet (1966) produced animals that, when awake, appeared to be hallucinating.

Jouvet considered REM sleep "the organizer and programmer of the innate behavior patterns that occur at each stage of the individual's development" (cited by Dell 1975). Dell considers that "one of the more attractive hypotheses" accounting for REM sleep, depicts it as a "sorting out and restructuring" of data recalled from daily life—a process resulting in "consolidation of engrams, the selective forgetting of nonmeaningful material, and a combination of the new elements with similar ones already stored in memory."

It appears that REM sleep may have some of these effects, possibly not including "selective forgetting of nonmeaningful material." However, it may favor conservation of the brain's working structure, or even on occasion lead to informational gains (problem-solving). Such informational gains appear to be quasi-random and accordingly undependable. We

37

cannot *count on* solving a problem of the day before in our sleep, though the more urgent it is, the more that may be likely to happen. The reason is that the *prime* function of REM sleep may be homeostatic in a much broader sense. That it acts in a nonspecific way to conserve central nervous information can result in some of the functions Dell ascribes to it, but these may essentially be side effects.

ENTROPY LEVELS IN THE CENTRAL NERVOUS SYSTEM

To understand in what sense REM sleep is homeostatic, it is helpful to consider the brain in more general terms, as a biochemical or bioelectric machine. As such, it is an open system, depending, for maintenance of its own activity, upon energy input from the body via the vascular bed.

In still more general terms, we can equate the negentropy of the system (availability of its energy for useful work) to the aggregate of its working structures. (On the relation of passive structure to system entropy in classical thermodynamics, see Lewis and Randall 1923). These are divisible into two general classes.

The first is represented by structures internal to the component cells of the system, and negentropy here relates to basal metabolism and maintenance of internal (intracellular) order. The second class is represented by structures external to the component cells, and negentropy here is a function of connectivity, or the degree of order in neuronal networks.

System structure dependent on connectivity is then roughly divisible into two types. One type is genetically fixed, and so subject to minimal further change (though often to some) at maturity. The other comprises those neuronal connections which have been genetically left open, subject to a variety of constraints (e.g. the degree of "hard wiring" in receptor systems such as the retina or the cochlea). Structures of this type then take more or less enduring shape as a result of the organism's experience, some very early, during developmental learning, others over an indefinite period after maturation. These are the structures lumped under the term memory, although as we have seen, they include some not usually classified that way.

Following Brillouin's (1956) definition of information, we may regard structures of this last type, or memories, as equivalent to the brain's acquired negentropy. We may then define the brain as a whole as a system having two functionally interrelated, but nonetheless thermodynamically distinct components. One is intracellular, and the measure of its negentropy (available energy) is metabolic. The other is intercellular, and the measure of its negentropy is the extent and efficiency of its connectivity.

There is a practical reason for making this distinction. For while the network cannot function efficiently when intracellular entropy (fatigue) has greatly increased beyond the normal range, the converse is not necessarily true. Intracellular entropy may be within normal functional limits, and losses of connectivity, or entropy increases, can still occur in the network.

This point appears to be illustrated by the Creutzfeldt-Heggelund experiment. The increase in "uncommitted" cells in that experiment can be interpreted as a loss of working structure, or an increase in entropy at the network level. The acquired imbalance in unitary responses to horizontal and vertical bar-orientations in these animals can then be interpreted as equivalent to some degree of perceptual deficit or distortion. Taken together, both results amount to some loss in central nervous efficiency.

Note that these changes occurred at the network level, with nothing to indicate any comparably great change at the intracellular or systemic level. The animals were not reported as showing gross behavioral effects from sensory deprivation—were apparently neither disturbed nor abnormally somnolent. In other words, we may infer that an entropy increase can occur at the level of connectivity while entropy at the intracellular level remains within the normal range. This distinction may be of some importance, since it has direct parallels in our need for two, electrocortically quite different, forms of sleep.

NATURE AND FUNCTIONS OF REM SLEEP

Sleep is a homeostatic response by which both brain and body periodically correct for the increases in entropy we call fatigue—fatigue being a state in which our mental and physical resources become progressively less available. In the body, including the musculature, sleep is effectively a single-phase reparative process. Energy output or catabolism is for a period reduced, and energy intake via the bloodstream (anabolism) is relatively increased. The locus of recovery is primarily intracellular.

In the brain, however, the situation is complicated by the fact that conditions which make for entropy-reduction intracellularly do not do so intercellularly. Indeed, processes making for entropy reduction at one level may increase it at the other. Protraction of the slow-wave phase of sleep, while permitting metabolic recovery of neurons and glia, may also lead to losses of connectivity, and hence to increases in entropy, in the network. An analysis of the electrocortical components of the various sleep stages makes it clear why that may be the case.

In slow-wave sleep (SWS), there appears to be a general decrease in focal patterned activity, as evidenced by widespread synchrony in the EEG, and by a decrease in the *variance* of neuronal mean firing rates (Evarts 1963). This is accompanied by an apparent, but perhaps nonsignificant increase in the firing rates of single neurons in sleep as compared to waking (Evarts 1962).

Evidence reviewed in chapter 3 suggests that, during SWS, the general fall in metabolic rates may differentially affect those laminae whose metabolic turnover during waking is the highest—namely I–IV. Reference is to the report of Lund (1981) that the concentration of inhibitory cells is somewhat higher in II–III than in other layers; and to the bicuculline experiment, indicating a predominance of GABA A units, or postsynaptic GABA receptors, in I–IV. The result, in slow-wave sleep, may be some "release" (disinhibition) of cortical units, especially of I–IV, with some consequent increase in unit activity of the column(s) as a whole. In other words, the rise in overall unit activity is accompanied by a proportionate decrease in the (inhibitory) patterning of that activity. Or as Evarts put it: "Differentiation within the group has fallen away." (Evarts 1966.)

All forms of sleep involve sensory deprivation, by definition. Consequently, continuation of relatively less patterned neuronal activity during SWS, especially Stage 4, can be inferred to produce some gradual, as it were thermal erosion of acquired action-patterns. The result is that, if SWS is sufficiently prolonged, appreciable losses of functional structure, perhaps particularly affecting "processing" assemblies (of I–IV), may begin to occur.

The function of REM sleep is then periodically to reverse such losses in connectivity, by pro tem reinstatement of some of the conditions of alert waking. (In human adults, up to old age, REM sleep recurs at intervals of about ninety minutes.)

Whereas SWS favors recovery at the intracellular (metabolic) level, REM sleep uses some of that accumulating energy to counteract entropy gains (losses of connectivity) simultaneously occurring at the intercellular level. It can apparently be triggered from the pons, and mediated by rostrally-running noradrenergic projections of the locus coeruleus. (Stockmeier et al. 1985; Jouvet 1974.) However, it can also be triggered from other levels of the central activating system, notably the pontine or mesencephalic. (Drucker-Colín et al. 1986. See below.).

The similarity of the REM sleep and waking-state EEG reflects the fact that they may have common origins, and produce a similar inhibitory/excitatory balance in the neocortex. The nonspecific "shotgun" inputs to the forebrain, occurring during REM sleep, may also activate parts of the long-term memory system, possibly with differential effect upon those parts in which some facilitation has persisted from the previous waking state. The result is that dreams sometimes reflect our immediate concerns, and more rarely include logical extrapolations equivalent to the solution of some current problem.

The reason that dreams, even when relevant, are apt to be metaphors—

analogical transforms of our concerns—may be related to the architecture of memory, discussed in chapter 14.

SWS, in which output of the locus coeruleus and the raphé nuclei decline together, acts in the forebrain to lower inhibition-to-excitation ratios, making the system *more* perturbable than it is in the waking state, an effect that is offset and somewhat masked by lower energy turnover, making the network less generally "tuned in" to inputs from the periphery. However, Winson (1982; Winson and Abzug 1978) showed that in the rat, the population spike elicited in CA1 by stimulation of the perforant path was much greater during SWS than during REM sleep, or "still-alert" states, or "locomotion." Prestimulation of the median raphé (without effect separately), greatly augmented the response during slow-wave sleep but did not affect it in the "still-alert" condition.

Nonspecific activation of the forebrain during REM sleep, as it probably increases the ratio of inhibition to excitation, by definition increases the patterning of forebrain neuronal activity. It mimics waking, in which Evarts found "an increase in the number of units showing evoked decreases in activity, as well as of those showing evoked increases." (Evarts 1963.) As inputs, e.g. from the reticular activating system (RAS) appear to carry little information,[1] they chiefly serve to remobilize information that is already there.

Therefore in the first few months of life, or when synaptogenesis is passing from the overproduction to the economization phase (Rakić et al. 1986) and memory formation is in the early developmental phase, human infants pass enormous amounts of time in REM sleep. Becker and Thoman (1981), in a study of REM sleep "storms" in infants, conclude that there is a significant negative correlation between the frequency of such storms at age six months, and scores recorded at twelve months on the Bayley Scales of Mental Development.

In such infants, we might interpret the persistence of paroxysmal REM sleep episodes as a homeostatic overresponse. Being proportional to the extent to which forebrain functional structures have yet to take shape, the response will remain exaggerated in proportion as that process is delayed.

The function of REM sleep, in short, may be to conserve forebrain negentropy at the intercellular level. Whereas SWS acts to reverse the effects of fatigue at the intracellular level, REM sleep, occurring as a reflex, perhaps triggered biochemically[2] when intracellular recovery has passed a certain point, borrows some of that renewed energy and, in the form of nonspecific activation, intermittently produces an inhibitory tightening in the network. The function of the latter is to reverse the effects of a kind of sensory deprivation; essentially, it acts to maintain connectivity, and in that way to protect the forebrain's stores of acquired information.

That neuromuscular junctions may not require this sort of maintenance (being in the nature of fixed connections) is suggested by the fact that intervals of REM sleep are accompanied, not by rises in skeletal muscle tonus, but by flaccidity.[3] (The twitching seen in animals during apparent dreaming, and the sleepwalking or violent awakening from nightmares that occasionally occur in man, may be spillover effects, in which the motor systems become atypically involved. Some "night terrors" reportedly occur in SWS.)

One might expect that in chronic depression, more particularly of the monopolar type, there might be waking-state entropic changes (connectivity losses) similar in principle to those occurring during sensory deprivation. In turn, these might result in a homeostatic increase in the frequency or duration of REM. Cassem (1983) reports that the onset of REM sleep in depressive patients occurs within an hour (vs. ninety minutes, on average, for normal subjects), and that eye-movement "density" is also greater than in the normal. (See also Puig-Antich and Rabinovich 1986.)

A study by Shapiro et al. (1981) illustrates the distinction made here between the functions of SWS and REM sleep, in that it shows the differential role of SWS in general (systemic) recovery. Sleep recordings made on runners on four nights following their participation in a 92-kilometer race, showed a statistically significant increase in SWS on nights 1 and 2. The increase was greatest for stage 4 (the deepest stage) on night 1, and more evenly divided between stages 3 and 4 on the second night after the race. The authors connect these increases with rises in "metabolic load," noting that "the increase in SWS on nights 1 and 2 is more remarkable because of the extended sleep period, and is accompanied by a decrease in . . . REM sleep particularly."

As a reflex mechanism, REM sleep seems only rarely and incidentally to entrain the cognitive side effects mentioned by Dell (1975). Its basic function is not to *add* anything to the system, but to keep in being what is already there. That it may sometimes push to completion a train of thought begun during waking is a bonus.

ADDED COMMENT

It should be emphasized that although sleep is here described as "mediated" by structures such as the locus coeruleus and the dorsal and median raphé nuclei, the intention is not to suggest that they are sleep "centers." (The role of these structures in maintaining baseline states or "climates" during sleep and waking both is discussed in chapter 11.)

In fact, sleep deficits can be produced by *p-chlorophenylalanine*, a tryptophan hydroxylase inhibitor, or by lesions to the raphé nuclei. But although REM sleep can be induced from the pons by local application of carbachol, destruction (by kainic acid) of the same pontine area had no effect over eight weeks on REM sleep. (Drucker-Colin et al. 1986.)

These data suggest that whereas the 5-HT system of the raphé may be necessary to SWS, it is rostral output, perhaps from several levels of the reticular activating system, that is responsible for REM sleep. Drucker-Colín et al. (1986) report that REM sleep cycles and cycles of increased protein synthesis in the pons and midbrain RF tend to run synchronously.

This is as we would expect if REM sleep arises when intracellular metabolic recovery, for instance in the structures mentioned, reaches some critical level beyond which there are significant rises in unit activity. Such rises in pontine and reticular firing rates were shown by these authors to occur in the transition from SWS to REM sleep.

Perfusion into the same areas of chloramphenicol (CAP), a protein-synthesis inhibitor, diminished or blocked this rise in unit firing rates. Similarly, antibodies prepared to medial midbrain reticular protein are reported to prevent REM sleep. Thus part of the RF at this level may be a necessary link in the activating system involved, while still not being *the* system responsible—the REM sleep "center."

The authors cite other evidence showing that bacitracin, a peptidase inhibitor, can produce 60% increases in REM sleep. Although intra-ventricular VIP reportedly increases REM sleep in rats and cats, the suppressive effect of pre-administered CAP is reversed by VIP in rats, but not in cats. The excitatory action and local vascular effects reported for VIP would make it a likely participant in rises in central activation generally.

Finally, if REM sleep has the function I have proposed here—if it acts to maintain "connectivity" or acquired functional structure in the fore-brain—it implies a CNS having some minimum of assemblies which are not pre-programmed.

The need for REM sleep, in other words, should be proportioned to the organism's memory capacity or its potential for acquiring a repertoire of learned behavior. It should consequently be characteristic of higher verte-brates, and become less evident or disappear as we look down the phyletic scale. According to Hobson (1967), that is the case.

He cites evidence from the literature that birds and reptiles sleep, but states that "sleep with desynchronized EEG activity is confined to the mammals and young birds, and is not found among adult birds or frogs." (Hobson 1967, p. 120.)

There are, however, several interesting details in Hobson's study, some relating to the effects of sensory deprivation, described in the next section.

He divided frog behavior into four categories:

1. "Activity" (swimming, crawling, jumping)
2. "Sitting up"
3. "Reclining" (floating, limbs flaccid)

4. "Withdrawal" (pulmonary respiration suspended, nares closed below the water, eyes sometimes closed.)

Withdrawal could be produced by unavoidable "painful" cutaneous stimuli, and included eye closure and limb flexion.

"Activity" was accompanied by a lower-frequency (6–15 cy/sec) high-amplitude EEG, especially from frontal leads. In general, high-amplitude bursts appeared to be synchronous with or to precede respiratory movements, and be followed by desynchronization (12–25 cy/sec) in apneic periods. Frontal desynchronization was somewhat more evident in "sitting" than during "reclining," but maximal (12–30 cy/sec) during "withdrawal." The respiratory rate declined from maximal during 1) to minimal during 4).

During continuous recording, over periods from 24 hours to a week, "the state of withdrawal, initially considered to be a possible analogue of sleep, never occurred spontaneously." (It may in fact represent an alarm or nociceptive response, simultaneously involving inhibitory functions of the interpeduncular nucleus. See chapter 11.)

And although, with continued isolation, the animals spent more time "reclining," they "remained responsive, reacting promptly and vigorously to minimal stimulation." There was no suggestion of isolation-induced functional losses, of the kind described in the next section here.

Hobson concluded that though his frogs "did not appear to sleep at all, the state of rest which occurs in association with desynchronized-EEG activity might nonetheless be an analogue of that desynchronized phase of sleep which occurs periodically in all mammalian species. But no other hallmark of that state (rapid-eye movement and inhibition of muscle tone) is to be found in the frog, so that this suggestion may be discounted. . . .

These results suggest that the desynchronized phase of sleep is thus . . . not an 'archisleep' as its apparent origin in the lower brainstem . . . had originally suggested, but is rather a more recent acquisition in phylogeny." (Hobson 1967, p. 120.) That is also the conclusion reached on theoretical grounds here.

A MODEL OF SENSORY DEPRIVATION

If we hypothesize that some minimum daily rate of sensory input is required to maintain acquired working structures in the forebrain, that hypothesis leads to the following account of events during prolonged sensory deprivation (SD).

In human subjects, following early stages of adjustment, SD should be accompanied by a progressive slowing of the EEG, essentially as a result of reduced collateral input from the sensory pathways to the reticular activating system (RAS). This decrease will act as a slow positive feedback loop, driving forebrain activity down towards the level at which, in slow-wave sleep, the REM sleep reflex is triggered.

As noted above, we have treated that reflex as a kind of alarm reaction. At the physiological level, it appears to be mediated by the rostrally-running noradrenergic system, and produces an arousal-like EEG. At the psychological level, the parallel events are dreams, almost always with an emotional tinge, the latter often describable as fearlike or fear related.

In sensory deprivation, then, as slowing of the EEG begins approaching the critical low-frequency range, there should be a turnaround. Subjects should show signs of an imminent self-protective response (which is basically what REM sleep is, though we don't directly experience it that way). They should become increasingly restless, and parallel indices (fall in GSR; increases in urinary volume) should indicate onset of an arousal or defence reaction. Episodes of desynchronization in the EEG should then occur.

In some subjects, roughly in proportion to the degree of prior fall in EEG frequencies, a waking-state equivalent of dreaming may follow. That is, as the EEG desynchronizes, "shotgun" nonspecific activation of parts of the primary cortical receiving apparatus may become so intense that the subjects will experience these "dreams" as as-if-real sensory events; i.e. they will hallucinate.

Finally, we would predict that the functional losses due to some destructuring of working assemblies in prime receiving cortex and adjacent areas, will result in EEG abnormalities and cognitive disturbances carrying over into the immediate postexperimental period.

DATA FROM SENSORY DEPRIVATION STUDIES

All of these findings have in fact been made in sensory deprivation studies. For example, Heron et al. (1961) published data showing the sequence of EEG changes just described, in one of his subjects before and during an episode of hallucinating. The episode occurred after 48 hours of semi-immobilization, in a sensory environment consisting of patternless light and white noise (arrangements were also made to limit body-sense input). A high percentage of subjects in this experimental condition (25 out of 29) experienced hallucinations, most of them visual.

The controls in this case were picked for nearly matching pre-experimental performance in 7 tests (Kohs Blocks, Digit Symbol, Thurstone-Gottschaldt Figures, Copy Passage, Delta Blocks, Picture Anomaly, Mirror Tracing). Postexperimentally, after isolation for periods up to 96 hours, the subjects (N = 12 to 20) did significantly worse than the controls on all but the last test. (Significance based on t-scores.)

On first emerging from isolation, when the translucent goggles were removed "nearly all subjects reported gross disturbances in visual perception." These lasted from a few minutes up to several hours, and included phenomena such as the walls of the room seeming to move in and out, or "abnormally strong" positive and negative afterimages.

The experimenters replaced translucent with opaque goggles on three Ss who had been hallucinating "persistently." Within two hours, two of the three stopped having hallucinations, and the third had fewer. Restoration of the translucent goggles brought back the hallucinations.

From the foregoing, it might be concluded that the destructuring effect of patternless illumination was greater than that of none. This, in fact, is the outcome predicted by the thermodynamic model outlined above. In visual area 17, for example, the structures most vulnerable to drastic reductions in "expected" input are presumably those also most vulnerable to disorganization by bicuculline blockade of GABA-mediated inhibition. These were structures of the external lamina or layers I–IV. (chapter 3.)

Particularly in the latter, reduction of input to near zero (in near-total darkness) can be supposed to result in passive decay of functional organization. However if input is maintained at near-daylight levels, but kept unpatterned, the rate of decay should theoretically be accelerated, because the input is random with respect to all patterns previously established in that cortex. The relatively high energy of the input (as compared to input in the darkness condition) then produces a higher rate of thermal degradation of primary visual receptive structures. For this reason, exposure to white light rather than darkness is more effective in triggering the REM sleep reflex, and the intensity of the latter is such that hallucinations are then more apt to occur.

Movement of the subjects in bed, during isolation, was monitored by tambour. After early restlessness, all subjects (except those who opted out) "adjusted" and settled down. There followed a trend towards greater average daily movement, as isolation continued. This increasing movement, accompanied by a fall in the GSR, represents the stage of building towards an overt REM-sleeplike rebound.

It should be noted that Heron et al. 1961, reported that their subjects showed no significant changes in blood pressure or basal metabolism, throughout. The implication clearly is that the observed effects of SD chiefly involved the CNS and (to repeat the distinction made earlier here) may have depended more upon changes in connectivity than upon changes at the intracellular level (though of course the two are never separable in any absolute sense). In other words, the observed EEG changes were primarily due to reduced sensory input, and only secondarily to changes in neuronal metabolic rates.

Mendelson et al. (1961) published data showing increases in urinary volume in subjects during sensory deprivation. There were also increases in the urinary levels of epinephrine and norepinephrine, the latter rising still further in the immediate postexperimental condition.

Zubek et al. (1963; 3 Ss), using arrangements closely resembling those in the Heron study (including translucent goggles) obtained quite similar results. Deprivation lasted 14 days. Visual hallucinations were rare in these subjects, and those that occurred ("a black dot racing across (his) field of vision"; "flickering pinpoints of light lasting 10 to 15 seconds") did so late in the experiment.

However "frequent references were made to repetitive auditory events noted throughout the entire 14-day period—birds chirping or singing, waves splashing, water dripping . . ." The tendency of subjects in this study towards auditory rather than visual hallucinations may have been a function of the level of noise-input in the two modalities (as compared to the two in the Heron study). In this study, as the authors' description suggests, a relatively higher auditory noise input (white noise) may have been the critical variable.

The significant finding in the Zubek study (in which deprivation time was far longer than in the one reported by Heron) was the long-lasting aftereffects, as reported by the subjects and shown in the EEG records. Figure 5–1 shows the frequency analysis of the EEG for subject A, recorded before, during, and at the week following the experiment.

Two of the three subjects reported "severe motivational losses, which they described as 'an inability to get started doing anything,' a 'loathing to do any work requiring even the slightest degree of physical or mental exertion . . .' " —a state lasting 6 days in one subject, 8 days in the other.

Zubek interpreted the foregoing as a loss of "motivation." The hypothesis proposed here would interpret it as reflecting the drain on central nervous energy produced by the work of reinstating partially degraded functional structures. Since this was not work consciously done by the subjects, they experienced it, not as fatigue, but as an unaccountable disinclination to do or think about much of anything.

In sensory isolation, according to the Heron report, subjects go essentially through three stages:

1. An anxious "adjustment" phase,
2. a period of adaptation, in which subjects try to devise strategies to keep mentally busy, and
3) a late stage, in which these strategies begin to fail, and subjects (to quote one) become unable to "think of anything to think about."

In a second study (Zubek and Wilgosh, 1963; 22 subjects) Zubek used a primarily somesthetic form of deprivation (body-restraint), the experimental period being a week. Analysis of intellectual test results showed that experimentals scored lower on all 12 tests than did controls with whom

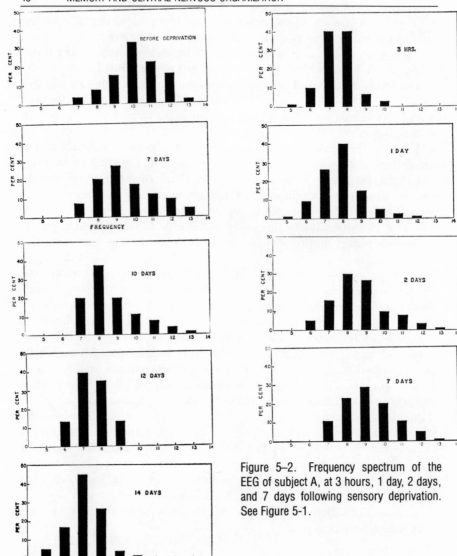

Figure 5–1. Frequency spectrum of the EEG of subject A before sensory deprivation, and at 7, 10, 12, and 14 days after the start of deprivation.

The ordinate indicates the percent of time that each frequency shown in the abscissa, appeared in the occipital EEG over an epoch of 5 minutes. (*From Zubek et al. 1963, reprinted with permission.*)

Figure 5–2. Frequency spectrum of the EEG of subject A, at 3 hours, 1 day, 2 days, and 7 days following sensory deprivation. See Figure 5-1.

they had shown nearly matching pre-experimental scores. Statistically, three of these results were significant—for cancellation ("picking out a particular number from pages of random numbers"), recall, and verbal fluency.[4]

The occipital EEG, recorded post-experimentally in 10 subjects, showed significantly lowered frequencies versus those recorded in controls. Three out of the 22 subjects reported hallucinations. In two subjects, these were visual; in the third, auditory.

The importance of this experiment is that it shows the interdependence of sensory inputs in respect of the maintenance of cortical organization. This is as one might expect, given that auditory, visual and somesthetic data are cross-modally represented, e.g. in parietal 7b, or in the region of the angular and supramarginal gyri.

The extent of this interdependence implies that the crucial factor for maintenance of functional integrity in the cortex is the gross amount of patterned input in all modalities. No one modality may be dominant in the sense that patterned input via it can maintain the status quo, in the near absence of such input via others. Thus, Sprague et al. (1961; 1963) reported that bilateral lemniscal section in cats, sparing the RAS, resulted in "marked sensory deficit" affecting even vision and olfaction, modalities not directly implicated. The animals were "mute" and apparently affect-less, showing "an incessant stereotyped wandering, sniffing and visual searching, as though hallucinating."

This is not to say that deprivation in one modality (only) may not favor hallucinations in the same modality. The Bonnet syndrome, or visual hallucinations in the blind (discovered by Charles Bonnet in 1769), is well known, and may occur in patients with dense cataracts (Levine, 1980.)

HALLUCINATIONS OF OTHER (NON-ORGANIC) ORIGIN

It is known that drug or alcohol abuse alters sleep patterns, such that withdrawal or acute alcoholic crisis tend to produce great, as it were compensatory, increases in REM sleep-time. Return to normal sleep cycles can then take six weeks to two months (Oswald, 1967). At the crisis stage, in withdrawal, hallucinations often occur, the reason perhaps being that cortical disorganization triggers the REM sleep reflex during waking.

Data reviewed in chapter 6, indicate that there are two types of serotonin receptor in the forebrain, S1 and S2, the S1 type being inhibitory. In the animal "serotonin syndrome," which is characterized by hyperactivity, hypertonus and tremor, the evidence is that excitatory S2 receptor types may be responsible (Peroutka, Lebovitz and Snyder, 1981).

The syndrome is suppressed by the neuroleptic spiroperidol, which binds selectively to S2 receptors. LSD, a hallucinogen in man, binds to both. In this connection, one might note some early work of Marrazzi's, showing the effect of psychotomimetic drugs on transcallosally evoked cortical potentials (Marrazzi 1958, 1960). The results led him to conclude that drugs such as LSD may be inhibitory for prime receiving areas and excitatory elsewhere.

Under this hypothesis, the net effect of LSD was to produce a mixture of central excitation and partial sensory isolation. This would be a situation in some degree paralleling the conditions in SD, in which hallucinations may result not from active (tonic) inhibition of cortical prime receiving areas but from passive decay of working structure in those areas.

It might then follow that radical, artificially induced increases in central drive states, brought on in the absence of the sensory inputs that would normally trigger them, can reproduce the conditions obtaining in REM sleep. Essentially, these consist in the activation of the contents of memory as if randomly from within, rather than nonrandomly, over the usual sensory pathways from without. The result may then be waking-state dreams. (For a model of the effects of high-level central activation, see Appendix.)

Wagner reports that dopamine-mimetic drugs can not only aggravate schizophrenic symptoms but may also produce hallucinations in "over-medicated" nonpsychotic patients. Disulfiram, which is used to treat alco-holism, evidently blocks the beta-hydroxylation of dopamine (its conversion into norepinephrine), and can also cause transient psychosis. (Wagner 1984.)

In some of Heron's subjects, onset of hallucinations followed a sequence consisting of

1) a period of gradual slowing in EEG activity
2) a period of reversal, with increasing restlessness accompanied by EEG desynchronization, ending in
3) an interval of hallucinating.

This suggests that in 1), sensory inputs had dropped below the level needed to maintain normal wakefulness (e.g. via the brainstem RF and locus coeruleus; see chapters 9–11). There was therefore some release of serotonergic units of the raphé from inhibitory catecholaminergic control. As a result, EEG frequencies slowly dropped until, at 2), the REM sleep reflex was triggered, a rebound activation resulting in 3), the occurrence of waking-state dreams. The essential element in 3) is that a sharp rise in central activation was not met by a corresponding increase in the flow of incoming sense data (as would normally tend to happen).

In other words, hallucinatory episodes may have the common feature that they involve rises in central excitatory states superimposed upon a critically low baseline of activity in higher-level sensory and processing systems such as the thalamocortical. This essentially seems to have been

Marrazzi's hypothesis—that LSD was hallucinatory because it reduced the flux of sensory input while raising central excitation.

It is not inconsistent with the hypothesis suggested here that the central activation characteristic of REM sleep may act, by injections of noise, to produce the hallucinatory states known as dreams. The latter, equivalent to evoked, semi-random patterned activity, may then serve to reverse the passive decay of working structures tending to occur in the forebrain during slow-wave sleep.

CHAPTER 6

Behavioral Effects of Serotonin; The Kandel-Schwartz Model of Memory Formation; Implications of the Model; The Model of Lynch and Baudry

Of all the major neurotransmitters, serotonin is functionally, perhaps, the most paradoxical. This chapter will begin with a brief review of data concerning its behavioral effects and the properties of S1 and S2 receptors; and go on to consider the model of Kandel and Schwartz (in which serotonin plays a major role), and that of Lynch and Baudry (in which it does not).

BEHAVIORAL EFFECTS OF SEROTONIN

Woolley (1967), noting the chemical resemblance of serotonin to psilocybin and ergot alkaloid (hence to LSD), pointed out that "serotonin analogs in which the hormone-like action is prominent cause symptoms of excitement and agitation in normal persons." These states may include "visual or auditory hallucinations, sometimes accompanied by sensations of pleasure and often by mental aberrations."

Increases in brain serotonin produced e.g. by a precursor such as 5-OH-tryptophan can also bring on "elation" or "euphoria." An earlier report (Pollin, Cardon and Kety 1961) indicated that in iproniazid-treated schizo-phrenics, 1-methionine or tryptophan brought on episodes of "insight," depressive reactions, or a form of logorrhea called "word salad."

Serotonin antagonists "tend to cause mental depression." (Woolley 1967.) A considerable recent literature (some of it discussed in the Appendix, final sections) reports an apparent connection between serotonin deficiency and monopolar depression, explosive aggression, and "violent" or "nonviolent" suicide. (Mann et al. 1986; Stanley et al. 1986.)

Meltzer (1984) reports that the serum cortisol elevation produced at 60–90 minutes by oral 5-OH-tryptophan was significantly greater in subjects with uni- or bipolar depression, or "mania," than in normal controls. The rise in serum cortisol was also significantly greater in 4 depressed and 3 manic patients who had attempted suicide, than it was in 20 depressed and 13 manic patients in the same study, who had not.

Peroutka, Lebovitz, and Snyder (1981), noting that serotonin "elicits both synaptic inhibition and excitation," describe a behavioral syndrome produced in experimental animals by elevated brain serotonin ("hyperactivity . . . with head-twitching, resting tremor . . . splayed hindlimbs, snake tail . . . and hypertonicity"). They report that tritiated spiroperidol and serotonin bind to "physically distinct populations" of serotonin receptors, whereas ^{3}H LSD (lysergic acid diethylamide) binds to both.

They conclude that the sites that bind serotonin (S1 receptors) "are regulated by guaine nucleotides", and appear to be "related to adenylate cyclase" and to synaptic inhibition. The sites that bind spiroperidol (S2 receptors) are not nucleotide-regulated, and mediate excitation. Spiroperidol (but not haloperidol) blocks tryptophan-induced head twitches.

Mann et al. (1986), in a pilot study using up-regulation of 5-HT receptors (as indicative of a compensatory response to serotonergic underfunctioning) report a significant (28%) increase in S2 binding sites, in suicides versus matched postmortem controls.

Aghajanian (1987) notes that "in general, serotonin has an inhibitory effect on sensory relay nuclei (e.g. in the dorsal horn of the spinal cord and in the lateral geniculate nucleus) and an excitatory (facilitatory) effect on motoneurons." (The synergic action of locus coeruleus and the raphé nuclei in the maintenance of forebrain "climatic" states is discussed in chapter 11.)

In the relatively simple nervous system of the mollusc Aplysia, the excitatory functions of 5-HT provide what may be a blueprint for effector or "procedural" learning, as it occurs in systems close to the final motor pathways in higher vertebrates. See, for example, the model for two-stage excitatory 5-HT transmission in the cord, outlined by Hökfelt et al. (1985; see also chapter 7). Learning of this type appears to depend upon functional modifications that were latent in the network *ab initio,* and in this sense more limited or predictable than the sorts of memory-formation of which the vertebrate NS is capable. (For a similar hard-wired system in *Hermissenda,* see Alkon 1982, 1983.)

In contrast, the type of postsynaptic learning proposed by Lynch and Baudry (1985) may correspond to what we call "declarative knowledge," and as such may have paralleled the phylogenetic appearance of REM sleep. Both imply the evolution of a central nervous system in which increasingly large areas have been left "open," pending preferential changes in connectivity that derive from experience and are equivalent to new path formation.

THE KANDEL-SCHWARTZ MODEL OF MEMORY FORMATION

These authors (Kandel and Schwartz 1985) describe sensitization as a process "in which an animal learns . . . to respond vigorously to a variety of previously neutral or indifferent stimuli after it has been exposed to a potentially threatening or noxious stimulus." Sensitization, in other words, has a focal origin—the "noxious stimulus"—but amounts to a CR which can be triggered by almost any sensory input temporally associated with the UCS.

"Whereas habituation is limited to the stimulated pathway, sensitization has a more widespread distribution, involving both stimulated and unstimulated pathways." (Kandel 1974.) As an example, in Aplysia, he reports a "noxious" head stimulus that generalized to block habituation to an innocuous stimulus to the siphon.

One of the critical steps resulting in a sensitized response appears to be a threshold lowering, or shift towards depolarization, resulting from blockade of one or more K^+ channels in neuronal membrane. These authors present experimental evidence suggesting that serotonin has this effect. "The facilitatory transmitter decreases K^+ current rather than influencing the Ca^{2+} channel directly." (Kandel and Schwartz 1985 p. 388)

They list four K^+ channels, found in both vertebrate and invertebrate neurons:

1. An "early" channel
2. A "delayed"
3. A Ca^{2+} dependent channel
4. An M channel modulated by ACh at muscarinic receptors.

Other studies appear to show serotonin does not affect these, thus presumably acting on a fifth, the S channel. They define serotonin's action on this channel (as) "decreasing the probability of its opening, not by altering its conductance or selectivity"—an effect which, by retarding repolarization, acts as a positive feedback.

"By decreasing this K^+ current, serotonin and cyclic AMP cause the action potential to broaden by 10 to 20 percent, allowing greater influx of Ca^{2+} and increased release of transmitter." (Kandel and Schwartz 1985, p. 389.)

The whole model then works something like this:

1. Serotonin acts to stimulate cyclic AMP synthesis.
2. Cyclic AMP inactivates the regulatory subunits of a protein kinase in neuron terminals.

3. The catalytic subunit of the same kinase then phosphorylates "a novel species of the K^+ channel protein or regulatory protein that is associated with it. This phosphorylation inactivates the channel and thereby slows repolarization . . . which allows more Ca^{2+} to flow into the terminals. This allows more synaptic vesicles to bind to release sites, and consequently more transmitter to be released."

These relations are shown schematically in figure 6–1, from these authors.

They conclude that short-term sensitization may not involve new protein synthesis, but that "its conversion to a long-term process might require the expression of new genes."

Their model for the long-term process, including the explanatory caption, is shown in figure 6–2. Notice that this process depends upon induction (synthesis) of a new regulatory subunit, R1, which produces a new protein kinase described as "site-specific." The net result is that "lower concentrations of cyclic AMP are required to phosphorylate these target proteins."

They cite behavioral and electrophysiological evidence that, in fact, short-term sensitization "grades into" long-term, as well as other evidence that in long-term sensitization, sensory neuron terminals "undergo strik-

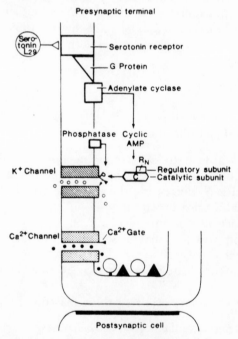

Figure 6–1. Molecular model of presynaptic facilitation underlying sensitization. (*From Kandel and Schwartz 1985, reprinted with permission.*)

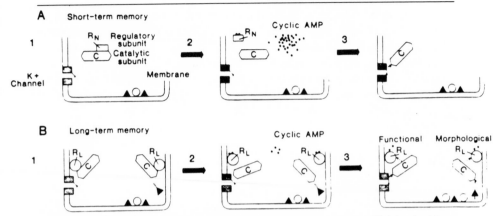

Figure 6–2.   A model for the biochemical basis of long-term memory. (A₁) In short-term sensitization the cyclic AMP-dependent protein kinase is proposed to have a normal regulatory subunit (R_N) and no particular orientation with respect to a substrate membrane protein associated with the K⁺ channel. In naive terminals, relatively high concentrations of cyclic AMP are needed to activate (C) the catalytic subunit (A₂) to phosphorylate (P) the membrane protein (A₃) which brings about enhanced release of transmitter, the neurophysiological event underlying sensitization. The memory is brief because the concentration of cyclic AMP diminishes soon after stimulation with serotonin.

(B₁) In trained neurons, a new class of regulatory subunit (R_L) has been induced. As a result, the protein kinase differs from the native enzyme in being site-specific, and thus being advantageously oriented both to the channel and to the mechanism that governs the organization of dense projections at the active zone where synaptic vesicles line up to release transmitter. In addition, this new kinase has higher affinity for cyclic AMP. (B₂) Consequently, lower concentrations of cyclic AMP are required to phosphorylate these target proteins. (B₃) Functionally, as in (A₃), the K⁺ channel is inhibited as long as the channel protein remains phosphorylated. Morphologically, protein phosphorylation leads to the stable enlargement of the synapse. In this form of sensitization, the memory persists for longer periods of time because it is embodied in R_L, a protein molecule. (*From Kandel and Schwartz 1985*, reprinted with permission.)

ing morphological changes. Transmitter vesicles are released from varicosities of the axon terminals called active zones. In naive animals, only 40% of the varicosities ... have active zones. In long-term sensitized animals, 70% of the varicosities have these release sites." The areas of active zones in sensitized animals are also increased. (Kandel and Schwartz 1985, p. 393.)

IMPLICATIONS OF THE MODEL

The important feature of the Kandel-Schwartz model is that it is presynaptic and primarily based on studies of an invertebrate (Aplysia). There is a logical difficulty with such models which may not become apparent so long as one is dealing with relatively simple (minimally branched) pathways. The difficulty is that in more complex systems, with widely branched inputs, the model itself becomes divergent. Unless we invent special mechanisms, limiting the processes Kandel and Schwartz describe to certain neuronal subpopulations and pathways, it is hard to see what prevents sensitization at a few sites from resulting in almost global diffusion of the process throughout the network.

Such global diffusion is, however, characteristic of responses we lump under the term nonspecific activation; and activation responses do, under certain conditions, show enhancement with repetition of noxious stimuli. They have the effect of speeding up trial-and-error behavior, and in other ways, e.g. by a reticulocortical sharpening of perceptual resolution (Lindsley 1958), may favor development of stimulus-specific CRs. However, in vertebrates activation itself may involve short- or long-term learned components, representing a survival, at higher neuraxial levels, of the type of unitary presynaptic learning or "sensitization" found in invertebrates.

Consequently, in situations which the organism finds inescapable, but in which it is unable to develop an effective CR (for instance because of the complexity of the problem confronting it), activation tends to spread, resulting in responses to cues which are purely contextual. A change of this type occurred, for example, in one of Pavlov's dogs, during an experiment in which food reward was made contingent upon its distinguishing between a circle and an ellipse. When the axis and semiaxis of the ellipse were reduced to a 9:8 ratio, the dog could still solve the problem, but evidently the difficulty of it caused his performance to deteriorate after three weeks. In the same period, the animal, having formerly been docile, became increasingly turbulent and resistant. When tested later, on simpler previously learned discriminations, it appears to have lost those too. (Pavlov 1927).

Pavlov described this behavior as "neurotic," and Liddell produced neuroses of the same kind in pigs and sheep. (For a review of this and similar work, see Maier 1949.) What these forgotten experiments demonstrate is that sensitization can be a form of longer-term learning in itself. Usually serving as a preliminary to development of responses tied to definite CSs, it can, if sufficiently augmented, override such defined responses and reinstate fight-or-flight behavior triggered by (any one of) a *set* of cues. (Sensitization is discussed further in chapter 13.)

The point is that learning which depends upon presynaptic changes tends to have this behavioral result because it leads to divergent spread of corresponding changes throughout the network. What Kandel and Schwartz describe, then, is a model suited to the learning of *activation*. But the latter, in vertebrates, may merely *prepare for* new learning in the more usual sense—CRs cued by specific CSs, with steady diminishment of central activation as the response approaches criterion.

One can call this last the second, or phasic stage of learning, and for it a model based upon changes in postsynaptic membrane seems better suited.

THE MODEL OF LYNCH AND BAUDRY

The model of Lynch and Baudry (1985) is of this type. For example, they report that binding sites for glutamate (glutamate/aspartate being a major transmitter in the hippocampus) are found in postsynaptic membrane of hippocampal neurons. High-frequency stimulation of hippocampal slices reportedly leads to increases in the numbers (rather than the affinity) of glutamate receptors.

The increase in glutamate binding induced by long-term potentiation (LTP) was found, in another study (using whole rats, pre-subjected to LTP) to be accompanied by morphological changes, notably "a rounding of dendritic spines and an increase in certain classes of synapse." These changes apparently do not occur if stimulation frequencies are below some minimal rate.

"It now appears that LTP is a more complex phenomenon than was originally thought. Three forms of potentiation, distinguishable by their half-lives (90 minutes, several days, indefinite) have been reported to follow the high-frequency train." (Lynch and Baudry 1985, p. 406.)

Another phenomenon, "kindling," they describe as "a persistent seizure-proneness brought about by repeated widely spaced bursts of intense, high-frequency electrical stimulation." Kindling is accompanied by an increase in glutamate binding sites. However, "Racine et al. (1983) found that the short-lasting form of LTP was intact after kindling, but that the more persistent form was not." The interpretation of this result is not clear.

Because of the temperature dependence of Ca-induced increases in glutamate binding sites, Lynch and Baudry speculate that it may be absent in poikilothermic animals (and report negative findings in the frog and the newt, as well as in reptile- or bird-brain membrane assayed at 30° or 35° C.)

Figure 6-3 and the caption are from these authors, and give the principal elements of their model.

Its essential feature is that it is postsynaptic, meaning that the longer-term to very-long-term memories formed e.g. in distal association cortex represent a focal residue of the much more generalized activation initially accompanying the process. In inferotemporal cortex, for example, what is "remembered" in a given assembly will correspond to certain patterns of presynaptic input. A similar relation will then tend to be found in units downstream to them, forming, in effect, a pathway.

In other words, a neuron in such an assembly will become predisposed to respond to inputs at *certain* dendritic or somatic sites—possibly with

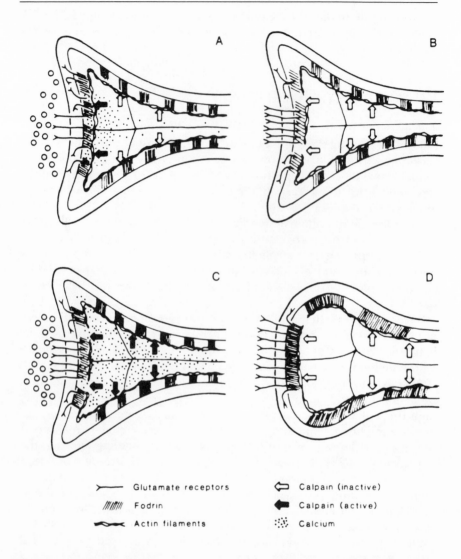

➤—	Glutamate receptors	⟸	Calpain (inactive)
///⫿⫿///	Fodrin	◀	Calpain (active)
∿∿◀	Actin filaments	⦂⦂⦂	Calcium

Figure 6–3. Hypothesis concerning the mechanism by which brief periods of high frequency activity produce long-lasting changes in synaptic efficacy. (A) Transmitter release causes an increase in calcium in the subsynaptic zone activating calpain, which degrades fodrin and uncovers occluded glutamate receptors. (B) Calcium is removed from the spine inactivating the calpain. (C) Subsequent episodes of high frequency activity produce a larger influx of calcium because of the greater number of receptors. This stimulates calpain throughout the spine and leads to widespread disruption of the fodrin network permitting shape change to occur. (D) Calcium is again eliminated from the spine but the structural and receptor changes produced by transient activation of calpain remain. (*From Lynch and Baudry 1985*, reprinted with permission.)

accompanying rises in threshold at others, as proposed by this author (Fair 1965). That the calpain-fodrin mechanism involves the cell's RNA apparatus seems likely, especially in view of Hydén's work showing the reversible base-ratio changes accompanying acquisition of a motor skill or a conditioned response (Hydén and Lange 1968; 1970).

The essential point is that the Lynch-Baudry model makes this selectivity in memory formation possible. By contrast, the model of Kandel and Schwartz does not. What it appears to describe are the preconditions of vertebrate learning—sensitization, or nonspecific responses having a tendency to spread and intensify, on repeated exposure to "motivationally" significant stimuli. Such responses, with their tendency to "build," appear well suited to produce LTP, thereby leading, as Lynch and Baudry suggest, to LTM formation dependent on changes in postsynaptic membrane.

In later chapters, I have tried to show how these two models may relate to what, in humans, are called "procedural" and "declarative" knowledge. I have also (in chapter 13) reviewed certain characteristics of chronic anxiety neuroses which run counter to current learning theory. These characteristics (and some of those reported in animal "neuroses") appear consistent with the hypothesis that, in higher mammals and man, sensitization normally occurs as a transient initial component of more focal long-term learning. If the latter cannot become stably established, but the external conditions demanding it are sufficiently repeated, long-term sensitization, with its apparently greater time-constant and more global central effects, may occur instead.

Cortical Organization: Two Basic Modes of Learning; Interareal Model of Memory Functions; Some Consequences of the Horizontal (Interareal) Model; A Hypothesis of Memory-Structure

CORTICAL ORGANIZATION: TWO BASIC MODES OF LEARNING

Graybiel's division of frontal and posterior association cortex into proximal and distal divisions (chapters 1 and 2) suggests two sets of pathways, or loops, connecting the posterior and frontal sectors.

The shorter loop involves prime receiving areas and proximal association cortex (e.g., 19, 7a posteriorly, and areas 6 and 8 frontally). It is concerned with responses definable as more "input specific" (STM dependent) than "experience specific" (LTM dependent). The shorter loop may depend chiefly on STM—which, at the unitary level, means neurons acting chiefly on Blakemore's Principle (chapter 1).

The longer loop involves distal association cortex (e.g. 20, 36, 37 posteriorly, and 9,10,11 frontally), and is concerned with responses more related to the organism's lastingly recalled experience. It is also related to new lasting memory-formation, for the reason that activity over this longer loop, as it involves more extensive participation of the limbic system, tends to be more directly related to the organism's basic drives and attendant feeling states. (The phylogeny of some of these limbic system functions is outlined in chapters 8 and 9.)

On the sensory side of the longer loop, cortico-limbic-cortical activity over the trisynaptic path can, given a sufficient "motivational" component, result in LTP, and hence apparently in LTM-formation. At the unitary level, this means in effect that Blakemore's Principle is overridden by a "fixing" process. The mechanism of fixation may depend upon site-specific changes in postsynaptic membrane, of the type described in the Lynch and Baudry model (chapter 6).

It is not yet known whether a similar mechanism figures in the fixation of memories in frontal distal association cortex—e.g. as a result of concurrent activity in the limbic, mesolimbic and extrapyramidal systems. This cortex may represent a system in which memory formation depends not only upon limbic feedforward but upon motor feedback, in particular from the basal ganglia. At neuraxial levels lying closer to the ventral roots, the biochemical or morphological changes underlying learning are also unknown; but at those levels, a "sensitization" model, based primarily upon presynaptic rather than postsynaptic neuronal changes, might be appropriate.

I suggested that such "presynaptic" learning might tend to spread very widely in divergent networks, making it disadvantageous except as part of a general activation mechanism whose function, e.g., in mammals, may be to establish preconditions for more discrete "postsynaptic" learning of the kind proposed by Lynch and Baudry. In other words, sensitization may be a concomitant of reticulocortical arousal or alerting responses, and usually (but not always) take transient form.

In systems closer to the effector periphery, short- or long-term sensitization may have survived as the primary mode of learning, since at the level of the ventral horn there is convergence of input upon final output assemblies, and the assemblies themselves can be activated only in genetically constrained ways, to accommodate the "idiosyncratic" requirements of various joint and muscle combinations (Nauta and Feirtag 1986).

Sensitization may, in short, be a phylogenetically old form of learning. It is possibly significant that 5-HT, the transmitter reportedly responsible for this form of learning in Aplysia, is also facilitatory for ventral horn units in the mammalian NS, and acts by a similar mechanism (a decrease in K+ conductance. See Aghajanian 1987.). Konishi (1986) considers the learning studied in Aplysia to be "procedural", and procedural learning "primitive."

The distinction between "procedural" (effector side) and "declarative" (cognitive, or receptor side) learning may be, in several senses, fundamental. The two forms evidently coexist, e.g. in man, but with separate overlapping representation in cortex and subcortically. The mechanics of "fixation" or LTM-formation may also differ in the two (in the way suggested above).

Motor feedback may figure in the consolidation in receptor-side (as well as "motor") learning (Held and Hein 1962). Moreover disruption of striatonigral projections (as in Huntington's disease) or of cortical projections from the nucleus basalis of Meynert (in Alzheimer's) either leads to, or is accompanied by, degeneration of cortical neurons, causing dementia or grave cognitive disorders, including progressive memory impairment (Coyle, Price, and DeLong 1985). At the same time, it is clear that this sort of subcortico-cortical input cannot *substitute for* loss of the capacity for LTM-formation that results if hippocampal-temporal lobe connections are cut, e.g. by bilateral ischemic loss of CA1 pyramids, as in Squire's patient, R.B. (Squire 1986.) For in that case, the evidence is that further additions to LTM have become impossible.

In other words, subcortical input, whether fed back or fed forward to the cortex, may facilitate cortical LTM formation. Such input, however, only takes effect if the LTM system it reaches is intact. As suggested, one reason for this odd dissociation of "motor" from "sensory" learning may be that the two forms of learning differ in phylogenetic age, and therefore in their biochemical mechanics. "Motor" or "procedural" learning, being, perhaps, much older, may depend upon a simpler (sensitization) mechanism, and so can collaborate in, but cannot replace, LTM-formation of the kind that depends upon synergic interaction of neo- and archipallium.

It should be noted that sensitization, as a general mechanism, must be distinguished from the phasic fine-tuning, e.g. of responses in the cord, that may be accomplished by means of firing-frequency-related release of endogenous neuropeptides (Black et al. 1985). It should also be noted that sensitization, if prolonged, might lead to RNA-mediated changes in the rate of synthesis of some of those neuropeptides. Montarolo et al. (1986) report that mRNA inhibitors in fact selectively block long-term sensitization in Aplysia.

At the level of the cord, such a (longer-term) mechanism might figure in motor learning, of the kind demonstrated by Chamberlain, Halick and Gerard (1963) who produced a postural asymmetry by cerebellar lesioning, the asymmetry surviving brainstem section caudal to the lesions. At higher neuraxial levels, as in the experiments of Pavlov, Liddell, Maier and Melzack (discussed in chapters 6 and 13) prolongation of sensitization, e.g., by the difficulty of a problem, may cause sensitization itself to become long-term.

In proportion as the networks in which that occurs are divergent, the effects of sensitization may tend to spread or generalize, thereby acting to obstruct or override learning of the more usual focal type. It is not impossible that some human anxiety neuroses involve a mechanism of this kind (chapter 13). In its normal role as a learning precursor, sensitization may also show some "savings." The latter may be what Wahler and Hann (1986) are referring to when they speak of those "antecedent events" which, in human experience " 'set the stage' for the occurrence of previously reinforced behaviors." Such "discriminative stimuli tend to increase the likelihood of responding, without demanding (eliciting) the behavior."

These "discriminative stimuli" are perhaps equivalent to the sensitization component of normal learning described here —a component which may be activated early, in parallel with the rises in aminergic output which accompany arousal or orienting responses. Like arousal, learned sensitization tends to be generalized, and may be essentially in the nature of a motor preparedness response. On the sensory side, it favors "selective attention" (Sara 1985) to stimuli only broadly associated with the CR. In this way, it may act to pre-facilitate more specific learned responses, pending the appearance of conditioned stimuli which may then definitely elicit them.

Sensitization may thus figure in the recognition of context, and so in cue-assisted or context-dependent recall (Sara 1985). This two-stage model of learning, and the role which aminergic activation may play in learning generally, are discussed further in chapter 13.

INTERAREAL MODEL OF MEMORY FUNCTIONS

In cortical columns close to or in prime receiving cortex, the shortest-term memory-formations—corresponding to our barest impressions of something just perceived—may be those which Peterson found, in human subjects, to have durations on the order of 18 seconds (Peterson 1966). In man, blanking-flash studies and other psychophysical data reviewed by Efron (1967), suggest a minimal perceptual "take" time on the order of 70 milliseconds.

Short-term memories surviving, e.g. on a scale of minutes, will tend to be more context dependent or "associative," and may consequently involve areas such as 20, 37, 39 or 40. (See figure 7-1.) Their duration will be directly related to the "holding" functions of III and V, and inversely related to the transaction rates—the amount of proactive or retroactive "interference"—in the same cortex. In Milner's (1963) bilateral hippocampal patient "Henry," the survival time of verbal STM (for instance, for people's names) was 10-15 minutes.

This short-term memory system, lying between prime-receiving areas and distal association cortex, was perhaps the one involved in the study cited by Coyle, Price, and DeLong (1985). In these experiments, young adult volunteers were given "low" doses of scopolamine (which blocks central ACh muscarinic receptors), and upon being tested, showed selective deficits in recent memory. LTM and "immediate registration" were not impaired. The authors note that the subjects' scores on the Wexler Adult Inventory Scale (WAIS) resembled those "seen in elderly drug-free individuals with a significant reduction in performance I.Q." (The fact that verbal I.Q. was not affected is of interest, since words, though not all of their associations, are part of LTM.)

I should quickly add that the evidence on which these risky inferences are based—the bicuculline, Creutzfeldt-Heggelund, and Berlucchi-

Sprague experiments, the scopolamine study just mentioned—is extremely indirect. The studies by Gabriel et al. (1980) and Orona et al. (1982), reviewed in chapter 8 provide more direct evidence for the differential involvement of layers V–VI in cingulate cortex of the rabbit during acquisition of two types of conditioned response.

It is important to distinguish the horizontal and vertical aspects of this model. The horizontal (interareal) aspect, considered in the next section, involves uncertainties of its own, particulary as to the processes underlying consolidation. The vertical (intracolumnar) aspect, at least in respect of layer V–VI, has some evidential support. And as will be seen in chapter 14, this vertical stacking of memory functions leads to an interesting account of certain logic-functions which may be integral to memory itself.

SOME CONSEQUENCES OF THE HORIZONTAL (INTERAREAL) MODEL

The model suggests that in posterior cortex, there is a kind of polarity of memory functions, such that units acting on Blakemore's Principle are concentrated in prime receiving and circumjacent areas (e.g., 17, 18, 19) whereas units that are memory-forming on the Lynch and Baudry Principle are concentrated in distal association cortex (e.g. of the temporal lobe).

We know, from several lines of evidence, that areas classifiable as proximal association cortex have two-way connections with both "poles" of this system. (See Lund 1981; Graybiel and Berson 1981.) These connections are both interareal and cortico-thalamo-cortical, and, beginning in prime receiving areas, follow a pattern of progressively shifted overlap (Graybiel and Berson 1981), such that areas at the far ends of the system are the least directly connected with one another.

Moreover some of the relay of sense data is in parallel (from thalamic nn. to N cortical areas concurrently) and some in series (from one area to another, sequentially). This is an arrangement suggesting error correction via redundancy in the case of perception, or reinforcement-by-repetition in the case of memory formation. Typically, both types of process will run concurrently; or, stated another way, the same arrangement serves two purposes.

We can infer, from the work of Flexner, Flexner, and Stellar (1963) that consolidation of a CR begins in distal association cortex and works backward, to involve larger cortical territories, for instance of the proximal division, or possibly closer still to prime receiving areas. That these workers were able to block consolidation, or cortical "irradiation" of the trace, by puromycin, implies that consolidation involves protein synthesis (Flexner et al. 1963).

While this conclusion is in agreement with the findings of Hydén,

mentioned earlier, it leaves open the question as to what is being synthesized. As we have seen, LTM functions—meaning, specifically, the capacity
to form new lasting memories of the "declarative" type (Squire 1986)—are
evidently *not* supported in either distal or proximal association cortex if
limbic connections of the latter are bilaterally cut.

The specific involvement of the hippocampus in this type of memory
deficit (which remained in doubt in the Scoville and Milner patients
because of involvement of the amygdala; Scoville and Milner 1957) was
demonstrated in Squire's patient R.B. At postmortem, it was found that
R.B. had bilateral ischemic lesions of the CA1 fields, extending the rostro-
caudal length of the hippocampus. There was minor involvement of the
left globus pallidus, right postcentral gyrus, and "patchy" loss of cerebellar Purkinje cells. The amygdala was not involved. The patient had
"marked" anterograde and little if any retrograde amnesia.

That in man, the temporal lobe is the more cognitively important structure, is shown by the effects of bilateral-temporal ablation (Terzian and
Ore 1955). The patient showed Klüver-Bucy signs, some transient sexual
release (as in amygdalectomized monkeys; Pribram 1958), often
addressed his mother as "Madam," and appeared "cognitively cut off"
from the world. Similar results of bilateral temporal lobectomy were
reported much earlier by Burckhardt (1890–91).

(A recent study, reviewed in chapter 8, indicates that bilateral amygdalectomy impairs formation of visual-tactile—i.e. intermodal—associations while minimally affecting intramodal associations—here visual-
visual or tactile-tactile. The authors suggest that disruption of intermodal
associations may be a factor in the Klüver-Bucy syndrome.)

The implication of the foregoing data is that during consolidation,
increased protein synthesis in areas outside posterior distal association
cortex may not bring about changes such as underlie LTM formation in
distal cortex proper. "Irradiation" may rather involve localized increases in
the production of certain neuropeptides such as CCK or VIP.

Such a mechanism might act, in response to posterior sector playback, to
prolong and make more selective the response preferences of neurons, e.g.
of proximal association cortex (chapters 3 and 4). In general, the development of such probabilistic response biases may depend on second-order
transmitters. Black et al. (1985) conclude that sympathetic neurons, e.g. of
the superior cervical ganglion in mature animals, may exhibit this type of
neuropeptide-modulated plasticity. That such changes may involve "post-
transcriptional" activity of the neuronal RNA apparatus was shown by the
in vitro conversion of preganglionic sympathetic units from adrenergic to
cholinergic. (Chikaraishi 1986; Black et al. 1985.) Chikaraishi reports that
in the brain, mRNA concentrations are three to five times higher than in
other tissues, a fact she relates to the brain's "cell heterogeneity."

Black et. al. note that "a change in transmitters may alter the target cell response," citing as an example recent work indicating that substance P, by interfering with cholinergic stimulation of nicotinic receptors, may inhibit release of epinephrine from the adrenal medulla. "Thus the effective ratio of substance P to acetylcholine at the synapse may critically alter effector responses." (Black et al. 1985, p. 39.)

A two-stage modulatory model, given by Hökfelt et al. (1985) involves a ventral horn neuron, 5-HT and two neuropeptides, TRH and substance P. In an early stage of the response, presynaptic uptake of 5-HT acts as a negative feedback, shutting it down. However if input to the unit is maintained at a sufficiently high level, larger vesicles containing TRH and substance P are released. TRH acts with 5-HT to increase postsynaptic facilitation, while substance P blocks the 5-HT autoreceptors, and so acts as a positive feedback—the result being "profound postsynaptic activation."

The report of Krnjević and Lekić (1977) that substance P acts selectively on Renshaw cells suggests that (as in the Hökfelt model) it may be mobilized at high stimulation frequencies and participate in the excitatory driving of the motor apparatus, occurring at high levels of reticular activation.

AN HYPOTHESIS OF MEMORY STRUCTURE

It seems entirely possible that by neurochemical mechanisms of this type, primary sensory inputs and playback from distal to proximal association cortex may combine to reinforce certain memories of the short-term system, giving them half lives which are, in effect, a function of their rates of input from two directions. Such memories would then become part of the longer cortical pathways established by playback from distal association cortex during consolidation[1].

Memories of this sort might thus be selectively activated when portions of LTM in the distal system were called into play, e.g. by events in the present. They would also remain subject to activation from the other side—the thalamocortical sensory projection system. That is, they would be components of a lasting memory as a result of one set of connections, but also remain liable to change on Blakemore's Principle, as a result of another.

Note, however, that I have presumed they are not fixated by any special mechanism (as those in posterior distal association cortex may be). Consequently, if such newly formed memory structures are not reinforced by parallel processes in and feedback from the temporal-hippocampal system, their survival time (as shown in the case of Milner's patient, Henry) appears to be on the order of 10-15 minutes.

Thus STM may differ from "registration," or primary cortical sense reception (which tends to stereotype through repetition), and from LTM (which relies on special fixation mechanisms). STM may depend upon dynamic maintenance—a function originally suggested by Lorente de Nó's (1938) work showing that the neocortex consists essentially of vertically organized internuncial chains. Within what were later called vertical columns, or between them, over interareal or cortico-thalamo-cortical relays, short-term recall was thought to be maintained by "reverberatory circuits." As such, it is highly sensitive to "interference" effects and to anticholinergic drugs such as scopolamine.

The selective effect of scopolamine on STM is consistent with the recent discovery that Meynert's n. basalis of the substantia innominata has extensive cortical projections, in particular to temporal and motor cortex, with lesser concentrations in prefrontal, and least in occipital cortex. (Nonhuman primate; Price et al. 1985.) It appears that the diagonal band and substantia innominata include the largest magnocellular groups found in the basal forebrain jointly supplying the chief, possibly the sole, cholinergic afferentation in neocortex (Nauta and Feirtag 1986, p. 243). In Alzheimer's disease, absolute cell loss in the nucleus basalis may amount to 75%, with correspondingly devastating effects on memory and cognition. Coyle, Price, and DeLong (1985) noted the parallel between STM deficits in Alzheimer's patients, and those induced in young adult volunteers by scopolamine.

In computer language, LTM of posterior distal association may have addressing functions which "call" certain of the contents of the STM system. These same contents I have supposed to be more or less continuously updated, in a statistical sense, from the thalamocortical (sensory input) side. The fact that the far ends—the "poles" of this system—are the least directly connected with each other may then serve as a means of preserving the integrity of primary perception. In the first (cortical) stage, sensory input is protected from revision in the light of long-term recall.

This cortical distribution of memory functions, which finds some support in known neuroanatomical connections, has interesting implications. It might explain the importance, in man, of junctional cortical areas such as 40 and 39 (see figure 7–1), to functions such as naming. Memories formed in this cortex, being activated by inputs from either end of the system, are perhaps more generalized than either the input patterns at one "pole," or the root patterns of long-term memories established at the other. Being resultants of inputs representing both the organism's continuous present and selected portions of its more distant past, traces of this type, established during consolidation, represent the "general-purpose" components of memory discussed earlier.

In other words, after consolidation, a given long-term memory will have a (possibly small) core of "fixed" elements which, when activated, will in turn activate a remainder of distributed cortical components, some lying

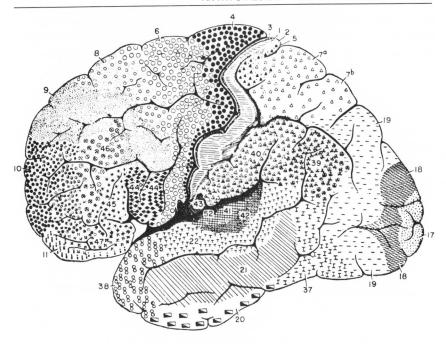

Figure 7–1. Cytoarchitectonic fields in lateral neocortex. (*After Brodmann.*)

in the "shorter loop" or proximal association cortex. These components, because of other inputs from the prime receiving side, may continue to change due to the flux of everyday sensory experience. Consequently, the proximal cortical components of a given long-term memory can alter considerably, while remaining part of the same pathway.

In some cases, probabilistic changes may be so extreme that even on a relatively generalized match-mismatch basis, the fit fails; the component ceases to be included in the LTM pathway. The more usual statistical result of prolonged exposure to experience may be that these generalized components of LTM become more so, causing the memories of which they are part to grow simpler or less detailed.

Luria (1976) said: "As investigations. . . have shown, the storage of traces in memory had nothing in common with the storage of unchanging copies or prints. *In the latent state, traces undergo further transformations and sometimes become more generalized and schematic. These changes naturally begin to distinguish old traces substantially from those recently imprinted.*" (Italics added.

The view of memory structure outlined here has the consequence that the "same" memory, however fixed and vivid it may seem, will tend to change over time, often in ways subjectively invisible to us (since we have no internal measure of the change). That will occur in proportion as the

general-purpose elements of which it is composed have themselves
changed, as a cumulative result of day-to-day experience. Hence the
details of our most detailed recollections often prove, on objective testing,
to have drifted into error, and some details may have dropped out alto-
gether.

In other words, if concious "declarative" memory has the structure
proposed here, the net result will be the one Luria describes; a tendency
for our more lasting memories to become not only less accurate but also
more schematic with the passage of time.

Phylogeny of the Limbic System and Cortex; Divisions of the Olfactory System in Mammals; Organization of the Distal System; Stimulation and Ablation Studies; Functions of the Amygdala and Hippocampus Compared; Conclusion; Historical Footnote

In this chapter, I will take up the limbic components of distal association cortex, as defined by Graybiel (1975) and discussed in chapter 2. The opening sections concern the comparative anatomy of the rhinencephalon. The remainder has to do with the structures and evident functions of its principal components.

PHYLOGENY OF THE LIMBIC SYSTEM AND CORTEX

Figures 8–1 and 8–2, from Herrick (1948), show the arrangement and approximate boundaries of major neuronal fields in the brain of Necturus or (in 2 A) of the tiger salamander. Note the close association of the amygdala with the striatum and strio-peduncular tract, and of the primitive striatum with the laterally-lying pyriform pallium. In reptiles, and still more so in birds, this "strio-amygdaloid complex" becomes greatly enlarged.

Herrick describes the stria terminalis in amphibians as "a massive connection passing downward from the amygdala medially of the basal forebrain bundles." Some fibers project to the septal area but "most of them turn posteriorly in the dorsal fascicles of the medial forebrain bundle to

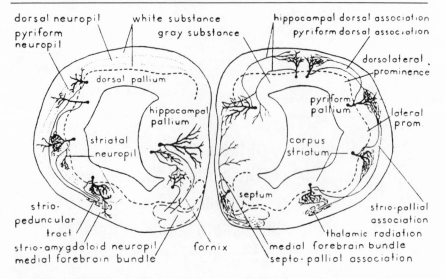

Figure 8–1.   Diagram showing in cross-section some of the projection- and association-fiber tracts in the cerebral hemispheres of Necturus, "a short distance rostrally of the lamina terminalis." (*From Herrick 1948,* reprinted with permission.)

reach the preoptic nucleus and dorsal part of the hypothalamus." (Herrick 1948, p. 256.)

The medially-lying hippocampal pallium is associated with the septum and medial forebrain bundle ventrally, and with "general pallium" dorsally. (Herrick's Figures 99 and 100 show the latter connections quite clearly. Herrick 1948, p. 377.) In structure, the hippocampal area "is evidently a first step toward differentiation of superficial (i.e. laminated or true) cortex." (Herrick 1948, p. 55.) There is a beginning of the mammalian fornix which "in other urodeles. . . has been described as reaching the hypothalamus" (Herrick 1948, p. 255). The precommissural fornix ("an ancient system") is well developed. It projects to the septum, and the connection, as in mammals, may be two-way.

At this evolutionary stage, then, the amygdala and pyriform pallium appear to be closely related to the forebrain final effector pathways and more distantly to dorsal general pallium. The *primordium hippocampi* is closely related to dorsal general pallium, but more distantly to the forebrain effector pathways.

Van Hoesen (1985) notes that, in mammals, "amygdaloid output is very much directed toward the origin of effector systems that influence motor, endocrine and autonomic areas along the full extent of the cerebral neuraxis. In this regard, it is very unlike the hippocampal formation whose output to such areas is either less strong or more indirect, and instead shifted more toward the association cortices."

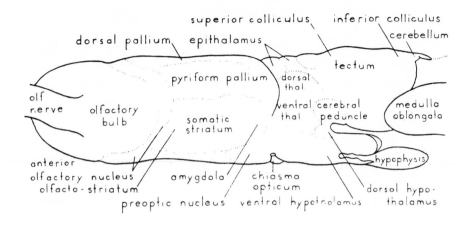

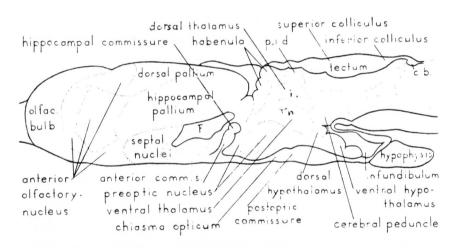

Figure 8–2.   Lateral (upper) and median (lower) aspects of the cerebrum of Necturus. (*From Herrick 1948, reprinted with permission.*)

In Amblystoma, as in higher forms, the influences of the amygdala and hippocampus converge on the hypothalamus, effectively the head ganglion of the system. There is a subthalamus, or "motor zone," homologous to the corpus Luysi. The habenula (epithalamus) forms the head ganglion of the olfacto-habenular-interpeduncular motor system. The thalamus proper apparently has far fewer receptor functions than it does in mammals. It receives visual system fibers, but the pars dorsalis, which is the primordium of the mammalian specific sensory system, has unknown or uncertain pallial projections. (They were, at least, unknown to Herrick.)

DIVISIONS OF THE OLFACTORY SYSTEM IN MAMMALS

Pribram and Kruger (1954) defined three major anatomic divisions in the mammalian olfactory system, as follows:

> The first system consists of the olfactory tubercle (anterior perforated substance), area of the diagonal band, prepyriform cortex and the corticomedial nuclei of the amygdala. This system has direct connections with the olfactory bulb.
>
> A second system has only secondary connections with the olfactory bulb. It consists of the basolateral nuclei of the amygdala, the septal nuclei, the frontotemporal (and possibly subcallosal) juxtallocortex, and probably includes basal parts of the striatum. . .
>
> The third allo- and juxtallocortical system, composed of Ammon's formation and cingulate and entorhinal cortex, has abundantly demonstrated electrographic as well as histological intraconnections and is only remotely related . . . to the olfactory bulb.

It now appears that the hippocampus, which might be taken as the major structure in the tertiary system, does receive projections from primary olfactory cortex via the entorhinal area, a path which Nauta describes as "more direct than the path from sensory surfaces such as the skin." (Nauta and Feirtag 1986, p. 129.) The inferred sensory "integrative" functions of the tertiary system in amphibians (dorsal pallium and *primordium hippocampi*) have evidently been greatly enlarged in the temporal-hippocampal system of mammals, in parallel with the appearance of the thalamocortical (specific sensory) projection system.

One can visualize the specific projection system, and frontally-lying pyramidal motor areas, as inserted into and splitting association cortex, the supposed descendant of the dorsal pallium in amphibians. Association cortex is then itself split, according to whether its connections are chiefly with the cortical prime receiving and frontal motor areas, or with the limbic system and the thalamic dorsomedial nucleus (DM). These are, respectively, Graybiel's proximal and distal divisions of association cortex. (Graybiel 1974).

Finally, frontal cortex of the distal system appears more closely related to DM and Pribram and Kruger's primary and secondary olfactory systems, in particular the amygdala, whereas posterior distal association cortex is more closely related to the tertiary olfactory system, in particular the hippocampus. It is of interest in this connection that while noradrenergic and serotonergic projections distribute widely to neocortex, dopaminergic projections reportedly reach frontal association fields only. (Nauta and Feirtag 1986, p. 127.)

The cingulate follows an antero-posterior plan of organization such that area 24, in the monkey, is a projection area of the midline and intralaminar nuclei, and receives afferents from the basolateral nuclei of the amygdala. Posterior cingulate cortex (e.g., 23) is a projection area of the anterior thalamic nuclei, and receives afferents from "the subicular division of the hippocampus." (Vogt, Rosene and Pandya 1979.) These authors report two-way connections between the anterior and posterior parts of this cortex, in part presumably via the cingulum bundle.

These are the major subcortical components of what I described earlier as the "long" (distal) loop into which posterior and frontal association cortex are organized. In contrast to the "short" loop, or Graybiel's proximal association cortex, this one is more closely linked to the limbic system—which is to say, the basal olfactory apparatus of the forebrain and the motivational-affective functions it has come to serve.

ORGANIZATION OF THE DISTAL SYSTEM

As in amphibians, the amygdala appears to be more directly related to effector outflows than does the hippocampus, and in structure is quite different from it, being not an extended cortical system but chiefly a cluster of nuclei. Evidence from stimulation and ablation studies indicates that, vis-à-vis the reticular activating system, it has important facilitatory and inhibitory functions both. (Pribram 1971. Pribram and McGuinness 1975.)

The tertiary olfactory system and its mammalian extensions (posterior cingulate and posterior distal association cortex) have what might be called observer-recorder functions. In contrast to the frontal-amygdaloid system, which is action-related and therefore prospective, the system involving posterior distal cortex appears to be less directly action-related, and the influence it exerts on behavior is more retrospective—more based upon lasting recall. It was perhaps the "computerlike" structure of the hippocampus (Olds 1975) that fitted it to act as a key structure in this system.

The cytoarchitecture of the hippocampus (as well as that of entorhinal cortex; see Lorente de Nó 1934: pp. 159-164) is much the same in all mammals. And as suggested by this writer (Fair 1963, p. 170) its tendency to repetitive firing may have made it uniquely useful as a means of fixating memories in posterior distal association cortex. Although the cortex in which this fixation occurs is very different from the amphibian general pallium, it may nonetheless stand in the same functional relation to the hippocampus as did its supposed predecessor. (Not all neuroanatomists accept Herrick's phylogenetic scheme on which this analysis is based.)

The enormous expansion undergone by the mammalian neopallium as a whole seems to have resulted in a medialward rolling-under of the hippocampus. If one performs this rotation mentally, it looks as though a portion of neuropil, perhaps not originally hippocampal but lying ventral to it in the amphibian brain, had broken away, so as to form a V-shaped cap on the leading edge of the rolled-under segment.

This cap is the dentate gyrus or fascia dentata (FD); and in relation to the hippocampus—CA3 in particular—it may have taken on receptor-processor functions analogous to those of layers I-IV in neocortex. For this reason, although the hippocampus is very old, there is embryological evidence suggesting that parts of it are phylogenetically new—that the system as a whole has continued to evolve, *pari passu* with the expansion of neocortex.

In the mouse, as indicated by autoradiography (Angevine 1965), prenatal neuron formation in the hippocampus, FD and related areas begins on the 10th embryonic day. In all areas except FD, elaboration follows an "inside-out" sequence (as it does in neocortex, where the basal layers are laid down first). By embryonic day 15, in entorhinalis, the parasubiculum, retrosplenial area (29e), subiculum, hippocampal CA2, and the molecular and hilar (CA4) layers of FD, the process is reportedly complete.

"In sharp contrast, the pyramidal cells of hippocampal sectors CA1 and CA3 continue to arise until birth (embryonic day 19) and granule cells of area dentata until postnatal day 20." (Angevine 1965, p. 34.) A study by Bayer, Yackel and Puri (1982) indicates that postnatally, in the rat, there is a linear increase in dentate granule cells (at a rate of ~ 1100 cells/day) which continues through the first year of life.

Apropos of his finding that "the stratum granulosum of area dentata and sectors CA3 and CA1 are among the last structures of the brain to reach completion of neuron formation," Angevine noted that they form an anatomical system, knit together by the mossy fibers projecting from FD to CA3, and by the Shaffer collaterals which project from CA3 to CA1 and the subiculum.

Angevine pointed out that these structural data were "of crucial importance to any analysis of hippocampal function," and concluded by mentioning "Elliot Smith's interpretation that the fascia dentata represent a localized hypertrophy of the superficial cortical layers." (Angevine 1965, p. 35.) The interesting feature of this arrangement is that it suggests a kind of evolutionary improvisation, such that instead of developing a columnar architecture, the hippocampus had added a displaced external lamina (FD) whose major efferents project not to a basal layer lying immediately beneath (as in cortical columns), but to a magnocellular layer (CA3) at some distance away.

In the same evolutionary process, the perforant path came to form a massive two-way connection, seemingly punched through from posterior distal association cortex into the rolled-under hippocampus and FD. In Nauta's language, "cascades of corticocortical fibers converge on the entorhinal area" which projects to the CA fields but principally to the fascia dentata. (Nauta and Feirtag 1986).

In entorhinalis (28a and 28b), the cortex becomes four-layered with a fifth, partially empty layer (the lamina dissecans) between the bottom two. In the presubiculum, it fuses to become two-layered; and in the subiculum, as in the hippocampus, it becomes one-layered. Over this polysensory pathway, a compression or statistical smoothing of data, such as I have attributed to magnocellular arrays in neocortex, may be carried to an extreme.

Axons in CA1, and those in CA3 which give off the Shaffer collaterals, pass to the alveus and fornix. Projections from the CA fields via the fornix reach the septum and contralateral CA fields. (Nauta and Feirtag 1986.) Efferents from the subicular area have wider distribution through the fornix, projecting to nucleus accumbens, the anterior and lateral thalamic nuclei, the lateral and preoptic areas and ventromedial and preoptic nuclei of the hypothalamus, and the bed nucleus of the stria terminalis. (Isaacson 1987.) In several of these structures, including the last, the influences of the amygdala and hippocampus converge. And as just mentioned, the cingulate forms a cortical bridge between the two.

Hippocampal fibers reach the lateral septum via the precommissural fornix; return projections over the same route arise from the medial septum, and horizontal and vertical limbs of the diagonal band. These are part of the cholinergic system of the basal forebrain discussed in chapter 10.

In addition, the hippocampus receives noradrenergic and serotonergic afferents. The neurotransmitter of the hippocampus proper is thought to be glutamate (or aspartate). It has also been found to contain CCK, substance P, somatostatin and histamine, and binding-sites for corticosteroids and mineralocorticoids. (Isaacson 1987. See also Sloviter 1987.) As mentioned in the next section, it is low in opioid activity, relative to the amygdala, though it appears to have a controlling effect on the brainstem endorphin system (chapter 12).

And interestingly enough, the hippocampus has been reported, in the rat, to produce two nerve-growth factors, one of which causes neurite extension in chick ciliary ganglion fibers (parasympathetic), the other causing neurite extension of lumbar chain (sympathetic) neurons. (Crutcher and Collins 1982. In vitro.)

STIMULATION AND ABLATION STUDIES

Studies in which animals could either self-stimulate electrically in a given locus at will, or were stimulated at various rates and able, by pedal-press, to shut stimulation off, resulted in maps roughly defining "reward" and "punishment" areas, and the proportion of "mixed" responses apparently obtainable from these. Not surprisingly, the highest rates of response in the forebrain involved the limbic system and related structures, in particular the preoptic area, lateral hypothalamus and medial forebrain bundle (MFB). The MFB, a two-way path linking the ventral tegmental area of Tsai to the hypothalamus and limbic system, is "the only place where the main conduction lines for the three monoamines (dopamine, norepinephrine and 5-HT) commingle." (Nauta and Feirtag 1986, p. 126.)

In an early atlas of site-specific effects, Olds and Olds (1963) reported more "escape" than "reward" responses from two hippocampal sites and from the *fimbria hippocampi* in the rat. Almost the reverse of this pattern was found for the fascia dentata (FD), the hippocampal commissure and the fornix. The lateral mammillary nucleus gave positive responses on balance, the dorsal mammillary nucleus negative. The *nucleus posterior hypothalami* yielded nearly equal positive and negative responses. Although the Olds's found about the same balance of "reward" and "escape" reactions in the medial and lateral septal nuclei as they had in FD in rats, Lilly (1960) obtained different results in the monkey. Septal stimulation in these animals was accompanied by penile erection, and by self-stimulation rates suggesting intense "reward."

Whether the monkey could turn on the current at will, or was passively stimulated and able to shut the current off, it ended up taking stimulation at about the same rate. At least at the intensities used, stimulation at this limbic site did not seem to produce motivationally "mixed" results. Lilly reported: "If one stimulates this particular system within the septal region. . . (the monkey) will stay awake on either schedule apparently without need for sleep, up to an unbelievable 48 hours. . . The sexual system here seems to be combining the effect of the powerful energizing avoidance system and the extreme pleasure of the rewarding system."

Evidence of this "energizing" function is provided by Sweet (1980), who reported that while stimulation in the septal area produced long-lasting relief from intractable pain (2 to 4 weeks in one patient), it also resulted in "temporary rage reactions." The septum is the only brain region from which Heath reportedly obtained "pleasure" responses, with electrical stimulation in human subjects (Heath 1964).

FUNCTIONS OF THE AMYGDALA AND HIPPOCAMPUS COMPARED

In contrast to the hippocampus, the amygdala may be less a processor than a switching system. The Olds's study showed it as giving about 50/50 "reward" and "escape" responses in the rat. In other animals or man, a great range of responses can be evoked by stimulation of different sites in it, or by different rates of stimulation at the same site.

In the cat, for example, one can elicit eating automatisms, eye closure, bradycardia, pupillary dilatation, acceleration or inhibition of respiration, piloerection, snarling, licking, shivering, gagging, or salivation (MacLean 1959). Many of these effects—e.g. bradycardia—were elicitable from several sites, and some, elicited from the same site, were opposite in "sign"— for instance bradycardia (parasympathetic) and pupillary dilatation (sympathetic). The principal pathways involved in this case would presumably be the stria terminalis, or the shorter ventral amygdalofugal path (to the hypothalamus) described by Nauta and Feirtag (1986).[1]

In man and animals, electrical stimulation of the amygdala reportedly can have graded effects, described by Pribram (1981) as "orienting (interest), avoidance (fear), or attack and escape (pain), as a function of ascending stimulus intensity." According to Nauta and Feirtag (1986), the diagnostic use of amygdalar stimulation in conscious patients often results in "undirected feelings of fear or anger ... accompanied by abdominal or thoracic sensations—for example the sensation that the stomach is churning."

Sweet (1980) reports a patient in whom stimulation of the amygdala produced 1½ days of relief from intractable pain, accompanied by a "mild detached euphoria." There is an interesting contrast here with the hippocampus, whose influence on the brainstem beta-endorphin system is discussed in chapter 12. Briefly, the hippocampus, together with medial and basal nuclei of the hypothalamus, appears to be capable of mediating central analgesia via the periventricular and periaquaductal gray. (Izquierdo and Netto 1985.)

According to Pert (1980), microinjection of opiates into forebrain limbic structures does not evoke analgesia, leading her to suggest that some of the other effects of morphine (euphoria, sleepiness) may be mediated in these structures. Hence perhaps the euphoric effect of amygdalar stimulation reported by Sweet. In the monkey, opiate receptor binding is 3 to 5 times greater in the amygdala than in the hippocampus or the frontal pole, and 1 to 2 orders of magnitude greater than that found in the inferior temporal gyrus or the occipital pole. (Pert 1980.)

Ablation of the amygdala bilaterally in the monkey has been reported to cause some release of sexual or aggressive behavior; it also appears to impair a sequence of responses often following evocation of primary fear. That is, the amygdala (as shown by some of the stimulation studies cited above) may have important affective switching functions, by which primary fear can be converted into proportionately intense rage, fear-induced paralysis into action, or flight into fight.

(May the high opiate-receptor levels in the amygdala relate to these rebound mechanisms? May concurrent opiate output mediate the temporary indifference to pain that sometimes accompanies rage responses and fighting, or help to convert a sense of acute danger into something like elation?)

Bilaterally amygdalectomized macaques show some behavioral disin-hibition (including transient hypersexuality). But when seriously chal-lenged by their cagemates, they seem unable to respond adequately, and so tend to fall in the dominance hierarchy (Pribram 1955). It is as if the fear induced by challenge had been blocked from turning into rage, thereby reducing or precluding the animal's normal defensive response.

Similar findings have been reported for the vervet, or African green monkey. It can survive in a cage following bilateral amygdalectomy, but cannot, in the wild, apparently because "it exhausts itself evading its peers. It can no longer distinguish between friendly and unfriendly gestures . . . and perceives all approaches as a threat." (Nauta and Feirtag 1986.) As in Pribram's macaque, a circuit by which primary fear results in affective contrecoup and so in a state more conducive to effective action (anger, aggressiveness) has evidently been cut.

"Novelty" or "orienting" responses appear to form a continuum with more intense, more overtly fearlike states (chapters 11 and 12), so habitua-tion to these may involve essentially the same mechanism. In the monkey, bilateral amygdalectomy has been reported to cause a failure of novelty responses to habituate. (Pribram and McGuinness 1975.) In its apparent ability to inhibit the arousal accompanying novelty responses, the amyg-dala is, however, acting in a way opposite to that just described in the case of rage-rebound. On receipt of signals from forebrain structures (e.g. distal association cortex) identifying the external input as "familiar" and "non-significant," it evidently turns down the gain on central activation (rather than up, as in the transition from fear to rage).

It is in this capability for resetting the whole course of behavior—motivational, affective, autonomic and extrapyramidal components included—that the amygdala is switchlike. This is not to say it may not have some processing capability. It has a "modified paleocortical structure" (Price 1987), and cross-modal sensory "hold" functions apparently similar to those of frontal association cortex. I have emphasized its switchlike functions because these appear to reflect its phylogeny as an action-related or quick-adjustment system. The fact that the amygdala can mediate transitions to forms of behavior whose underlying physiology is often so different has led to some uncertainty as to how it should be classified functionally.

As noted below, the amygdala has a substantial input from inferotem-poral cortex—one source from which a concurrent sensory input might be identified as having a learned significance (or nonsignificance, as the case may be). It also projects to n. accumbens and structures of the basal forebrain cholinergic system (substantia innominata; n. basalis) and has viscero-autonomic control functions similar to those of orbitofrontal cor-tex (the only part of neocortex with direct projections to the hypo-thalamus: Nauta and Feirtag 1986).

Bilateral amygdalectomy is reported to impair cross-modal (visual-tactile) but not intramodal (visual-visual; tactile-tactile) associations in macaques. This result was not obtained in a second group of animals following bilateral hippocampectomy. Postoperatively, intramodal associations were minimally affected in both groups. However, in the course of 500 trials on the cross-modal task, bilaterally hippocampectomized animals reached ~ 90% correct scores, the amygdalectomized animals only about 55%. (Murray and Mishkin 1985.) The fact that the amygdala plays a major role in cross-modal associations, whereas the hippocampus apparently does not, relates to the phylogeny of these two structures outlined at the start of this chapter.

To repeat: Herrick considered amphibian hippocampal pallium "a first step toward differentiation of superficial cortex." With its "computerlike" structure (Olds 1975), it perhaps marks the emergence, in mammalian evolution, of a second learning capability—the "declarative." One can regard this as essentially an auxiliary to the more ancient, more directly action-related forms of learning we call "procedural" (chapters 13 and 14). The hippocampus is characterized by its tendency to prolonged massive action (as in LTP), with similarly prolonged effects, for instance on plasma levels of 17-OH-corticosteroids.(Mason 1958. See Appendix.)

In contrast, the amygdala, in amphibians, forms part of the "strioamygdaloid complex" (Herrick 1948), and earlier in this century was classed as belonging to the basal ganglia in mammals. (The tail of the caudate is "continuous" with the amygdala, which is "dorsally contiguous with the putamen." Nauta and Feirtag 1986.) Its reciprocal connections with inferotemporal cortex, provide the amygdala, in primates, "its single most massive input." (Nauta and Feirtag 1986.)

The amygdala may act in parallel with frontal association cortex in issuing "hold" orders on sense-data currently in the registers. The determinants in this case presumably include the organism's motivational set and drive-level of the moment, and the learned significance, if any, of concurrent inputs in the several modalities. Its connections with the hypothalamus and extrapyramidal system, together with its inputs from higher-level sensory systems, make the amygdala central in establishing those temporary cross-modal associations likely to figure in the guidance of incipient behavior.

In a "million-sided world" (to use Sherrington's phrase)—an environment in which no combination of adaptively important signals is ever exactly repeated—it is of obvious importance for an animal to be able to attend to whatever combination may present itself. The temporary cross-modal associations established via the amygdala, together with the rapid motivational or affective shifts it is evidently capable of mediating, appear to fit it for that role. Similarly, the structure and input-output relations of the hippocampus fit it to mediate the type of "aftermath" learning described in chapter 12 and the Appendix. It acts, retrospectively, to add to the organism's store of more lasting information. The amygdala uses whatever may be to hand, prospectively, to produce behavioral results.

CONCLUSION

It is remarkable that, in man, structures of the primary olfactory system—notably the substantia innominata—should recently have been found to have such profound influence upon activity in the neocortex. It suggests an evolutionary principle similar to that proposed by Dumont and Robertson (1986). Citing the anomalously located (abdominal) interneurons that form part of the locust flight-system, or the conversion of the lung in lung-fishes to the swim-bladder in teleosts, they conclude that these are examples of "pre-adaptation." By that they mean "a characteristic that has evolved as an adaptation to one set of conditions" and "subsequently been co-opted" to conform to another.

Herrick's view was that "especially in the corticated mammals, the olfactory sense, lacking any localizing function of its own, co-operates with other senses in various ways, including . . . the activation or sensitizing of the nervous system as a whole, and of certain . . . sensorimotor systems in particular, with . . . differential reinforcement or inhibition of specific types of response." (Herrick 1948, p. 99.)

When compared to the visual, auditory, somatosensory or vestibular modalities, olfaction seems the most climatic—the sense most dependent upon other senses for the location of its external sources. Perhaps for that reason, and because of its great development in pre-mammals, the olfactory system in mammals has been "co-opted" to become a generator of those climatic states we call emotion.

In the relation of the hippocampus and posterior distal association cortex to the fronto-amygdalar system—which is to say, of retrospective ("declarative") to prospective ("procedural") knowledge—we may see another evolutionary principle, namely, that the CNS has evolved in such a way that higher cognitive functions tend to remain closely tied to the basal apparatus of motivation, and thus to the main business of life.

HISTORICAL FOOTNOTE

Apropos of the recently discovered importance of the nucleus basalis, it is interesting that nearly thirty years ago, when polysensory and cortical activation functions of the reticular formation were a kind of vogue in neurophysiology, Sir Geoffrey Jefferson, at the Henry Ford Hospital Symposium in Detroit, presented evidence for what he called an "anterior critical point" necessary to the maintenance of consciousness in man. He pointed out that bleeding from aneurysms of the anterior cerebral and anterior communicating arteries in this mediobasal forebrain area could produce hypersomnia passing over into coma.

He commented that "the interesting thing physiologically is the profound effect that lesions at this anterior site have on consciousness, *despite the fact that the better known arousal pathways are intact.*" (Jefferson 1958. Italics added.) Figure 8-3 shows in frontal section the area he was talking about. Figure 8-4 is the schematic of Nauta's frontal section 98, made at approximately the same level. It shows the relation of the anterior cerebral artery to the diagonal band and substantia innominata. (Nauta 1986.) Sir Geoffrey's finding came a generation ahead of the evidence needed to interpret it.

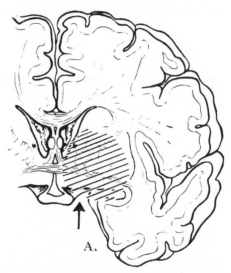

Figure 8–3. Schematic frontal section, showing the area of hemorrhage or infarction involved in some anterior communicating aneurysms. (*From Jefferson 1958,* reprinted with permission.)

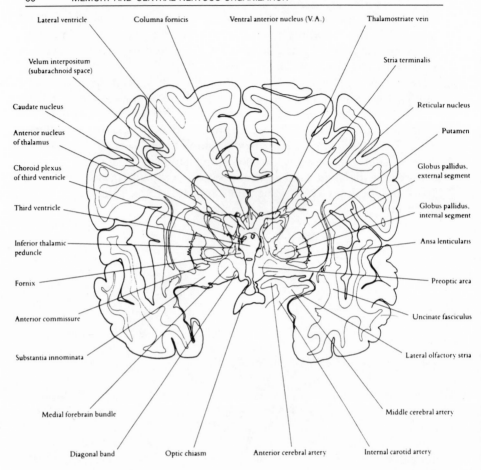

Figure 8–4.   Schematic of frontal section No. 98 (*Nauta and Feirtag 1986*, reprinted with permission.)
    Original material from the collection presented to Harvard Medical School by the late Paul I. Yakovlev.

The Reticular Activating System: Then and Now; The Ventral Tegmental and "Limbic Motor" Areas; Limbic-Mesolimbic Connections; Emergency Functions and N. Gigantocellularis: Reticular Organization; Overview: Anterior Limbic Structures

THE RETICULAR ACTIVATING SYSTEM: THEN AND NOW

In Sir Geoffrey Jefferson's day, although some studies suggested reticular gating of sensory input (Hernández-Peón 1961), and others showed that highly organized movements could be obtained from stimulation of the brainstem reticulomotor system (Ward 1958), the nonspecific system appeared not to exert phasic control over cortical activity. That was thought by some to be due to the fact that the neocortex and the RF were not truly compatible systems, because of their great differences in phylogenetic age and fine structure.

Projections of the midline and intralaminar nuclei, which were reported to distribute mainly to cortical layers I and VI (Lorente de Nó 1951), were not found to be modality specific. Studies of split-brain animal preparations (Meikle and Sechser, 1960) and of callosally sectioned humans (Sperry 1974) indicated that at the brainstem level there was no transfer, e.g., of patterned visual input, from the "informed" to the "uninformed" hemisphere. It was concluded from these results that reticular influence on the cortex was tonic.

The RAS, in other words, was a kind of power supply, supporting waking-state cortical activities, while the newer specific projection system provided the data for cortical processing. In the same period, evidence as to the routes of propagation of subcortically versus cortically induced seizures (Adey 1959; Gloor 1957; Poggio et al. 1956), suggested that cortical projections *to* the limbic system might functionally outweigh those reaching the cortex from that system. The conclusion seemed to be that as vertebrates had become more highly corticated, control of basal functions in the CNS had tended to be increasingly mediated from the top of the neuraxis down.

Recently, however, the trend of the evidence has been the other way, suggesting a more conservative model according to which cortical activity is controlled in major ways subcortically, or from the bottom up. This view finds some support from neuropathological studies indicating the importance, to normal cortical functioning, of striatonigral pathways (implicated in Huntington's disease)[1] or of projections of the nucleus basalis (implicated in Alzheimer's). Further support is provided by Iversen's report (1986) that 6-hydroxy-dopamine lesions to n. accumbens in the rat severely affect "motivational arousal" and therefore the animals' capacity for organized adaptive behavior.

The data now available suggest that the reticular formation, acting synergically with the limbic and mesolimbic systems, plays a more complex, more departmentalized role in the modulation of cortical activity than had been thought. This conclusion was, in fact, implicit in Nauta and Kuypers' (1958) neuroanatomical definition of the limbic midbrain (presented at the same meeting at which Jefferson described the "anterior critical point"). For what their study indicated was that a part of the reticular system, distinguishable from the main ascending pathways of Forel's tract, figured in the support and modulation of activity in the basal motivational systems, and so in the modulation of cortical activity over pathways other than those of the reticular activating system then known. The next sections have to do with the neuroanatomy of these systems, including the neurotransmitters evidently characteristic of some of them.

THE VENTRAL TEGMENTAL AND "LIMBIC MOTOR" AREAS

According to Nauta and Kuypers (1958),

> "a main pathway of ascending conduction through the brain-stem reticular formation is incorporated in Forel's tractus fasciculorum tegmenti ... Its component bundles occupy a large part of the cross-section of the bulbar tegmentum ... At the level of the isthmus, this major ascending pathway shifts lateralward, and thus comes largely to leave free a paramedian zone of the tegmentum of the lower midbrain ... apparently related more specifically to the hypothalamus and limbic system."

This "paramedian zone" is the ventral tegmental area of Tsai. (For the classification of deep midbrain tegmentum as reticular, see Crosby et al.

1960, p. 246 ff.) Forel's tract, continuing cranialward, is then displaced (by the decussations of the brachium conjunctivum and the rubrospinal tract) into a dorsal position, most of its bundles "corresponding to the 'central tegmental tract' of primates" (Nauta and Kuypers 1958. See also Nauta and Feirtag 1986, Figures 83-85.) It represents the old main highway of the RAS, sending projections to the periaqueductal gray, the deeper layers of the superior colliculus, and the pretectal area. It finally bifurcates to distribute to the subthalamus "with a considerable offset" of fibers to the thalamic intralaminar nuclei. The nucleus gigantocellularis of the medial medulla provides an ascending component of Forel's tract.

The ventral tegmental area of Tsai is dopaminergic (in the Dahlström and Fuxe nomenclature, A10), and lies in the caudal midbrain, a region which includes Gudden's dorsal and ventral tegmental nuclei, the interpeduncular nucleus, paramedian reticulum and periaqueductal gray. According to Corti et al. (1963) the dorsal longitudinal fasciculus of Schütz arises in Gudden's dorsal tegmental nucleus. Crosby et al. (1962) describe it as projecting both caudally and rostrally. Its rostrally running fibers form part of the periaqueductal-periventricular system, of which the medial hypothalamus is a continuation (Nauta and Feirtag 1986).

The interpeduncular nucleus (IPN) is a principal mesencephalic structure in what Papez (1958) called "a primitive motor path." The latter arises rostrally in the anterior perforated substance (or olfactory tubercle), and via the habenula projects to the IPN. A major link in this system, the stria medullaris, includes fibers from the septum, the nucleus of the diagonal band, the lateral hypothalamus and the ventral GP of Heimer and Wilson. (Nauta and Feirtag 1986.)

The stria medullaris, which projects to the habenula, is evidently a one-way conduction system (Nauta and Feirtag 1986). The fasciculus retroflexus of Meynert, connecting the habenula to the interpeduncular nucleus, is reported to contain cholinergic fibers (reflecting some of its sources). Projections of the IPN, via Ganser's tract, reach the mesencephalic raphé—i.e., presumably elements of the globally-projecting 5-HT fiber system.

The interpeduncular nucleus appears to figure in learned avoidance responses in the rat. Bilateral electrolytic lesions to this nucleus, while blocking the motor response to the CS, did not block the animals' distress responses to it (squealing). The CS (a warning light) preceded footshock by 5 sec. On delivery of shock, the animals then responded normally (Thompson 1960).

Thus, there was no impairment of (other) motor pathways involved in direct response to shock. What seems to have been affected was, specifically, a motivationally driven anticipatory motor response, one of whose stations, en route to the ventral horn, was the interpeduncular nucleus.

Consequently, lesions to this nucleus dissociated the motor component of a learned response from its "emotional" component. That the IPN projects to the raphé suggests that such responses may include an analgesic contrecoup phase. Evidence suggestive of a role of the raphé nuclei in "stimulus-produced analgesia" is given by Liebeskind (1980). (Data indicating a related role for the periventricular-periaqueductal β-endorphin system are reviewed in chapter 12.)

For these reasons, the olfacto-habenulo-interpeduncular system might be described as "limbic motor." The key point is that its activation may depend upon what might be called motivationally- or emotionally-colored anticipation. Note that this does necessarily imply aversive coloration. (The Olds's 1963 atlas shows the interpeduncular nucleus as giving, on balance, "reward" responses, but the lateral and medial habenular nuclei as giving, on balance, "escape.") Nor does it mean that the anticipatory response is necessarily learned. (Some may be innate, relating, e.g., to food odors. The olfacto–habenulo–interpeduncular system, as Papez noted, is very old.)

LIMBIC-MESOLIMBIC CONNECTIONS

The MFB, a major bidirectional pathway from the ventral tegmental area, includes noradrenergic and serotonergic fibers (the latter arising in the raphé nuclei), and dopaminergic fibers arising in the ventral tegmental area itself. These last form a "remarkable adjunct to the projection from the substantia nigra to the striatum," projecting to the amygdala, entorhinal area, frontal association cortex, and "to a large ventromedial sector of the striatum." (Nauta and Feirtag 1986.) Its input and output arrangements, and related physiological evidence, mark the ventral tegmental area as, effectively, the core of the motivational system.

Moore (1977) distinguishes two ascending noradrenergic fiber-systems. One, a lateral tegmental system, arises "diffusely" in the subcoeruleus region and (more caudally) in the (parvocellular) lateral and dorsal tegmentum of the medulla, (which has connections with the medially-lying n. gigantocellularis). The second originates in the locus coeruleus. A third arises in the region of the dorsal raphé nucleus (Lindvall and Björklund 1974).

Fibers of the lateral tegmental (LT) group first ascend in the central tegmental tract. They then merge with the ventral bundle (of Ungerstedt) where, with fibers of the locus coeruleus, they travel a short way together. At the level of the nn. pontis, LC fibers separate off, travelling in the dorsal noradrenergic bundle; at the level of the mammillary nucleus, some but not all then turn ventralward and rejoin those of the LT in the ventral bundle. (Moore 1977.)

The distinction between these two projection systems may be important in that it relates to the discussion, in chapter 11, of the "climatic" (usually low-level arousal) functions of LC. In contrast, more massive emergency responses arising, e.g., at the level of the medullary RF, may entrain rises in output both of LC and the lateral tegmental system. It is perhaps significant in this connection that, according to Routtenberg (1978), the dorsal noradrenergic bundle yields "reward" on stimulation, but the ventral bundle does not. (However, see Stein 1977.) Fibers of both of these systems travel with dopaminergic fibers in the MFB, those of LC having extraordinarily wide distribution.

Besides descending projections to the cord, the LC sends fibers to the dorsomedial, periventricular, paraventricular and supraoptic nuclei in the hypothalamus. LC fibers also project to the amygdala, hippocampus, septum, the cingulum bundle, external capsule[2] and the olfactory nuclei. Turning caudally, they reach the fornix, stria medullaris and stria terminalis. LC fibers also "reach all of the neocortex." (Moore 1977.)

The total cell population of the locus coeruleus is estimated at 20-30,000 neurons per side (Nauta and Feirtag 1986; Scheibel 1987b), making it extraordinarily small relative to the numbers of neurons whose activity it is likely to influence. Unlike those of the medullary n. gigantocellularis, the somata of LC neurons are not exceptionally large, a feature which, along with their small numbers, argues against their having major driving or pre-emptive functions in areas to which they project.

Their very wide distribution, along with that of fibers of the dorsal and median raphé nuclei, suggests that a principal function these two systems may be the joint maintenance of what I have called ground-states, i.e., they may act homeostatically to maintain the forebrain "climates" characteristic of normal waking (chapter 11); or during sleep, may figure in the periodic alternance of slow-wave and REM stages, whose homeostatic functions were outlined in chapter 5.

A related synergy is suggested by the fact that noradrenergic and serotonergic afferents converge on "a restricted region," the zona limitans of the dentate gyrus. (Moore 1977; see also Winson 1982.) This convergence may be functionally quite significant, given the role of the dentate gyrus in the temporal-hippocampal circuit mediating one type of LTM formation in man, as well as the role which has been inferred for noradrenergic arousal, e.g., in context-cued recall (Sara 1985), or in reinforcement responses leading to memory formation (Stein 1977). In other words, during aminergic arousal, a shift in the balance of NE and 5-HT inputs (in favor of NE) may act to favor participation of the dentate gyrus in the memory-forming process.

The third noradrenergic system (Lindvall and Björklund 1974) has dorsal and ventral divisions which project rostrally in the dorsal longitudinal fasciculus of Schütz (whose origin in the dorsal tegmental nucleus is mentioned above). This system, evidently *en passant*, receives input from the periaqueductal and periventricular gray. The dorsal division of

Schütz's fasciculus reaches the pretectal area, habenula, and midline and medial nuclei of the thalamus; the ventral division reaches the dorsomedial hypothalamus, and from there sends a second set of projections to the midline and medial thalamic nuclei.

Epinephrinergic fiber systems appear to have a more restricted distribution. Hökfelt et al. (1985) mention two major E-cell groups in the medulla and caudal pons. Some E fibers travel in the central tegmental tract and in the MFB, the latter group "innervating primarily the periventricular regions such as the periaqueductal central gray and various hypothalamic nuclei—for example, the paraventricular and the dorsomedial nuclei. The most rostral fibers are found around the olfactory ventricle and medial to the anterior olfactory nucleus."

E neurons occur in "the dorsal vagal complex,[3] with the majority of cell bodies in the solitary tract nucleus." They also occur in the retina, along with amacrines of several other types (chapter 14). Descending E-fibers of the dorsal lateral funiculus "innervate almost exclusively the lateral sympathetic column." (Hökfelt et al., 1985.)

EMERGENCY FUNCTIONS OF N.GIGANTOCELLULARIS: RETICULAR ORGANIZATION

The reticular n. gigantocellularis of the medial medulla, appears to play an important part in pain and escape reactions. For example, Casey and Jones report that in the awake, active cat "pain related behavior has been directly correlated with the activity" of single units in this nucleus; they note also that Olds and Olds (1963) and others have "consistently found" stimulation of the midbrain RF to be aversive (Casey and Jones 1980).

In that it is capable of mediating extremely quick emergency responses, the n. gigantocellularis suggests a rough homology with the Mauthner cell fast-response system in teleosts. When activated by pain stimuli, its rostral output parallels, and may act collaterally to augment, nociceptive responses mediated, e.g., by concurrent spinothalamic input to rostral and lateral areas of the central gray. (Kerr 1980. The periaqueductal system described by that author, and by Nauta and Feirtag 1986, includes a more medial, more caudally-lying division, stimulation of which produces analgesia—a counter-response mechanism, evidently entrained by primary pain or discomfort. For contrecoup effects of the same type, involving the β-endorphin responses found to accompany "orienting," see chapter 12.)

Over pathways of the classical RAS, n. gigantocellularis may act as a major "booster" system, amplifying reticulocortical input to the point that, in extreme pain or fear, higher-level control of behavior is effectively disrupted. A mechanism of this kind is perhaps the basis of Denenberg's observation that behavioral efficiency tends to be an inverted U function of the level of central activation. (chapter 11 and Appendix.)

The net result of massive two-way output from this medullary level may then be to cause release of fight-or-flight mechanisms of the brainstem, and simultaneously to activate parts of the spinal reticulomotor apparatus likely to figure in the corresponding behavior.

In fact, the axons of some of these large medullary neurons bifurcate into rostral and caudal segments. One of these is shown in material presented by the Scheibels (1958; p. 46, figure 12). Both segments emit collaterals to the adjacent RF. The caudal segment collateralizes to n. gracilis (hence modulating sensory input), and apparently terminates in the ventral horn. The rostral segment sends collaterals to the RF and periaqueductal gray, and terminal branches to the ventromedian hypothalamus (associated with "stop" functions in the stimulation and ablation literature), the zona incerta, and several nonspecific thalamic nuclei including CM.

It might be noted, in this connection, that paleospinothalamic projections from the cord reportedly reach centralis lateralis, parafascicularis and lateral DM, but not CM (Kerr 1980). In contrast, n. gigantocellularis provides "direct excitatory input" to thalamic nonspecific nuclei, in particular to parafascicularis, but also to CM—a nucleus providing access to the extrapyramidal system (Casey and Jones 1980). Such access perhaps represents the priority often given lower-level systems during behavior arising out of intense fear or pain. The connections of CM may be significant here; for while it receives input from motor cortex and from the globus pallidus (via the ansa lenticularis), it projects "mainly to the putamen" but not back to motor cortex (Nauta and Feirtag 1986).

N. gigantocellularis has descending projections to the cord which are "known to influence spinal reflex and motor function" (Casey and Jones 1980). Parvocellular portions of the lateral medullary RF have connections with this nucleus (making the relation bidirectional).

Spinoreticular fibers project to the mesencephalic central gray. The latter in turn projects to the midbrain RF and (via the dorsal longitudinal fasciculus of Schütz), to the dorsal and posterior hypothalamus, the zona incerta of the subthalamus, and to the midline and intralaminar nn. in the thalamus (Casey and Jones 1980), thus overlapping reticular projections to the same areas.

This type of circuitry, in which the ascending RF sends input to, and, at the same or higher levels, receives input from, systems such as the periaqueductal and periventricular gray, suggests an amplifying system, the activity of whose circuits is very readily perturbed by any change in the existing pattern of exteroceptive or interoceptive inputs. The extreme of this perturbability is then exemplified by inputs, e.g., from the substantia gelatinosa, which activate magnocellular assemblies lying at the base of the system as a whole. Such assemblies, in effect, represent its reserve driving-capacity.

Precisely because the RF—defined by Bishop (1958) as a "linked system running throughout the length of the neuraxis"—has retained something of the diffuse character of primitive nerve-nets, it has the multi-modal sentry functions and the capacity for massive central nervous activation we find in higher vertebrates today. Although regionally differentiated, as in LC, the raphé nuclei or the ventral tegmental area, it remains a system whose functions are essentially modulatory, and in that sense, vehicular. It supports or regulates functions, many or most of which it could not handle unaided.

The *range* of these vehicular functions, from maximally to minimally dynamogenic, is illustrated by the contrast between functions of n. gigantocellularis and those of the structures just mentioned. Nauta and Feirtag (1986) describe LC as "a caricature of the reticular formation" embodying "the extreme expression of a prominent reticular trait, an apparent diffuseness and nonspecificity of synaptic connections." The same nonspecificity seems to be characteristic of its transmitter, norepinephrine.

The norepinephrinergic system represented by LC, although there is evidence to indicate its entrainment along with other NE projection systems during massive activation, appears in itself only moderately dynamogenic. (Its joint action, with the dorsal and median raphé nuclei in the maintenance of forebrain "climactic" or normal baseline states is discussed in chapter 11.)

Whereas the rostrally running 5-HT system is similarly diffuse, its caudally running projections appear to be more differentiated. In the cord, 5-HT innervation appears to be inhibitory for sensory input via the dorsal horn but facilitatory for units of the ventral horn (Aghajanian 1987). The latter function is possibly related to the antiquity of excitatory serotonergic transmission, for instance as described in Aplysia by Kandel and Schwartz (1985).

If, as seems justified on various grounds, we regard the ventral tegmentum (VTA) as a differentiation of the RF, it is clear that (in comparison to the rostrally running NE and 5-HT projection systems) the dopaminergic projections of the VTA are the most selective—witness the distribution of DA terminals or receptors in parts of the striatum, the limbic system and in frontal (but not posterior) cortex. A further, quite remarkable, quite unreticular feature of the DA system is the diurnal stability in output rate of ventral tegmental neurons. Taken together with the narrow range of burst-frequencies these units show when excited, this seems to say that at the level of the caudal midbrain, the motivational system is the least perturbable of any. (The details of this surprising finding and its implications are discussed in chapter 11.)

OVERVIEW: ANTERIOR LIMBIC STRUCTURES

Perhaps the most striking feature of the limbic system is its Wheatstone bridgelike structure. Beginning with the lateral olfactory stria, which distribute to the amygdala, and the medial stria, which distribute to the septum, it is as though action-related switching functions of the amygdala (chapter 8) were systematically balanced off against sensory recording-related functions of the hippocampal-septal system.

This primary arrangement suggests a functional relationship that is synergic but also, under appropriate conditions, competitive. As described in chapter 8, these relations are mirrored in the functional differences between frontal and posterior distal association cortex, as well as in the projections of the amygdala to anterior cingulate, and those of the subicular area to posterior cingulate cortex. And in the anterior forebrain area, which by phylogeny was concerned primarily with olfactorily guided behavior, output of the amygdala, hippocampus, and frontal association areas converges on a primary motor structure, the nucleus accumbens.

Likewise, the amygdala, hippocampus and septum have reciprocal connections with substantia innominata—the hippocampus and septum by way of the diagonal band. The substantia innominata, including the nucleus basalis, also receives input from n. accumbens. N. accumbens projects to the hypothalamus, the ventral globus pallidus, the substantia nigra, and via the medial forebrain bundle (MFB) to the ventral tegmental area.

The substantia innominata projects to the hypothalamus, to mesencephalic and pontine motor areas, and (via n. basalis of Meynert) to large areas of neocortex. The ventral GP, besides having reciprocal connections with the amygdala, projects to the subthalamus and provides some of the output carried by the stria medullaris.

As already mentioned, the stria medullaris receives other input from the septum, lateral hypothalamus, anterior perforated substance and the nucleus of the diagonal band. It projects to the habenula which, via the fasciculus retroflexus, reaches the interpeduncular nucleus. By Ganser's tract, fibers from this nucleus project to the mesencephalic raphé.

Because of these connections, some of whose functional implications are discussed elsewhere here, Nauta and Feirtag (1986) have suggested that the ventral GP be regarded as forming part of a "limbic striatum" or motor system. We should also recall that the hippocampus, besides its reciprocal connections with the nucleus of the diagonal band and septum, projects (via the post-commissural fornix) to the mammillary bodies. The latter project caudally to "small" medial nuclei of the caudal midbrain tegmentum, and rostrally, to the anterior thalamic nuclei which, in turn, project to posterior cingulate cortex, not to area 24, as was formerly thought. (Vogt, Rosene and Pandya 1979.)

The following are some of the features that warrant our regarding the ventral tegmental area of Tsai and the web olfacto-hypothalamic structures just described as motivational, or indeed, as a *system*.

At both ends it contains subsystems related to feeding or (in the case of the septum) rage reactions (Sweet 1980) or sexual behavior (Lilly 1959). Its ancestral relation to olfaction, rostrally, is reflected caudally, in its apparently close relations with the nucleus of the solitary tract, and hence with gustation. (Crosby et al. 1962.) Norgren (1977) notes that the locus coeruleus and the pontine taste area are very close to each other in the dorsolateral pons, and give rise to remarkably similar ascending pathways. Fibers of both types travel in the dorsal noradrenergic bundle (of Ungerstedt) and evidently have overlapping distribution, e.g., in the central nucleus of the amygdala, the bed nucleus of the stria terminalis and the substantia innominata.

Finally, along the length of the limbic-mesolimbic system, self-stimulation studies at a number of sites have given maximal response-rates, suggesting that this system also mediates internal states equivalent to intense pleasure or satisfaction. While some of the highest rates have been obtained from tegmental core-structures, very high rates have also been elicited from the MFB or its continuation in the lateral hypothalamic-preoptic area, notably n. supraopticus. These are hypothalamic areas that Hess long ago classed as trophotropic (Hess 1954); they are functionally related to what I have defined (in chapter 11) as normal maintenance activities. That most of these should involve an inner climate equivalent to "reward" seems only logical.

In more rostral olfactory-system structures, n. accumbens and the diagonal band were found by Olds and Olds (1963) to give moderately strong, mixed (~4:1, 3:1) reward/escape ratios. Nauta and Feirtag (1986) report that the substantia innominata has been found to yield "reward" responses. Apropos of the connections between the nucleus accumbens and the amygdala, hippocampus and frontal cortex, data presented by Iversen (and reviewed in the chapter which follows) lead her to conclude that n. accumbens may be "a core structure in the generation of central motivational states." (Iversen 1986.)

Given that the substantia innominata reaches large areas of neocortex via cholinergic projections of the nucleus basalis and is evidently of critical importance to human mental functions, we might also surmise that it represents a core structure in the generation of centrally motivated cognitive processes.

The chapter which follows concerns that question.

CHAPTER 10

The Reticular and Olfacto-Cortical Projection Systems; N. Basalis, the Nucleus of the Diagonal Band and N. Accumbens; N. Basalis and the RF as Complementary; Recapitulation

THE RETICULAR AND OLFACTO-CORTICAL PROJECTION-SYSTEMS

Jefferson's (1958) observation that ischemic lesions involving the diagonal band and substantia innominata can mimic the effects of damage to the central activating system suggests the obvious conclusion that the two projection systems are complementary. The reticular formation contains cholinergic cell groups which may figure both in cortical activation via the nonspecific thalamic nuclei, and in modulation of cortical and limbic activity via structures of the basal forebrain.

Scheibel (1987b) notes that the core RF contains ascending "ACh-rich" systems. The nucleus cuneiformis of the dorsal midbrain projects to the tectum, thalamus and globus pallidus, the latter projecting in turn to the pedunculopontine nucleus (Nauta 1986). These nuclei form part of the brainstem Ch5 system described by Mesulam (1987). More ventrally-lying cholinergic cell groups of the mesencephalic and pontine RF reportedly reach the thalamus, hypothalamus and basal forebrain—a system including the nucleus basalis, and the septum and diagonal band (which have cholinergic projections to the hippocampus).

It is worth noting that the cuneiform nucleus is in fact a region extending from the lower border of the inferior colliculus to the rostral border of the superior colliculus. Medially it is bordered by the periaqueductal gray, and laterally by the medial lemniscus. It is essentially parvocellular, with a magnocellular area, the subcuneiform nucleus, lying ventral to it. The tegmental pedunculopontine nucleus lies ventral to both, and as noted receives return projections from the pallidum. (Crosby, Humphrey and Lauer 1962.)

These details suggest a typical reticular structure having collateral inputs (e.g. from the medial lemniscus), a magnocellular "effector" division, and very probably bidirectional outputs, to the forebrain and cord.

Scheibel (1987) distinguishes a dorsal and a ventral leaf of the ascending RF. The first projects to the nonspecific thalamic nuclei, including the nucleus reticularis, which appears to have global influence intrathalamically (Nauta 1986). The ventral leaf projects via the subthalamus and parts of the dorsolateral hypothalamus, to the septum and basal forebrain.

The significant point here is that projections of the brainstem Ch5-Ch6 RF reach the nonspecific thalamic nuclei, and also structures such as the diagonal band and the nucleus basalis. This branching of its lines of influence means that the RF can affect cortical activity both directly (via the thalamus) or indirectly, by modulation of cholinergic cortical input from the nucleus basalis. The same arrangement may also make possible the global "override" functions of the reticular system discussed in the next chapter.

An estimated 90% of nucleus basalis units are cholinergic. (Mesulam 1987.) DM and VL in the thalamus are noradrenergic, the intralaminar nuclei dopaminergic (Nauta 1979). Frontal cortex contains both noradrenergic (NA) and dopaminergic (DA) fibers, the former being thicker and having more pronounced beadlike swellings. DA fibers are thinner and "more sinuous." (Routtenberg 1978.)

NA fibers are reported to have more even frontal distribution, both by area and by layer. DA units, in contrast, are concentrated in medial and sulcal frontal cortex, and in "islands" of entorhinal cortex, all of these being areas from which "reward" responses are obtainable. (Routtenberg 1978.) Iversen (1986) notes that frontal DA neurons have been found to lack autoreceptors. Since the latter may mediate negative feedback via transmitter reuptake, the lack of autoreceptors may be a feature conducive to the "driving" of frontal units during high-level excitatory states. In turn, this might be a feature consonant with the reported role of frontal DA units in avoidance conditioning (during reactivation of such CR's, or during their formation). They are also reportedly activated by stress produced by (unavoidable) foot-shock (Roth 1984).

Bloom (1981) reviews evidence indicating that in rat frontal cortex, β-adrenergic receptors are concentrated in layer II, with "dopaminergic responses predominating in deeper layer V test cells." Peterson also reports that DA neurons are found in the deeper layers of frontal cortex and figure in learned avoidance responses (Peterson 1985). In cingulate cortex, according to Moore, DA projections are "limited to" layers II-III (Moore 1977). Bloom cites single unit studies showing that locus coeruleus stimulation resulted in post-stimulus inhibition of about 50% of all cingulate neurons tested. Other workers reported noradrenergic innervation preferentially in posterior cingulate cortex, and similar innervation for the anterior thalamic nuclei.

This finding is consistent with an important discovery reported by Vogt, Rosene, and Pandya (1979)—namely that, in the monkey, only posterior cingulate cortex receives projections of the anterior thalamic nuclei. Area 24, by contrast, receives most of its thalamic input from the midline and intralaminar nuclei, and afferents as well from the basolateral amygdala. Posterior cingulate cortex receives fibers from the "subicular division" of the hippocampus. Area 24, the amygdala, and the midline and intralaminar nuclei have relatively high affinities for binding opiates.

Routtenberg's report of the laminar distribution of frontal NA fibers appears to conflict with other studies showing a "strong tangential orientation" of noradrenergic afferents in layers I and VI of neocortex, a pattern "common to most cortical areas" (Bloom, 1981). This distribution, it should be remarked, is the same as that described in the older literature as characteristic of the nonspecific cortical projection-system. (Lorente de Nó 1951.)

Noradrenergic fibers of the locus coeruleus, as mentioned in the previous chapter, project widely in neocortex, but whether the laminar distribution of these fibers differs from that of fibers of the classical nonspecific system, and if so, how and in what cortical areas, is, I believe, not yet known. Such differences could, however, account for the apparent discrepancy between the reports of Routtenberg and of Bloom just cited.

N. BASALIS, THE NUCLEUS OF THE DIAGONAL BAND AND N. ACCUMBENS

Recent evidence suggests that these three structures, essentially of the primary olfactory system (Pribram and Kruger 1954) may be as important as the amygdalar and hippocampal-septal systems in the regulation of adaptive behavior.

Iversen reports that in the rat, 6-OH-dopamine lesions to n. accumbens result in a "profound disorder" of the hoarding behavior which these animals normally show when exposed, after a period of deprivation, to ample food supplies. The disorder evidently manifests itself as a generally low level of "motivational arousal"—the animals, during food hoarding, performing "sloppily," as if unable to keep their minds on the task. She notes that these results are not obtained from similar lesions to A9 dopaminergic units of the nigrostriatal system (Iversen 1986).

N. accumbens has powerful connections with the basolateral amygdala and thus, via these nuclei, presumably with cingulate area 24. Apropos of the functional relation of the limbic system with distal association cortex (Graybiel 1974), Iversen points out that those parts of the striatum which have connections to sensorimotor cortex are "conspicuously devoid" of projections from the amygdala. In turn, this underscores Nauta's differentiation of "limbic" striatum (Figure 2a) from nonlimbic (Nauta and Feirtag 1986).

As mentioned, Iversen concludes that n. accumbens is a "core structure in the generation of central motivational states." As such, it appears to be responsible for "organized motor behavior," including exploration, responses to "contact stimuli," and consummatory acts. A part of the reason for this central influence lies in the connections of this nucleus with the substantia innominata.

The latter, as noted, has been reported to give "reward" responses. Some of its large cells are evidently interposed between the external and internal pallidal segments, and between the external GP and the putamen. These cells nonetheless appear to be "physiologically distinct" (Nauta and Feirtag 1979), a conclusion supported by the post mortem findings of Coyle et al. (1985) in five patients with Alzheimer's disease. (There were "no consistent" changes in cell density in parts of the pallidum examined. The nucleus of the diagonal band showed some losses, the greatest losses, outside of n. basalis, being in the cortex and hippocampus.)

N. BASALIS AND THE RF AS COMPLEMENTARY

The nucleus basalis of the substantia innominata contains "the largest magnocellular group found at the base of the forebrain." (Nauta and Feirtag 1986.) The nucleus of the diagonal band, although smaller, also contains very large cells. Both structures are cholinergic. Indeed, they provide the neocortex its "only known source of cholinergic afferentation." (Nauta and Feirtag 1986; p. 243; Price 1985.) Davies (1985) describes them as supplying "about 80%" of cholinergic input to the neocortex and hippocampus. Apparently the connections are not reciprocal; there is no direct cortico-subcortical feedback.

Note also that the output of these large-celled units to the neocortex probably represents great presynaptic convergence—implying considerable "integration" of inputs and consequent loss of information. Thus what was found true of nonspecific (reticulocortical) input in the 1960s may, with some qualification, also prove true of cortical input from the nucleus basalis.

The "fairly orderly" topographic projections of n. basalis (Nauta and Feirtag 1986) may mediate effects, selective for certain cortical sectors and corresponding to certain basal "motivational" states. One way to conceptualize this influence would be to see it as a succession of cortical "high-

lighting" effects that shift as behavior itself unfolds, and are comple-
mented by inhibitory "contrast" effects resulting, e.g. from concurrent
dopaminergic or noradrenergic input.

Such a mechanism would have obvious utility. By selectively facilitating
those cortical sectors most likely to be implicated in a given class of
adaptive behavior or a given train of specific actions, it would accomplish,
in effect, two things. In psychological terms, it would establish the outer
boundaries of an attentional field (shifting these, as behavior and its
consequences developed). And in proportion as the aminergic activating
systems participated (see below), the resulting combination of inputs
might be conducive to the early "sensitization" phase of learning.

As described in chapters 6 and 13, that phase perhaps corresponds to a
type of generalized or wide-focus learning which in general may serve as a
precursor to more focal learning. In those chapters, I have reviewed
evidence suggesting that when the task presented was beyond the organism's capabilities, the result was either a failure or an actual loss of learning
at the focus, and a broadening of sensitization. The latter then took the
form of a strong primitive undifferentiated response, triggered by a variety of CS's equivalent to peripheral features of the learning situation.

Such a mechanism (which conceivably figures in some floating anxiety
or chronic phobic reactions in man) represents an exaggeration of the
early "contextual" stage of learning. This stage, taking the (usually transi-
tory) form of a "novelty" response, is perhaps initially mediated by forebrain noradrenergic input and the corresponding states of arousal. Under
normal conditions, such learning may persist sufficiently, as generalized
"savings," to provide a basis for cue-facilitated or context-dependent recall.
(Sara 1985; Deweer and Sara 1985; Mactutus and Wise 1985.)

One of these investigators (Sara) presented evidence suggesting that this
type of contextual recall depends critically on forebrain noradrenergic
input from the locus coeruleus, adding that in patients with Alzheimer's
disease (AD), the LC was found to be involved. However, Coyle, Price and
DeLong (1985) report that the locus coeruleus "remains relatively intact"
in patients who have died with the senile form of AD. These authors
suggest that LC degeneration may be a concomitant of an earlier onset
form of the disease, of possibly different etiology. Hence memory deficits
in the more elderly AD cases must evidently have had other origins.

More to the point, what we refer to as states of arousal may always have a
conjoint origin. So damage to one transmitter-system may impair arousal
responses and related functions—for instance memory-formation—and
still not be *the* system responsible for those functions.

The reticular formation of the brainstem has long been supposed to
control the level of general activity of the cortex. The tendency of the
inhibition-to-excitation ratio to increase as the central activation level is
raised was suggested as a general principle by Purpura (1959). A number

of studies at the time showed that reticular stimulation acts to increase "contrast" or perceptual resolution (Brooks 1963; Fuster 1961; Lindsley 1958).

What has only recently become apparent is that cortical activation may involve a major cholinergic component whose effect is chiefly excitatory. Desmedt cites data which indicate that "cerebral arousal" may be "associated with a diffuse muscarinic action" arising, in part, in n. basalis. He reviews other data indicating that ACh effects are mediated intracellularly via cyclic GMP, and are facilitatory (for pyramidal neurons, in the rat), whereas norepinephrine effects are mediated by cyclic AMP, and inhibitory. (Desmedt 1981. See also Stone, Taylor, and Bloom 1975.)

Krnjević (1964) published a report concerning the areal and laminar distribution of "cholinoceptive" neurons in cat neocortex. While many of these cells were found "in or near primary afferent regions," particularly the visual or somatosensory, he concluded that "they are certainly not restricted in their regional localization."

"Within any one area" (the report continues) "the sensitive cells seem to occur in small groups ... One of the clearest characteristics of the cholinoceptive cells is that they occur very rarely within about 0.8 mm. of the surface; they are especially concentrated in a relatively narrow zone between 0.8 and about 1.3 mm, corresponding approximately to the fourth and fifth cortical layers, but many are also seen deeper." (Krnjević 1964, pp. 78-79.)

These findings have as yet not been duplicated in primates, in the sense that "intrinsic" cholinergic neurons have not been found in neocortex. Mesulam (1987) notes that in the rat, "at least 70% of the cortical cholinergic innervation is extrinsic." He adds that the nucleus basalis is "phylogenetically progressive," being maximally developed in cetacea and primates. These observations are interesting, in that they suggest an evolutionary trend the reverse of that represented by telencephalization in general.

The implied synergy of ACh and catecholamines in producing cortical arousal may be most important, since it may represent a mechanism underlying the generation of motivational states generally. An example would be the "motivational arousal" mentioned by Iversen (1986), in which the primary aminergic component appears to be dopamine, but which (via the projections of n. accumbens to the substantia innominata) presumably involves a frontal cholinergic component as well.

As I will presently try to make clear, the relations between these major transmitter-systems are not as clearcut as the foregoing might suggest. The underlying reason is that central activation is itself a portmanteau phenomenon; beside its dopaminergic component, corresponding to various types of "motivational arousal," there is perhaps always a leading-edge noradrenergic (-adrenergic) component (chapter 11).

The latter is guaranteed by the neuroanatomy of the brainstem, and its function is perhaps not merely dynamogenic. It may have important veto-powers as well. Its inclusion, as a supporting element in (often quite specialized) forms of "motivated" behavior, may serve to make these readily convertible into more primitive fight-or-flight responses, as circumstances may dictate (chapter 11).

The levels to which central activation levels may be raised will depend in part on the anticipated energy demands of incipient or ongoing behavior. To the extent that such anticipation is learned, it will tend to involve distal association areas of frontal and posterior cortex, the limbic system, and related structures of the caudal midbrain. (However there is evidence to suggest that in thoroughly learned or habitual responses, there is some disengagement of association cortex from participation in the response. See chapter 13).

In other words, the substantia innominata and the aminergic brainstem systems may be complementary in that the aminergic systems provide the cortex an input in which the proportion of inhibitory to excitatory activity increases as some function of the level of arousal. Within that framework, the cholinergic projections of the nucleus basalis may then provide a more largely facilitatory input which, being topographically organized (Nauta 1986), tends to be selective for certain cortical sectors. Nor need the sequence occur in that order. Either input-system may be capable of "calling" the other.

The important point is that it may be the areas of overlap of these two types of input which set up the boundary-conditions for more focal activity arising in the cortex itself. This is perhaps an essential reason why input of the nucleus basalis has been found to be as necessary as input of the classical RAS, to the maintenance of normal cortical functions.

Electrophysiological studies of the orienting reflex (OR) and of so-called event-related potentials (ERP's) suggest that the more usual sequence involves a leading edge of aminergic activation (roughly equivalent to the N100) and a trailing edge of cholinergic activation (roughly equivalent to the P300). If these slow potential events are followed, over post-stimulus intervals ranging from 400 msec (Skrandies et al. 1984, p. 273) to 4 sec (Deecke et al. 1984, p. 461), they clearly suggest a damped oscillation.

The further suggestion is that the two subcortical input systems represented by these sequences of surface-negative and surface-positive potentials may show this form of oscillatory interaction continuously, although the relation may only become obvious (readable in the EEG) under stimulus conditions which exaggerate it sufficiently to make it stand out from the background electrical noise.

It is probably unnecessary to point out that these slow potential changes are distinct from the shorter-latency primary positive potentials associated with inputs via the specific thalamocortical projection system to post central cortex or areas 17 or 41–42. Nor need I mention that they may include a tonic component, such as the CNV (contingent negative variation) often accompanying expectancy, or the *Bereitschaftspotential,* a slow-going surface-negative shift reported to precede an intended motor activity by ≈800 msec (Kristeva 1984).

That surface-negative shifts such as the N100 represent aminergic reticulocortical input is implied by several lines of evidence. As mentioned in chapter 3, Taylor and Stone (1981) report that NA fibers of LC have wide cortical distribution, but "with some predominance in the outer molecular layers." The classical account of nonspecific projection fibers describes them as principally reaching layers I and VI (Lorente de Nó 1951). Input via this fiber system could therefore be expected to result in negative-going potentials in the EEG.

Positive-going surface potentials imply focal activity in the cortical mid-layers, as illustrated by the primary positive response of specific sensory receiving cortex, reflecting focal activity in IV-lower III. The P300 epoch may consequently represent further processing of an input, e.g., in association cortex, with possibly concomitant STM formation.

These relations are rather strikingly paralleled in psychophysical experiments reported by Weichselgartner and Sperling (1987). Subjects were shown a stream of 25 numerals, displayed for 18 msec each, at intervals of 10–12.5 msec. A target numeral, highlighted or enclosed in a square, was randomly embedded in the sequence. The Ss' problem was to recall (and write down, at the end of the display period) the target and the next three numerals.

The authors report that "most numerals were recalled from two separated periods in time, the first mode between 0 and 100 msec after presentation, the second mode between 300 and 400 msec after target presentation." These were called "first glimpse" and "second glimpse" recall, respectively. Recall of the "critical numeral" (the target) was good (p > 0.9). This "first glimpse" recall was described by subjects as "effortless," whereas "second glimpse" recall, occurring at 300–400 msec, "required effort."

Note that first and second glimpse recall occurred in epochs roughly corresponding to the N100 and P300 epochs reported by encephalographers, and that these, in turn, may correspond to the aminergic-cholinergic sequence of subcortico-cortical input which I have proposed as a mechanism establishing the basic conditions of attention in the cortex.

The early aminergic component, resulting in "effortless" (automatic) registration of the critical numeral, may be taken as a prototype of the primacy effects seen in serial learning. In raising the level of facilitatory and inhibitory activity in the cortex, the RAS is acting in its "dynamogenic" role—as an external power source. By contrast, the cholinergic component, being perhaps more largely facilitatory, is more "permissive"; it does not add to the inhibitory tightening of ongoing activity. It corresponds to a further processing stage in which registration demands conscious effort—meaning that in this stage, the cortex is left to finish its own work. (See Desmedt 1981, for a similar interpretation of the P300.)

Repetition of this experiment with concurrent recording of the EEG should produce findings of considerable interest. For example, subjects expecting to see the target numeral should exhibit a corresponding CNV which, in proportion to its amplitude and duration, should facilitate registration by carry-over of activation into the "second glimpse" stage. In fact, the experimenters report that when the target occurred late in the numeral stream, "second glimpse responses sped up with this increased expectancy; first glimpse responses were unaffected."

If, as proposed here, the second glimpse or P300 stage reflects input from the nucleus basalis, such input, by definition, involves a limbic or "motivational" component. It has been shown that if a perceptual event is accompanied by a payoff, even a modest one (in the case reported, it was 25 or 50 cents), the P300 is significantly increased in amplitude (Sutton and Ruchkin 1984). Deficits both in the P300 and in slow negative waves, have been reported in schizophrenics. Similar findings for clinically normal subjects classed as "anhedonic" are reported by Miller et al. (1984)

The cerebral vascular correlates of these psychophysical events would presumably resemble those reported for human subjects by Lassen, Ingvar and Skinhøj (1978). In general, areal bloodflow changes may tend to become increasingly focal, as sequential (aminergic-cholinergic) activation results in development of specific foci of cortical activity. At those foci, the vascular concomitants may themselves become more sharply localized, e.g., as a result of the intracolumnar synaptic release of VIP. (Emson and Hunt 1981. See chapter 2.)

RECAPITULATION

The foregoing amounts to a conceptual model of the sequence of events hypothetically involved when the cortex "focuses down," or "decides" what to attend to next. According to this model, a (chiefly facilitatory) cholinergic, and a (mixed, facilitatory-inhibitory) aminergic input-system determine, by their degree of areal overlap, which cortical sectors are mobilized, e.g., as the organism monitors its environment or commences the learning or carrying out of a particular train of actions. The final stage in focussing down may then, under most conditions, be left to the cortex.

(I am here overlooking the reciprocal aspect of this process, by which outflows from the cortex, e.g., to limbic and extrapyramidal systems, may shape concurrent activity at those levels. In fact, much central nervous activity seems to involve multiple recursive processes of this type—in effect, the circular computation of N interdependent variables, where N is very large and the degrees of interdependence, like N itself, cannot be specified).

The model just outlined, though obviously oversimplified, suggests a similar scheme of relationships, according to which the cortex and limbic system structures are influenced from the medullary, pontine and meso-limbic levels, over pathways described in chapter 11.

Forebrain Outputs of the Brainstem; Level One: The Ponto-Bulbar-Caudal Mesencephalic; Normal Maintenance Versus Emergency Functions; First-Line Emergency Responses; The Second-Line (Major) Emergency System; Locus Coeruleus and the 5-HT System of the Raphé; Locus Coeruleus: Major and Minor Afferents; The Mesolimbic Dopaminergic Projection System

FOREBRAIN OUTPUTS OF THE BRAINSTEM

In the brainstem, we may define three levels, distinguishable according to the ways in which their rostral output affects activity in the neocortex. The first level is the ponto-medullary, the second the mesolimbic, and the third the limbic-hypothalamic.

In chapter 10 we considered the sort of input the cortex "sees" as a result of input from n. basalis, that nucleus and n. accumbens being anterior olfactory-system structures which are themselves projection areas of more basal brainstem systems. What these nuclei "see" is consequently a complex resultant of inputs which (on the basis of anatomic and physiological evidence reviewed in chapter 9) can be inferred to represent the organism's *milieu interieur*—essentially, its drive- or motivational- or comfort-discomfort states of the moment.

Arising in the second (mesolimbic) tier, the crude information as to such states is then passed into the Wheatstone bridge-like structures of the third tier. Some of these data may be handled mainly by the hypothalamus, resulting in adjustments of the kind called homeostatic or "vegetative"—adjustments superimposed on those (such as respiratory or cardiovascular controls) mediated from the medulla.

Data not suited to this sort of automatic handling are more likely to enter the several loops that connect frontal and posterior (distal association) cortex with limbic structures and the hypothalamus. Such loops, in effect, bring to bear the most detailed information the organism may have on file, relating either to the learned significance of a given sensory input (posterior cortical?) or to the learned behavioral sequences it is likely to call for (frontal?), or both.

The sensory input referred to in this case is chiefly of internal origin, but is also co-ordinated automatically with inputs arising externally at the same time. The latter would include information relayed from distance- or body-surface receptors, and from the proprioceptive and vestibular systems. These represent parallel input lines, reaching the cortex via the specific and nonspecific (reticulocortical) projection systems.

The specific system is not only the newest, phylogenetically, but as compared to the limbic or reticular systems, the most motivationally or affectively neutral. This appears to be shown by the relative paucity of sites in it yielding "reward" or "escape" reactions, and the relatively low opioid concentrations found in prime receiving areas or in the specific projection nuclei in primates (Pert 1980).

On the cortical output side, we should note two pathways—the orbitofrontal, representing the only direct cortical projections to the hypothalamus (Nauta and Feirtag 1986); and cortical outflows to the extrapyramidal system (e.g. via the external capsule to the putamen), a part of which are then played back (via GP and the ansa lenticularis) to the thalamic VL-VA (motor) nuclei. The former outflows presumably relate to the organism's concurrent viscero-autonomic state, the latter to postural or readiness-to-act states.

The model outlined in chapter 10, involving the "steering" of attention by n. basalis, should consequently be made a recursive one, in which what the cortex "sees" in the way of input from the limbic system is partially the result of cortical output to the same system. The amount of information finally fed back over that loop is apt, however, to be small.

Essentially, what all such loops may involve is an iterative type of processing that serves several purposes at once. By an averaging down or smoothing of the transmitted data, it permits systems of very different internal complexity to communicate with each other. It reduces error through redundancy, and it accomplishes those final simplifications that may be necessary if higher-level cognitive processes are to eventuate in practicable orders to the skeletal musculature.

Thus cortical outflows, passing through the striatum and the pallidal "funnel" (Nauta 1979), and thence, in part, back to the cortex, might be supposed to act as a feedback trimming mechanism. Such a mechanism may not merely sharpen existing foci in motor cortex; its main function may be to simplify them—to impose innately determined constraints on incipient outputs of a higher-level, more complex system. The net result is to edit out details that the lower-level system cannot "see," and to increase (inhibitory) "contrast" for those it can. It is perhaps essentially by mechanisms of this kind that the cortex is prevented from issuing orders to the musculature that cannot be carried out.

Likewise, the relatively complex data which the cortex is capable of relaying to limbic structures, e.g. through "funnels" such as entorhinalis and the fornix system, may then interact, at several levels, with systems whose ascending inputs represent the organism's concurrent motivational state. The resultants of this interaction are then passed back, through the "funnel" of the nucleus basalis to the cortex itself.

As mentioned in chapter 10, the great convergence of inputs on that nucleus (e.g. from the septum, hippocampus, amygdala, and, via the MFB, from the ventral tegmentum), together with its magnocellular structure, imply a high degree of "integration" or loss of detail. In addition, its cortical projections, though reported to be more topographically organized than those of the noradrenergic systems, are cholinergic, and thus perhaps chiefly facilitatory (i.e. "permissive" rather than "restrictive").

What all this suggests is a guidance apparatus that allows the guided system considerable internal freedom—an arrangement of some adaptive value. For whereas the editing of motor outflows originating in higher-level systems may be a practical necessity, subcortical editing of the processes *leading* to those outflows should be only sufficient to keep them on track (i.e., adaptively relevant). Otherwise, lower-level control of higher-level activity could amount to functional decortication. (In fact, as will be discussed shortly, the lower brainstem contains a mechanism which on occasion can accomplish just that.)

So I have speculated that n. basalis may decide, in a general way, where the focus of cortical activity shall be, but not what shall be at it. The globus pallidus, by contrast, receives data from foci already existing, and may decide what shall be excluded from them. Lying on the sensory side, n. basalis establishes the conditions for processes which the cortex is left to complete; lying on the effector side, the extrapyramidal system imposes final conditions on some of the cortical effector outflows that result.

In that such recursive "integrating" or simplifying functions tend to confine forebrain attentional processes to the adaptively relevant and motor outflows to the physically possible, they perhaps represent a most basic principle of central nervous organization. Its prime exemplar is perhaps the cerebellum, a "time-chopping device" (Nauta and Feirtag 1986) whose major function may be to act as a simplifier of effector outputs handled minute to minute, *en bloc*. The evidence suggests that its influence reaches far into the forebrain, affecting sense reception, (Snider and Sato 1957) or by some reports, even memory processes. (Thompson 1986.)

It is tempting, and possibly heuristic, to suppose that the cerebellum acts as a universal translator. That is, its stereotyped structure may serve to reduce its diverse inputs to a relatively simple common-denominator code, making its corresponding outputs readable anywhere. If so, an understanding of that code would be a kind of passkey.

LEVEL ONE: THE PONTO-BULBAR-CAUDAL MESENCEPHALIC

A good deal of evidence suggests that structures of the caudalmost (first) tier are also those whose outputs have the most global effects in the cortex. I will call the corresponding states "climatic," meaning that they set the outermost boundary-conditions, equivalent to the constraints within which the other cortical processes described above must operate.

Structures chiefly implicated in establishing such "climatic" states appear to be n. gigantocellularis of the medial medulla, and the pontine and caudal mesencephalic projection systems of the locus coeruleus and the raphé nuclei.

In contrast to the latter systems, which have what one could call normal maintenance functions, as in the regulation of sleep cycles, n. gigantocellularis evidently figures in pain and escape responses (Casey and Jones 1980), and so has what can be called emergency dynamogenic functions. At neuraxial levels above the brainstem, perhaps particularly in the cortex, these emergency functions, mediated by the ascending RF, tend to include pro tem disabling (erase and reset) effects. This arrangement, in which reticular input ceases to have a "supporting" or synergic relation, e.g. to the cholinergic and dopaminergic cortical input-systems, is clearly related to certain principles upon which adaptive behavior seems to be organized.

NORMAL MAINTENANCE VERSUS EMERGENCY FUNCTIONS

There appear to be two major classes of adaptive behavior. The first includes actions or functions whose energy demands are graded, and which can therefore be anticipated, through natural selection, e.g. in the form of special consummatory mechanisms such as figure in mating, eating, or the killing of prey. Actions often connected with these—for instance, fighting among species members over food or mates—tend to be subject to innate constraints (Tinbergen 1951) which limit unadaptive side effects such as death or total exhaustion of the combatants.

Note that in contrast to consummatory behavior, which tends to be stereotyped, an animal's exploratory behavior is generally more unpredictable. (Tinbergen 1951.) In general, also, telencephalization appears to be most important to actions of this more flexible type. Hence the relation of exploratory behavior to "motivational arousal," which in turn is related to normal maintenance functions (such as feeding or mating) and mediated rostrally by n. accumbens, n. basalis, and projections of the latter to neocortex.

A second major class of behavior involves energy demands that cannot safely be provided for, except in the form of fast-acting, generalized mechanisms, calling upon whatever reserves of energy the organism has available. Behavior of this type includes actions arising in response to grave external threats or injury; and partly in the interests of speed, it tends to be extremely primitive. The latter result appears to be achieved via massive brainstem inputs to the forebrain, whose effect is temporarily to nullify higher-level behavioral controls.

In other words, there is one class of behavior (related to normal maintenance of the individual or the species) in which the organism can generally go at its own pace, in response to internal forces equivalent to its drive-state(s) of the moment. There is another class in which it cannot—in which the normal flux of motivational states is stopped short, and the pace of behavior begins to be forced from without.

Because, for most species in most habitats, unexpected external events have a nontrivial probability of being injurious, natural selection has provided two principal lines of defence against them. The first is preparatory—essentially a sentry system which treats *any* novelty as potentially dangerous. The second is a pre-emptive or override system, mobilized when sensory signs indicate that the danger is real.

FIRST-LINE EMERGENCY RESPONSES

Low-level (preparatory) emergency reactions take the form of the orienting reflex or what are called novelty responses. These work as if on the premise that any sufficiently sharp discontinuity in sensory input patterns may signal trouble, and must therefore command attention. As a system, par excellence, for the formation of "temporary connections" (Scheibel and Scheibel 1958), the reticular formation tends to lead in such responses, producing rises in central activation which are roughly a function of the amount and rate of change of sensory input patterns.

The forebrain recognition-systems may then act, in the way suggested by Sokolov (1960), to damp such arousal responses if it happens that the input changes triggering them correspond to recalled nonthreatening events. The important point is that novelty responses, though they can be damped, cannot really be precluded.

The tendency to treat any input change (above certain thresholds for intensity, type, and rate) as *potentially* dangerous appears to be built into lower-level core structures. In other words, besides their normal maintenance-of-consciousness functions, these act as a first-order sentry system. Consequently, novelty responses of some (graded) intensity tend to accompany even minor changes in sensory input configuration.

Hence the transient arousal apparently responsible for "primacy" effects in serial recall. (The first item in the series commands attention simply because it is first—because it marks a discontinuity.) At the cortical level, this process perhaps takes a biphasic form—aminergic activation evoking cholinergic contrecoup, both then setting the attentional field boundaries. (chapter 10.)

In other words, what gives those sense data preferred status in short-term memory, (as the initial items in a recalled sequence), may not *just* be aminergic activation but, via n. basalis, the synergic or sequential entrainment of cholinergic activation as well. This conclusion is suggested by the fact that whereas many studies have indicated that the catecholamines, including epinephrine (McGaugh 1985), play a role in memory formation, or that noradrenergic projection systems, for instance of the locus coeruleus (Sara 1985) figure in attentional mechanisms and retrieval. It has also been shown that scopolamine interferes with STM and mimics memory defects found in Alzheimer's patients (Coyle, Price, and DeLong 1985).

In human subjects, physostigmine, a cholinesterase inhibitor, did not significantly affect Digit Span (tested at 9 minutes, post-infusion). For a 15-item word list presented 30 minutes pre-infusion, and tested at 18 and 80 minutes post-, the testees' improvement in retention vs controls was nonsignificant at 18 minutes, but significant at 80 minutes. (Davis et al. 1978.)

Putting these ideas together, we might conceptualize STM formation, during serial recall tests, as beginning with a surge in aminergic input (the "orienting" phase of the response) followed by an answering rise in cholinergic input. Of these two "halves" of the synergy, the cholinergic may perhaps be the more important to maintenance (survival) of the corresponding short-term memories. But since some rise in aminergic input above normal waking-state levels may be necessary to trigger the whole sequence, and to a lesser extent may figure in its continuance, the two "halves" of the synergy may not really be separable.

The conclusion is that the low-level arousal produced by "novelties" and resulting in primacy effects, represents a first-line emergency response—the sentry system mentioned above.

THE SECOND-LINE (MAJOR) EMERGENCY SYSTEM

The second set of emergency responses comes into play when the organism is confronted by stimuli whose innate or learned meaning is "extreme danger"—stimuli which may or may not include externally inflicted pain. The core systems appear to be organized in such a way that in this situation, the organism has little choice; whether by flight or fight or freezing into tonic immobility,[1] it responds massively.

As suggested in chapter 9, the medullary nucleus gigantocellularis may be a key structure in such responses. In respect of pain, e.g., from bodily injury, it is a gate-keeper; and in respect of cell structure, it is suited to prompt powerful action. Caudally, its output can drive the skeletal musculature. Rostrally, its output, combined with others along the length of Forel's tract, can also drive the cortex.

In general, rises in reticular input may, in the cortex, result in an overall increase in the inhibitory/excitatory ratio. Up to a point, the result is also an increase in perceptual resolution (Lindsley 1958; Fuster 1961). Reticular activation may also, up to a point, permit rapid shifts in attention. Beyond that point, however, behavior may begin to go over the hump of the inverted U representing its efficiency as a function of central activation (Denenberg 1967).

Two models to explain that transition suggest themselves. One is that the continuing rise in the inhibitory/excitatory ratio leads finally to a breakdown in intercolumnar or interareal communication in the cortex. The other model (which seems preferable and is discussed in detail in the Appendix) postulates the reverse—a decline in the I/E ratio at high or "supramaximal" levels of activation. The result in either case is a loss in what Denenberg calls behavioral efficiency—essentially as a consequence of transient functional decortication.

This last is perhaps the physiological basis for the paralysis of rational functions sometimes brought on by extreme fear or pain. Such states lead naturally into panic behavior—that is, to release of primitive fleeing or back-to-the-wall fighting mechanisms. There is a residual advantage, in that such massive disruptions of higher-level function may act to clear temporary memory registers. They may consequently serve to facilitate appropriate new learning, in the immediate post-crisis stage, when central (aminergic) activation declines, and cholinergic activation, evoked by contrecoup, in effect catches up with it.

In physiological terms, the inhibitory-to-facilitatory ratio shifts rapidly in favor of facilitation, the equivalent motivational-affective shift being from intense fear to one, potentially at least, of equally intense rage. Recall that rage may be related to normal maintenance functions involving ferocity, as in the hunt. It therefore has limbic-mesolimbic representation, and as reported above, has been elicited in man by septal stimulation. (The role of the amygdala in rage-rebound is discussed in chapter 8.)

In his Civil War memoirs, General Phil Sheridan, describing how he had rallied his routed troops at Mill Creek, goes on to say that "enthusiasm" [ferocity] is a "potent element with soldiers" but "if it can be excited from a state of despondence" [i.e. on the rebound from intense fear] "its power is almost irresistible." (Commager 1950.)

It may be by a rebound mechanism of this kind that sudden extreme stresses sometimes result in "one-take" memory formation of the sort that, with no repetition of the external conditions or other reinforcement, may last a lifetime. "Clearing" of prior contents in STM may be a major factor in that process.

Because of the great importance of the central emergency system, involving n. gigantocellularis and the classical RF, the limbic-mesolimbic system has many input lines to it, not only at the midbrain level but more rostrally as well. Thus, as we saw, feeding and defensive functions are found at closely adjacent sites in the amygdala—an obvious safety feature favoring rapid behavioral and emotional switchover in the event of the sudden appearance of an enemy.

Many self-stimulating (or simply stimulating) studies suggest that "reward" systems are in general so linked to the emergency system that at many sites, sufficiently high stimulation rates may trigger the latter and so produce responses of opposite "sign." As might be expected, this is more the case for hypothalamic or tegmental sites (where animals will opt for moderate stimulus intensities) than for the septal region, in which animals may self-stimulate to the point of seizure (Olds and Olds 1963) or to the point of exhaustion (Lilly 1960).

Stimulation effects at a given site may also depend upon the existing baseline state of the organism. Some early work of Grastyán et al., apparently showed that stimulation of the thalamic nonspecific nuclei produced no characteristic effect, but rather seemed to "accentuate whatever the background tone" might be. (Olds and Olds 1963.)

Later work of Grastyán's stressed the importance of rebound responses. For instance cats, stimulated at hypothalamic sites, would not press a lever terminating stimulation, apparently to avoid hippocampal desynchronization which occurred as if by contrecoup when stimulation was stopped. (See Hall, Bloom, and Olds 1977.)

That norepinephrine (and epinephrine, to a lesser degree, in the forebrain) are the transmitters principally involved both in the maintenance of motivationally neutral waking states, and in massive emergency responses, whereas dopamine is principally involved in states relating to normal maintenance and "reward," is suggested by several lines of evidence.

For example, it is reported that self-stimulation in the MFB is greatly reduced by depletion of both norepinephrine and dopamine. When NE was maximally and DA minimally depleted, self-stimulation appeared to be unaffected. Another study showed that, following 6-OH-DA lesions to the ventral and dorsal noradrenergic bundles, self-stimulation in the substantia nigra (presumably the pars compacta) was increased. (Breese 1977.)

The foregoing implies some competition between the classical arousal system, which mediates general arousal (or, on occasion, massive activation related to extreme emergency behavior), and the limbic-mesolimbic systems which mediate (goal-specific) "motivational arousal" and "reward" responses (related to goal attainment or consummation).

Keene's single-unit studies in the midline and intralaminar nuclei suggest distinct populations of thalamic neurons that are selectively responsive, either to stimulation of the "aversive" midbrain RF, or to stimulation of the (usually rewarding) MFB. Intralaminar units that were "on" to RF stimulation were "off" to stimulation of the MFB—a reverse on-off pattern being found for units of the internal globus pallidus. (Keene 1975.)

These differences within the thalamic nonspecific system appear to reflect the differentiation of the brainstem RF described earlier here—the separation off of the ventral tegmental area of Tsai, to become a division whose principal transmitter is dopamine, and whose principal function is to provide aminergic support of normal maintenance behavior. To paraphrase a remark of Herkenham's (1986), differentiation of the transmitter here marks the differentiation of a functional system.

It is this ventral tegmental division which evidently supports forms of behavior dependent upon "motivational arousal"—which is to say, a repertoire of partially or wholly innate behavioral forms such as food hoarding in the rat. (Iversen 1986.) In general, these behavioral forms relate to the normal maintenance (including procreation) of the species, and accordingly have discrete representation.

More rostrally, this system includes "open" areas such as frontal association cortex or the posterior hippocampal-entorhinal-temporal complex which provide for the acquisition of motivationally relevant long-term memories. This cortex corresponds to the association areas which Graybiel classified as distal and, for many of the reasons given here, considered part of the limbic system. (Graybiel 1974.)

In contrast to the ventral tegmentum, the main division of the ascending RF appears to provide a type of arousal less directly related to specific forms of behavior and more related to sheer minute-to-minute survival. It thus supports a spectrum of low- to very high-energy states, ranging from the sentry functions represented by novelty or orienting responses, to the all-out activation triggered by extreme pain or fear. It may have norepinephrine and epinephrine as its principal transmitters, and employ structures and pathways of the classical RF as its principal route of access to the forebrain.

The reader will have noticed that the functional and internal-structural differences between these two systems—the one "motivational" in a multiple sense, the other chiefly in one—have parallels in the differences between the two main branches of the autonomic nervous system.

That the sympathetic branch has a relatively high ratio of post- to preganglionic units, and is capable of mediating fast-rising pressor responses, tachycardia and transfer of blood from the viscera to the skeletal musculature, are among the features obviously relating it to emergency functions of n. gigantocellularis and the classical RF. The parasympathetic system shows more discrete organization, related to what I have classed here as normal maintenance functions—for instance, feeding and reproduction.

The two branches, of course, act synergically in the control of basal functions such as heart rate, pupillary size, gastric motility or heat loss. The relation appears to be sequential, involving a variety of time courses. Thus the parasympathetic plays a major role in the vasodilator reactions related to coitus. But accompanying signs (e.g. pupillary dilatation, increase in heart rate) suggest sympathetic "support"; and the terminus of the process—ejaculation—appears to be mediated by sympathetic fibers of the hypogastric plexus.

It was study of the autonomic nervous system that, I believe, first led to the term contrecoup as physiologists use it. It arose from the observation of physiological events whose relatively long time course made their sequential nature obvious. The principle involved may, in fact, be a more general one applying to turnabout on-off relations between small assemblies on a scale of milliseconds, or to sequential entrainment of larger subsystems on scales ranging from hundreds of milliseconds to days.

I mentioned earlier that Olds and Olds had found stimulation of the hippocampus to be "aversive" (as, indirectly, did Grastyán). As also mentioned, the role of the hippocampus in memory formation seems solidly established. That learning in general may tend, in some degree, to be stress-related (and thus often experienced as a stress) perhaps follows from the account of emergency system functions outlined above. This amounts to saying that memory formation always tends to have an aminergic component—one which figures in a minor way in "primacy" effects, in a major way, for instance in the one-take memory-formation just mentioned, and to some extent in learning of any kind. Prolonged disturbance of the aminergic-cholinergic balance in the forebrain produced, for example, by learning situations that an animal finds very difficult but also inescapable, may lead to the "sensitization" discussed in chapters 6 and 13.[2]

Reticulocortical driving, during the onset stage of acute fear, may produce extreme excitatory states, coupled initially with massive inhibition, e.g. as a result of driving of GABA interneurons. As central activation reaches maximal levels, the tendency may then be for excitation to exceed inhibition. At this point (see Appendix), reticulocortical input may act as an erase mechanism on short-term memory, clearing all but the most recent contents.

A residual effect may also be persisting desynchronization in the hippo-campus—a structure notably prone to prolonged post-stimulus activity or seizurelike responses. Therefore, as fear subsides, and the cholinergic-aminergic balance in the cortex shifts (back towards the cholinergic) both long- and short-term memory formation may be facilitated, with short-term registers "cleared" for intake of new data.

The adaptive advantage of such a mechanism is obvious. It helps to insure that if the organism survives, it may very rapidly learn new things relevant to its survival in future.

It is the reserve activating capacity of the RF, represented by the nucleus gigantocellularis, which may produce these effects. They are special only in being a drastic exaggeration of the "climate" normally produced by reticulocortical input (including that of LC), and normally conducive to cortical functioning.

LOCUS COERULEUS AND THE 5-HT SYSTEM OF THE RAPHÉ

A less extreme set of states seems to be mediated at the pontine and mesencephalic levels by the locus coeruleus and the dorsal and median raphé nuclei. Their climatic nature is apparently correlated with the over-lapping and very large forebrain territories reached by the noradrenergic and serotonergic projections of these nuclei. As mentioned, the raphé nuclei and the locus coeruleus appear to take turn about in the mediation of slow-wave and REM sleep.[2] They may have a similar role in the mainte-nance of what one could call ground-states during waking.

Thus while LC has been shown to figure in arousal, other evidence indicates that the forebrain states maintained by it may, in general, be low-level ones, forming a background upon which, for instance, states of "motivational arousal," mediated by the limbic-mesolimbic system, may then be superimposed. This relation is implied, for instance, by the find-ing that "self-stimulation in the LC is accompanied by very little motor activity or general excitement, and differs markedly in this respect from self-stimulation of the MFB" (Hall, Bloom, and Olds 1977).

As mentioned in chapter 9, the raphé nuclei receive a massive input from the interpeduncular nucleus (IPN), via Ganser's tract. Evidence cited in that chapter showed the IPN to figure as a motor nucleus in avoidance responses in the rat. The fact that it projects to the raphé nuclei may relate it to inhibitory effects of the 5-HT projection system, e.g. in the neocortex. (Taylor and Stone 1981. These authors note that serotonergic inhibition appears to follow a different time-course from that mediated by nor-epinephrine.)

Herrick commented that "the unusually large size of the interpeduncular nucleus of urodeles may be correlated with the fact that in the normal behavior of these animals total inhibition [immobility] is a conspicuous feature." (Herrick 1948, p. 206.)

It seems reasonable that during waking the background states maintained, e.g. in the cortex, by the very widespread projections of LC and the raphé nuclei, might show periodic variation, but with shorter periods than those involved in SWS-REM sleep cycles. Such variations, occurring on a scale of minutes, might figure in attention-span.

This raises the possibility that in some children, diagnosed as having attentional deficit disorder (ADD), the problem may be of brainstem origin. For example, it might involve a heritable anomaly in transmitter balances similar in principle to that suggested by the findings of Sudak and Maas (1964) for BALB/cj "emotional" mice.

Comparison with "unemotional" (C57BL/10j) mice showed no significant differences between strains, in 5-HT concentrations in hippocampal-pyriform cortex. However the "emotional" strain showed significantly higher norepinephrine concentrations in those limbic areas, and also significantly higher brainstem concentrations of 5-HT, than did the controls. (This example is meant only to illustrate a possible *class* of heritable disorders, not to suggest a direct parallel with ADD.)

Data reviewed by Shaywitz et al. (1983) suggest that the anomaly responsible for ADD may not involve serotonin. A significant feature of the disorder may be underfunctioning of the dopaminergic systems, with a consequent lack of "directional" or motivated components in behavior. To the extent that noradrenergic-adrenergic system activity is normal in such children, it will amount to an all-directional component, adding to their motor restlessness and attentional instability.

That hyperactivity, when present, tends to pass at adolescence, may relate to the increase in noradrenergic activity, and the consequent rise in inhibitory/excitatory ratios (see Appendix) occurring during puberty. The authors review a study in which intracisternal lesioning with 6-OH-DA in rat pups later produced hyperactivity and learning deficits. The hyperactivity passed at maturity, the deficits (e.g. in avoidance learning) did not. These results resemble Iversen's (1986), who obtained behavioral disorganization and what she described as a defect of "motivational arousal" in the rat, by 6-OH-DA lesioning of the nucleus accumbens.

Both sets of findings relate to the two fundamental classes of adaptive behavior defined earlier in this chapter, and to the catecholaminergic systems that "support" them. Briefly, the dopaminergic system, as part of the differentiated RF of the ventral tegmentum and its limbic extensions, appears to subserve normal maintenance activities, which is to say behavior having definite direction or objectives.

The noradrenergic (-adrenergic) systems have, in general, more non-

specific functions. These include "climatic" functions of the locus coeruleus (e.g. in waking-alert states); "dynamogenic" functions of the classical
RF (e.g. in support of activities such as hunting or mating); and "override"
functions described here as involving magnocellular structures such as n.
gigantocellularis, and mediating massive emergency responses of the
fight-or-flight type.

None of these last directly gives rise to what might be called directional
or goal-specific behavior. The neurophysiological parallel is perhaps that
reticulocortical input establishes the *conditions* for focal activity—the facilitatory and inhibitory baselines. It may then be the dopaminergic and
cholinergic inputs that supply the directional component—effectively,
selection of those areas in which the foci of cortical activity will finally be
established. (chapter 10.)

In children with ADD, it may be this directional component which is
deficient (consequently the diagnosis of ADD without hyperactivity may
be a real category, contrary to some clinical opinion). It is significant, in this
connection, that d-amphetamine, which is reported to have more selective
effect than the 1-isomer on dopaminergic activity, has also been reported
to produce greater improvement in attention in children with ADD and
hyperactivity. By contrast, both isomers, which have about equal effect on
NE transmission, were reported to be equally effective in reducing "restless behaviors." (Zametkin and Rapoport 1987.)

The rise in noradrenergic activity-levels at puberty may then (because of
the accompanying increase in inhibitory/excitatory ratios) act to improve
motor control in these children. But partly, perhaps, from the cumulative
effects of higher-level functional impairment during their earlier forma-
tive years, "their associated cognitive difficulties persist." (Shaywitz et al.
1983, p. 334.)

In the foregoing, I have attempted to define essentially three tiers of
influences that the cortex "sees," over and above the inputs it "sees" from
the specific thalamic projection system.

The first tier, arising in the lower brainstem, involves motivationally
neutral supporting inputs, with an important reserve which can be
mobilized under circumstances the organism experiences as painful or
extremely dangerous. In that case, reticulocortical input is not necessarily
"supporting," since it may result in pro tem functional decortication. In the
same case, the cross-linkages of the classical RF mediating these responses,
with the brainstem "motivational" systems mediating normal maintenance
behavior, and the access which both have to the central gray, guarantee that
emergency responses are not motivationally or affectively neutral.

This must not be taken to mean that a reticular structure such as the n.
gigantocellularis is specialized, and a "pain center." As no doubt are other
reticular structures, it can be driven by inputs representing pain. Its

relations to the lateral parvocellular RF at the same level may be essentially similar to those between small-celled "receptor" and large-celled "effector" assemblies found elsewhere in the nervous system (chapter 2). What distinguishes it is the potential massiveness of its outputs.

Rostral to this nucleus, forming the second tier, lie the locus coeruleus and the raphé nuclei, which perhaps act synergically in providing the ground states equivalent to sleep and still-alert waking. Because of their cross-linkages with other systems, they may also participate in states involving higher levels of general activation—states they themselves possibly cannot bring on unaided. Their influence on the third tier—the limbic-mesolimbic—may be "climatic" as it is on the neocortex.

LOCUS COERULEUS: MAJOR AND MINOR AFFERENTS

Aston-Jones et al. (1986) report important data concerning afferents to the locus coeruleus. Using anterograde and retrograde tracing, and electrophysiological methods in other preparations, they have shown that in the rat, the locus coeruleus may not receive input from the amygdala, insular cortex, the nucleus of the solitary tract, or the dorsal horn (as had been reported earlier in the literature).

These authors' combined techniques indicate two major and two minor sources of input to LC. The major afferents are both medullary, arising in the nucleus prepositus hypoglossi and the nucleus paragigantocellularis. The minor afferents originate in the paraventricular hypothalamic nucleus, and in scattered neurons of the spinal intermediate gray, near the central canal.

The functional implications of this pattern of input are pertinent to the argument developed above. The least clear are those involving n. prepositus, which may figure in gaze control, but whose convergence of input suggests other functions as well. (Aston-Jones et al. 1986, p. 736.)

N. paragigantocellularis, as might be expected, has been implicated in pain responses. The authors point out that the paragigantocellularis area "is a crossroads for circuitry pertaining to" autonomic responses; that projections from it reach the interomedial lateral column in the cord; that rises in LC and sympathetic activity tend to occur in parallel; and that LC neurons in waking animals "exhibit pronounced excitation following painful or polymodal nonnoxious stimuli."

These afferents to LC illustrate what I have called its "supporting" role in emergency responses. That is, the projections it receives from paragigantocellularis represent a major route by which the normal "climatic" functions of LC may be overridden, making it, pro tem, one of a chain of reticular structures supporting massive central activation instead.

That afferents to LC arise in the paraventricular nucleus (PVN) is of particular interest since that nucleus probably receives noradrenergic efferents of the LC projection system. It is reported to be differentially responsive to intrahypothalamic injections of norepinephrine, which behaviorally elicit feeding (Stanley, Eppel and Hoebel 1982).

PVN is described in the older literature as receiving projections from orbital cortex (Fulton 1951) and, along with the supraoptic nucleus, as being part of the "parasympathetic" division of the hypothalamus (Hess 1954). The neurosecretory output of PVN and the supraoptic nucleus (of oxytocin and 8-arginine vasopression) seem clearly related to what I have called normal maintenance functions. The point of interest here is the cross-linkages of PVN with the nonspecific brainstem arousal systems.

Projections of PVN to LC suggest a feedback control-mechanism, such that the noradrenergic-sympathetic component involved, e.g. in the search for food or the initiation of feeding, is then damped back by inhibitory outflows (PVN→LC) during feeding proper or the onset of satiety. Like the parvocellular neurosecretory system of PVN reported by Zimmerman (1987) to contain CRF (released via the anterior pituitary), these PVN-LC connections perhaps illustrate the sequential auto-reversing dominance relations upon which much of the sequencing of behavior itself may depend.

The second minor input to LC appears to arise in Rexed's layer X—i.e., the central gray, whose pain functions were mentioned earlier—or in the adjacent layer VII, whose medial part, at the level of the canal (dorso-ventrally) includes the nucleus intermedio-medialis, described as having autonomic reflex functions (Rexed 1964; pp. 76 and 84).

Aston-Jones et al. (loc. cit.), noting that the "preponderance of afferent control over the LC emanates from the medulla" conclude that "it is unlikely that this nucleus is engaged in the complex processing of several types of information." The very small size of LC in man ($\sim$20,000–30,000 neurons per side; Nauta and Feirtag 1986; Scheibel 1987b) suggests a similar conclusion.

Taken together, these findings would appear to fit the description of the locus coeruleus as forming the dynamogenic component of a two-element regulatory system whose rostral projections determine the ground-state or "climate" in forebrain structures—perhaps most critically (because of its "delicacy of function") in neocortex. Thus while the locus coeruleus and the dorsal and median raphé nuclei respond to rises in central activation (see Appendix) they may have an essentially homeostatic or re-equilibrating function, providing the baseline to which forebrain waking activities return between episodes of more intense arousal.

It follows, perhaps, that a chronic imbalance in the serotonergic and noradrenergic output from these brainstem levels might lead to chronic abnormalities of mood. If sufficiently prolonged, or aggravated by external circumstances, such an imbalance might lead to episodically decontrolled behavior—for example, as a result of a sharp rise in central activation, occurring against a background in which the inhibitory component due to the 5-HT system was critically low. Evidence mentioned earlier (see also Appendix) suggests that underfunctioning of the 5-HT system may figure in major depression, monopolar depression, and certain forms of impulsive violence, including "violent" suicide.

THE MESOLIMBIC DOPAMINERGIC PROJECTION SYSTEM

Single unit studies have shown that the output of brainstem dopaminergic neurons is surprisingly constant and limited in its dynamic range. Neurons in the substantia nigra (rat, cat, monkey) and in the ventral tegmental area (rat) are characterized as showing long (2–5 msec) spikes, a slow tonic discharge-rate (2–7 spikes/sec) and a pattern of occasional bursting, with spike amplitude decreasing during the bursts (Jacob 1986).

Surprisingly also, Jacobs reports that "across the sleep-waking-arousal cycle, DA unit activity shows a remarkable stability in both rate and pattern." In the cat, for example, DA units of the substantia nigra showed a mean rate of 3 spikes/sec during quiet waking, slow-wave sleep and REM sleep. Overt movement or "behavioral arousal" resulted in a "slight (20%) overall increase in the activity of these neurons." Computer analysis showed this increase to be related to burst-activity. Jacobs adds that ventral tegmental unit activity in the rat shows a diurnal cycle "virtually identical" to that described for units of the substantia nigra.

He notes that this diurnal stability and narrowness in range of output-frequencies is "unique among the various groups of mammalian neurons that have been examined under similar conditions." The implication is that the apparently much wider range of central excitatory states involved, say, in hunting, feeding or mating (i.e. normal maintenance behavior) may depend upon facilitatory or inhibitory modulation of ventral tegmental output elsewhere, for instance, in the hypothalamus, nucleus accumbens, or structures of the classical limbic system.

Data implying support for this conclusion derive from studies of the central effects of neurotensin (NT). Using a conditioned place-preference response paradigm, Glimcher, Margolin and Hoebel (1982) concluded that cannular injections of NT into the ventral tegmental area in rats were "rewarding." These authors cite a study by Palacios and Kuhar (1981) indicating that NT receptors on DA units in this brain-region are on somata.

Nemeroff (1987) reports that presynaptic NT receptors are found on DA terminals (in humans and experimental animals) in nigrostriatal but not in mesolimbic units of the DA system. Intraventricular NT produces inhibitory ("neuroleptic-like") effects in part, apparently, involving the nucleus accumbens. Bilateral injection of NT into that nucleus blocks the locomotor effects producible by DA or d-amphetamine. He notes that "in contrast" neurotensin injected into the VTA results in increased DA turnover and hyperactivity; and that "predictably, intra-accumbens NT blocks" these effects. (See also Goeders and Smith 1983.)

These results, together with the data reviewed by Jacobs, imply that the DA system of the ventral tegmentum is relatively stable in its rostral output—so much so that it appears minimally affected by diurnal regulation e.g. via the retino-hypothalamic tract and suprachiasmatic nucleus.

Since the kinds of behavior it evidently figures in involve a considerable range of central excitatory states, the further implication is that the rostral output of this system depends heavily on modulation at the limbic-hypothalamic and cortical levels.

What all of this adds up to is that structures forming the rostral part of the dopaminergic system may "expect" a certain narrow range of input from the ventral tegmental area. When that input shows variations critically outside the expected range—when for example it is chronically below, and episodically at or above, the normal maxima and minima—two results may follow. Upregulation of frontal and limbic DA receptors may occur chronically; and this in turn may make the system potentially unstable when rises in midbrain DA output occur acutely. The reported absence of DA autoreceptors in areas of frontal or cingulate cortex may be an important contributing factor in such latent instability.

These may be some of the reasons for the connection which seems to have been established between dopaminergic dysfunction and disorders lumped under the term schizophrenia. The foregoing analysis suggests that whereas 5-HT underfunctioning may lead to relative overactivity of the brainstem noradrenergic systems, and thence to a chronic mood disorder—in some cases with episodes of eruptive violence—malfunctioning of the brainstem dopaminergic system in the way described is likely to have more grave results. In effect, it cuts at the root of adaptively motivated behavior.

In physiological terms, it may chronically diminish the subcortical "steering" of cortical processes (chapter 10). But from quite early in life, it may be this forebrain dopaminergic input which establishes the basic priorities according to which we note, recall and act on the data of experience. Psychologically, it may therefore determine the primary categories of relevance, and so the root-patterns, of our adult thinking. Impairment of this priority-system is essentially what we may be seeing in the idiosyncratic word-usage or atypical problem-solving techniques reportedly found in some schizophrenics. (Carini 1973. See Appendix.)

The same impairment may also contribute to the latent instability just described. In other words, atypical episodic rises in dopaminergic output, impingeing upon forebrain systems which are both sensitized (by DA receptor upregulation) and functionally somewhat underorganized, may easily result in bizarre thought-disorders (delusions; hallucinations) and behavioral breakdown.

It would be natural to expect that the overt form of this disease might be precipitated by the hormonal onset of adolescence, since the latter would greatly increase the probability of episodic sharp rises in DA output from the ventral tegmental level (hence dementia praecox, the older term for schizophrenia). One would also expect that in some cases, the disease would tend to follow a long-term degenerative course, in which the de-structuring effects of chronic undermotivation were gradually aggravated by episodes of more radical disorder. Such changes, though far more grave than those produced acutely by sensory deprivation (chapter 5), may nevertheless resemble them in principle.

It will be recalled that, in chapter 5, the conclusion suggested by several lines of evidence was that hallucinatory episodes have the common feature that they involve rises in central excitation superimposed upon critically low baselines of activity in higher-level sensory and processing systems. Jacobs's review (1986) of data on output of single neurons in the substantia nigra and ventral tegmentum suggests that the range of dopaminergic input forebrain systems "expect" from the mesolimbic level may be narrow and normally quite stable. It follows, perhaps, that dopamine-mimetic drugs are particularly apt to induce hallucinations—as for instance in non-psychotic patients "over-medicated" for Parkinsonism with DA agonists, or for alcohol abuse with disulfiram. (Wagner 1984.)

As also mentioned in chapter 5, a similar mechanism may underlie the dreams occurring in REM sleep—the triggering factor in this case being the decline in forebrain activity occurring during SWS. Beyond some critical point, such declines result in brainstem release, the forebrain activation which follows then producing the functional equivalent of hallu-cinations—i.e. dreams. Since the same basic conditions were established in subjects during prolonged sensory deprivation, some subjects tended to have waking-state dreams—i.e. hallucinations. Apropos of the basically different mechanisms which may be involved in depressions without a cyclical or manic component, it is of interest that hallucinations rarely seem to occur in chronically depressed patients of this type.

What is less clear is why the hypothetical underfunctioning of DA systems thought to figure in Attention Deficit Disorder does not lead on to psychosis. Perhaps the essential difference is in the neuraxial levels at which DA functioning is impaired in the two cases. In ADD, for example, (and contrary to the suggestion made earlier here), brainstem structures may not be involved; basal output from the ventral tegmental level may be within normal limits and normally stable, the problem lying in the more rostrally lying systems which modulate that output. Only further research is likely to settle these questions.

Methodological Note; Novelty Responses and the RF; Opioid Mechanisms and Arousal; The Beta-Endorphin System and Novelty Responses; Further Considerations; Conclusion

In the last chapter, discussing pain responses, I omitted mention of the extensive opioid systems which appear to act as feedback controls on such responses. In this chapter, I will review evidence suggesting that the β-endorphin system may be a general-purpose one, called into play whenever central activation is raised above the normal-alert waking range.

As such, its functions may only incidentally be analgesic. Its more basic function may be to damp back rises in central activation of whatever origin. It appears to act homeostatically to limit the outlay of gross central nervous work over a range of states from the acute arousal accompanying pain or fear to the milder fearlike arousal involved in "orienting" or novelty responses. It can thus, in some circumstances, have analgesic effects, and in others, an amnestic one, affecting retrieval.

METHODOLOGICAL NOTE

The reader will have noticed that in the text I have given relatively little attention to neurochemical data. In part, that is because in this study I hoped to establish a framework of intersystemic relationships, into which the more minute, more intricate relations involving neuropeptides, transmitters and receptor-types might later be seen to fit.

The immense amounts of new information concerning biochemical mechanisms in the brain have led to a certain pessimism as to the solubility

127

of some of the problems taken up here. However, the circuitry of the nervous system, and the larger-scale physiological relations known to exist in it, are not *contradicted* by the new data. Often what those data seem to show is that the reciprocal or competing "opposite-effect" relationships which exist between larger assemblies, such as the medial and lateral hypothalamus, are mirrored at the biochemical level—e.g., in the relations between substance P and the enkephalins (Hughes 1980); between thyrotropin releasing factor and somatostatin or neurotensin (Prange 1980); or between ACTH-like peptides and β-endorphin (Krieger 1985).

The discovery, by Vogt, Rosene and Pandya (1979), that cingulate areas 23 and 24 have different thalamic innervation and different limbic connections may be fully as important to our understanding of cingulate functions as the finding that in some cingulate areas, dopamine is concentrated in layers II-III (Moore 1977).

Neurochemical mechanisms, in short, do not invalidate circuitry; they are simply its microstructure. However complex the latter may turn out to be, the way it works adds up to the way we find the circuits work.[1]

NOVELTY RESPONSES AND THE RF

In chapter 11, I suggested that "novelty" or orienting responses represented "sentry" functions, which were mediated in the first stage by the RAS, and related to major emergency responses in the sense of being their potential first phase.

In man, novelty responses can consequently take a range of subjective forms, from the barest stirrings of interest or curiosity to feelings of uneasiness or outright panic (vide the literature on UFO sightings). The fact that at their extremes the subjective features of novelty responses can be so different does not mean, however, that the same basic mechanisms may not generate them.

Fundamentally, what may be involved in all such responses is a set of match-mismatch processes which begin at the reticular level and reach to the level of the cortical short- and long-term memory systems. The degree of reticular arousal that then results will be roughly proportional to the sum of mismatch signals, the first of which arise *en passant* in the RF itself. The psychological concomitants may vary from neutral to mildly stimulating to unsettling or acutely unpleasant, depending upon the level of central activation finally reached.

That in general, the feeling tone or subjective "sign" associated with RAS input is a function of the *rate* of input, is suggested, for instance, by studies showing that graded and finally opposite effects can be evoked from stimulation of a given site in the intralaminar nuclei—high frequencies producing fearlike responses, lower frequencies simply arousal, and lower still, sleep. (Casey and Jones 1980. Some of the earliest work involving RF stimulation gave similar results.)

In chapter 11, it was proposed that novelty responses and memory formation, e.g. in the cortex, were both in some degree stress-related. That is because the leading edge of those processes—aminergic arousal—is itself a graded stress, being part of the machinery by which, in emergencies, the organism's energy output is drastically elevated. In the latter process, many of its internal functions are thrown out of balance accordingly. Driving of the heart, disturbances of the gut and excretion, and "functional decortication" may be regarded as indices of the calculated risk which major emergency responses in fact are.

Novelty responses and learning, as they involve some or much participation of the same machinery, should have physiological features in common with these more extreme reactions. Primacy effects in general—including novelty responses to input changes of no adaptive significance—should, for example, involve contrecoup activity in the central analgesic system. Evidence reviewed below suggests that they do.

OPIOID MECHANISMS AND AROUSAL

The central gray is apparently important in the mediation of pain. At the mesencephalic level, in the periaqueductal system, there is a caudo-medial region which on stimulation produces analgesia, and more rostral and lateral sites at which stimulation elicits evident pain. Transection of a dorsolateral quadrant of the cord, which interrupts descending 5-HT projections from the nucleus magnus of the medullary raphé to the dorsal horn, appears to abolish analgesic effects ipsilaterally but not contralaterally. (Kerr 1980; Liebeskind 1980.)

That pain and analgesic contrecoup responses should be represented in adjoining parts of the same central system of course makes sense, as does the fact that the periaqueductal-periventricular system is extensively cross-connected with the reticular formation. A functional consequence of such cross-connections may be that increases in some non-nociceptive inputs from the RF may, if sufficiently massive, activate not only an opioid response but a part of the pain system, converting an initially neutral or pleasurable state into an "aversive" one. The absence of input from visceral or somatic nociceptors would then serve to distinguish these states of psychological pain from pain states proper. Some of the reversals (from reward to escape reactions) seen in stimulation studies may be due to such spillover effects, occurring for instance as the stimulus input rate is increased.

Spinoreticular fibers project to the mesencephalic central gray, which, in turn, projects to the midbrain RF and (via the dorsal longitudinal fasciculus of Schütz) to the dorsal and posterior hypothalamus, the zona incerta of the subthalamus, and the midline and intralaminar nn. in the thalamus. (Casey and Jones 1980.) Thus analgesia-producing systems of the periventricular, periaqueductal and lower raphé areas, and the pain fiber systems associated with them, have two-way lines with the RAS, and a partially overlapping diencephalic distribution as well.

Apropos of the "aversive" responses obtainable by stimulation of units of the intralaminar nucleus, it might be noted that the concentration of opioid receptors in midline and intralaminar nuclei, as compared to the specific nuclei, is quite high. Opiate binding is reportedly maximal for the "anterior" amygdala, exceeding that at the frontal pole or in the hippocampus by a factor of five, and that in the inferior temporal gyrus by an order of magnitude. (Pert 1980.)

THE BETA-ENDORPHIN SYSTEM AND NOVELTY RESPONSES

In contrast to the Met- and Leu-enkephalin, and dynorphin systems, which Izquierdo and Netto (1985) describe as "scattered all over the brain," these authors define the β-endorphin system as having "cell bodies in the medial basal hypothalamus [which] project to the periventricular region." (Nauta 1986 defines the medial hypothalamus as an extension of the periventricular system.)

Izquierdo and Netto conclude that hypothalamic regulation of β-endorphin activity may depend chiefly on input from the hippocampal-septal system, since their own work showed that the β-endorphin response to training was markedly reduced by fornix section but unaffected by other hypothalamic deafferentation. (It was also unaffected by adrenal medullectomy or dexamethasone.)

They describe the endorphin response in the rat as being elicitable by either aversive or nonaversive conditioning; specifically, by inescapable footshock, by passive and active footshock avoidance training; by exposure to "50 low-level 1 kHz tones" or by "simple exposure to the apparatus."

They list no paradigm which clearly involves reward. It would be of particular interest to know whether food reward training, occurring, for example, in a situation in which the animal could smell the food, would produce the same results.

Quite possibly it would. The model of CNS organization developed here implies that motivational arousal by way of the olfactory and ventral tegmental systems very probably entrains arousal not only via dopaminergic projections of the MFB but also via the noradrenergic common-carrier system, e.g. represented by the ventral bundle. A continuation of this synergic relation into frontal cortex is then suggested by the existence of dopaminergic fibers in the deeper layers and noradrenergic fibers, for instance in tangential layers I and VI.

The β-endorphin response reported by Izquierdo and Netto showed a primacy effect such that when any of the experimental tasks or situations was repeated (by implication, within minutes to hours) the endorphin response did not occur. However, the response apparently re-occurred "when animals were trained in one task and tested in another."

The response, equivalent by their estimate to a release of 20–40 ng of β-endorphin per brain, involves a depression of brainstem endorphin levels continuing for up to 2 hours post-training. This is then followed by a rise to higher-than-pretraining levels at 6 hours (apparently a period of overshoot), and an approximate return to baseline at 12 hours.

The fact that this change in endorphin levels had a primacy feature and was abolished by fornix section led them to conclude that it was, in fact, a "novelty" response.

FURTHER CONSIDERATIONS

The phenomenon reported by Izquierdo and Netto might better be described as a *component* of novelty responses—part of a contrecoup process which is essentially circular and takes the form of a damped oscillation. "Paradoxical" effects, such as a locking in one phase of a given sequence, with partial expression of the next phase, or "escape," occurring during prolonged postponement periods, may result when a given phase of such oscillatory processes is sufficiently exaggerated.

It is interesting, for example, to note the results, in rats, of increasing the dose of intraventricular β-endorphin, as reported by Segal (1980). At 0.01 μg, the animals reportedly showed excessive grooming—a reaction, I believe, often occurring, as it were on the downslope from highly activated states.

For instance, male cats, in the course of tense confrontations with each other, will sometimes break off the encounter momentarily and begin to groom. The basic mechanism involved may work as follows: β-endorphin levels, rising in response to high activation levels, tend to have a damping action, in effect causing a pro tem shift in central motivational state. The result, in the example given, is a shift from a high-energy fight-readiness condition (with corresponding emergency-system support) to a lower-energy condition whose behavioral equivalent is a low-level normal maintenance activity such as grooming.

In the rat, doses of 0.1 μg, β-endorphin, given intraventricularly, are reported to delay extinction of a pole-jumping (avoidance) task. In this case, the drug is perhaps interfering with the "new learning" phase which tends to follow activation generally (chapter 11; see also Appendix.) by bringing activation to too low a level too fast. Truncation of the new learning phase causes the animal to require more trials to extinction.

At 5 μg, there is "profound" immobilization, with muscular rigidity and loss of righting responses, suggesting a form of decerebration. Segal also reports having found "a biphasic pattern of locomotion," such that, with higher doses of β-endorphin "the rigid immobility phase is followed by a period of motor activation in which oral stereotypy is a prominent feature." This would correspond to a reactivation, or partial contrecoup stage, perhaps chiefly involving "escape" of lower brainstem mechanisms.

(He lists several possible neurochemical mechanisms that might account for this "sequential emergence of behavioral events," suggesting that "prolonged activation of receptors, even at the physiological site of action, might eventually result in the distortion of behaviors or in the induction of atypical behavior patterns.")

The doses producing these results (e.g. up to 300 μg) are far higher than the amounts Izquierdo and Netto estimated for normal β-endorphin release during novelty responses (20–40 ng per brain). It is perhaps significant that the time relations in the two cases are, however, quite similar.

In Izquierdo and Netto's study, peak depletion of central β-endorphin occurred at 2 hours, with overshoot at 6 hours and return to baseline at 12.

Segal describes the "rigid immobility" response in his animals as lasting "at least six hours"—the period of overshoot reported by Izquierdo and Netto. The later motor effects observed by Segal may then have occurred as a result of partial rebound-activation, during the stage when β-endorphin levels were dropping (from a peak, at 6 hours) and the whole oscillatory process was starting to return to baseline (at approximately 12 hours).

Di Chiara and Imperato (1986) present evidence (also obtained from the rat) indicating one of the aminergic components in this process. They note that low doses of alcohol, barbiturates, or opiates have "behavioral stimulating effects" paralleled by release of dopamine in n. accumbens, the ventral tegmental area of Tsai and (to a lesser extent) in the striatum.

Higher doses, e.g., of morphine (5 mg/kg s.c.) "produced frozen immobility, catalepsy and rigidity for about 1 hour, followed by behavioral stimulation for the next 2 hours and 20 minutes. DA released increased maximally by about 90% in the accumbens, and by about 30% in the striatum."

At a dose of 1 mg/kg, s.c., the period of behavioral "freezing" lasted ~30 minutes, with a peak in "stereotypy scores" occurring 1 to 1.5 hours, and tail-away at about 2 hours and 40 minutes post-injection. (Stereotypy these authors define as grooming and hypermotility, with sniffing and rearing—i.e. apparent nonspecific activation of the motivational system described by Iversen 1986.)

These time-relations are of some interest, since Izquierdo and Netto (1985) noted that 1 μg/kg i.p. β-endorphin, given a few minutes before testing, did not affect retrieval of a step-down avoidance task at 2 hours post-injection—the period during which endorphin depletion is becoming maximal, and dopaminergic contrecoup (Di Chiara and Imperato 1986) appears to be reaching a peak. The same avoidance response is then blocked (not "retrieved") at 6 hours post injection—the period in which Izquierdo and Netto also report β-endorphin "overshoot." (See Appendix.)

The graphic data of Di Chiara and Imperato show the presumed parallel—a return to baseline of dopaminergic activity (in n. accumbens, the striatum and the ventral tegmentum) occurring at 4–5 hours. The suggestion of an oscillatory or turn-about relation between the aminergic and opioid (β-endorphin) systems concerned is clear.

CONCLUSION

The foregoing is intended to illustrate the applicability of the several-stage sequential model developed here, to experimental data of the kind just reviewed.

Such models may, I believe, lead to better understanding of the behavioral-cum-biochemical anomalies found in various human mental or affective disorders. While many of these suggest disturbed cynbernetic controls, earlier attempts to account for them at the circuitry level—to correlate conditions such as schizophrenia with cytoarchitectural abnormalities found at postmortem—have, with some exceptions, not proved very useful.

Present evidence suggests that a number of disorders of this kind may arise from hereditary imbalances in transmitter output, or from anomalies in the density and distribution of related receptor types. (See chapter 13.) The same evidence appears to support Herkenham's observation (1986) that transmitters define functional systems.

Structural Invariances and Memory in the CNS; The "Effector" Model of Learning; Central Coexistence of Two Modes of Learning; Sensitization and Behavior; Pavlov's Dog; Maier and "Frustration"; Anxiety Neuroses and Sensitization-Learning; Stress-Reactivity and Heredity; Conclusion

In chapter 6, I outlined the Kandel-Schwartz presynaptic and the Lynch-Baudry postsynaptic models of learning in single units. I proposed that these two forms of learning might coexist, for instance in mammalian neocortex, and be, under some circumstances, competitive.

I proposed, further, that presynaptic learning might be paradigmatic for the acquisition of motor skills, or for what is called "procedural knowledge" generally. In contrast, learning which followed the postsynaptic model, I suggested might be paradigmatic for the acquisition of cognitive skills, or "declarative knowledge." These are the ideas explored in this chapter.

STRUCTURAL INVARIANCES AND MEMORY IN THE CNS

Especially in higher vertebrates, sensory inputs tend to diverge over several synapses, reaching neuronal populations much larger than those at either periphery. At central stations, the reverse trend begins; there is reconvergence en route to the ventral horn. The latter relationship appears to be duplicated, on a millimetric scale, in cortical columns, the

135

output of a given column representing a considerable convergence of input from smaller-celled aggregates in the same assembly.

On a larger scale, on the effector side, there is then complex cortico-subcortical convergence, for instance involving the basal ganglia and motor cortex, with final convergence of pyramidal and reticulomotor out-flows (with or without γ-system feedback via the dorsal horn) on motoneurons of the ventral horn.

The hypothesis that, in columns in the neocortex, memory-functions may differentially involve magnocellular output arrays (whether or not the columns themselves are in motor areas) suggests that the CNS is here doing on a small scale what it does on a larger one. It is learning outputs—ultimately actions. Hence learning, even in central subsystems far from the periphery, perhaps tends to follow an "effector" model.

(Sutherland, it should be noted, constructed a computerized model for conditioning in the rat, in which "attachment" of the CS occurred first to the "motor analyzer" and only later to the "sensory analyzer." The result-ing learning curves shown by his "stat rats" closely resembled those of real ones. Sutherland 1964.)

As I shall try to show in a later section, the notion that effector responses, including learning, tend to "lead," or closely parallel receptor responses, may have evidence to support it. It may also have led to much confusion as to the sequence of events involved in conditioned response-formation, and much debate as to where memory finally "is."

THE "EFFECTOR" MODEL OF LEARNING

The model can be generalized as shown in Figure 13-1:

	A	B	
	Parvocellular	Magnocellular	
	"processing"	"integrating"	
Input →	assemblies →	assemblies	→ Output
	High metabolic	Lower metabolic	
	rates	rates	
	Low hysteresis	Greater hysteresis	

Figure 13–1. The "Effector" Model of Learning.

In output arrays in a given assembly, for instance in the ventral horn, much of the "hysteresis" may be genetically predetermined; an arrange-ment relating to the special, not very flexible types of innervation required for various joint-and-muscle combinations, some of which Nauta (1986) describes as "idiosyncratic." In such assemblies, presynaptic learning or "sensitization" amounts to potentiation of already existing pathways, and may thus form the basis of "procedural" knowledge.

In type B (Output) arrays lying more centrally—for instance, in lower layers of temporal association cortex—the amount of genetic preprogramming may be much less than it is, say, in the ventral horn. In such comparatively open systems, postsynaptic learning should theoretically be the dominant mode, since it results in new path formation, and thus ultimately in specific learned elaborations of behavior.

CENTRAL COEXISTENCE OF TWO MODES OF LEARNING

Presynaptic learning, as it may lead, in diverging networks, to a diffuse spread of excitation, is possibly not the dominant mode. However, it may survive in such networks 1) because neurons of many types may tend to show lasting increases in transmitter output, given sufficient excitatory driving, and 2) because the diffuse sensitization responses that result are under certain circumstances adaptive.

Earlier, I proposed that high levels of reticulocortical input (as in acute fear reactions) may produce a transient functional decortication, accompanied by "clearing" of short-term memory registers, and some release of lower-level motor mechanisms. These are essentially episodic, or phasic states, one of whose adaptive functions is to promote prompt action. I have also supposed that they may be conducive, in the aftermath phase—on the "downslope" from extreme activation—to new postsynaptic learning. (See Appendix.)

Various lines of evidence suggest, however, that if such states of extreme activation are repeatedly brought on and closely enough spaced in time, they become, in effect, tonic. That is, presynaptic learning in higher-level assemblies may begin to consolidate, by way of a second-stage cyclic AMP mechanism such as the one outlined in the Kandel-Schwartz model (chapter 6).

By presynaptic learning, I mean the type described by Bailey and Chen (1983), involving increases in the area of "active zones" and in the number of vesicles at synaptic terminals. Since axons in neocortex typically distribute to sizable numbers of neurons downstream, the tendency, in this type of network, may be for long-term presynaptic learning to spread. That is, it may increase the probability and duration of diffuse excitatory states, with some consequent impairment of cortical function.

This is the learning of "sensitization" referred to in chapter 6. Operationally, it may cause once-specific learned responses to generalize to stimuli having only a distant relation to the initial CS(s). The excitatory component in such responses may increase rather than decrease with time, and the corresponding behavior will tend to reflect reduced cortical participation—for instance, by becoming more primitive and ill-directed, or stereotypically fixed and "superstitious."

SENSITIZATION AND BEHAVIOR

Long-term sensitization may particularly tend to occur in situations which the organism finds extremely difficult but also inescapable. The essential reason may be that in such situations, rises in reticulocortical activation are not adequately "answered" by increases of focal activity in the cortex (as would normally occur). Cortical outputs, including those to the brainstem, are disorganized accordingly.

This perhaps amounts to disruption of a cybernetic control mechanism whereby the cortex, by its outputs to lower levels, acts to produce an inhibitory damping of central activation. In the "difficult problem" situation, the failure of focal cortical activity to develop may result in some brainstem release. And since the drive state itself is "inescapable" (maintained by external circumstances), a positive feedback loop is set up. There is further de-differentiation of higher-level activity and, in proportion, control of behavior is shifted down the neuraxis. (See Appendix.)

This appears to be the basic sequence followed by Pavlov's dog (in the experiment described in chapter 6), by Maier's rats in the no-solution problem, and perhaps by many human neurotics. These questions are taken up in order, next.

PAVLOV'S DOG

Pavlov's dog could not reliably "focus down" (chapter 10) because the problem given it was at the limits of its perceptual resolution. Hence the patterning of cortico-subcortical output was unstable from the outset, since the outcome of the response itself remained close to chance level.

In turn, this meant there was no reliable relaxation of the underlying state—the "downslope" phase of central activation that I have supposed may be important in LTM formation. Correct responses, therefore, did not consolidate as they normally would, and repeated exposure to the experimental conditions, instead of leading to improved cortico-subcortical control, led to the reverse.

From trial to trial, central activation was not damped back by higher-level inhibition, but persisted at above normal levels, leading to long-term sensitization. As if in parallel with these hypothetical internal events, the dog, after a period of partial success in coping with the problem facing it, underwent a behavioral sea-change.

Its reactions to the situation suddenly generalized, becoming tense and aggressive. It began barking when brought into the lab, and "wriggling" or biting at its harness. It also lost the difficult discriminatory response it had partially learned, as well as similar, easier discriminations it had learned earlier. (Pavlov 1927; p. 290 ff. See also the experiments he describes on pp. 289–90.)

Melzack (1962) obtained a similar result, apparently by accident. He reported that during acquisition of a series of increasingly difficult visual discriminations (rewarded with food), one of three beagle littermates serving as normal controls "underwent a remarkable change. . . . It showed an increasingly high level of behavioral excitement and struggled violently when it was picked up. . . . It developed a strong position habit and 'superstitious' behavior patterns, such as turning two complete circles before responding to the stimuli" (suggesting some release of subcortically driven automatisms).

Its error scores and general behavior became comparable to those of the experimentals—littermates that had been sensorily deprived through being cage-raised in a lighted but otherwise blank environment from age 3 weeks to 9 months.

As with Pavlov's dog, the critical variable here seems to have been the difficulty (and inescapability) of the problem confronting the animal. As sensitization set in, its behavior deteriorated to the point of resembling the developmental deficits produced in the experimental animals by early sensory restriction.

Reactions of this type, though often inclucing maladaptive features (such as "superstitious" automatisms), probably are adaptive in the same sense that acute fear responses are. By calling upon the organism's energy reserves and mobilizing its general-purpose (attack or defence) mechanisms, they serve as a last-ditch means of extricating it from situations with which it cannot deal. Note that in Pavlov's and Melzack's dogs, the fight-or-flight response was not primary; it developed gradually, in proportion as normal learning failed to "take." And as it developed, the effect on the learned response was attritive.

In general, what makes such transitions possible is the fact that the nonspecific activating system, which mediates all-out emergency responses, also provides graded support for systems mediating "goal-directed" forms of behavior—normal maintenance activities such as hunting, feeding, or procreation (chapter 11). Hence the qualitative change from behavior of this type to that of the relatively crude, unlearned fight-or-flight type, is always potential, and also, perhaps, ultimately quantitative—a matter of the relative output of the supporting and the supported systems.

Pavlov's and Melzack's experiments (and some of Maier's, discussed below) appear to have dissected away one of these behavioral components (the specific or goal-directed), leaving the other (the nonspecific). Their data are consistent with the suggestion made earlier here that high levels of reticulocortical input have important "erase" functions, tending to clear memory registers of recently acquired data (chapter 11). Under normal conditions, as mentioned, this mechanism may act to facilitate new learning in the phase when central activation subsides—i.e., when it passes back over the hump of the inverted U representing "behavioral efficiency." (Denenberg 1967. See also Appendix.)

If central activation is too often raised and too continuously held above the theoretical maximum for efficient performance, much new (specific) learning that might have occurred may be minimized or aborted. In part this may be because STM "erase" functions, if sufficiently prolonged, act to preclude retention even of most recent, most relevant data.

Sufficiently repeated, such disruptions of STM should also, on the model of cortical-memory functions developed here (chapter 7), produce retrieval deficits affecting memories established prior to sensitization. (Note that Pavlov's dog showed retroactive memory losses, requiring 1½ months to relearn even the easiest discrimination in the series.) At the cortical level, essentially what may become impaired, in the course of sensitization, is the process of "focusing down" described in chapter 10. For it is to the integrity of that process that the neocortex may owe such power as it has to control other subsystems and behavior.

MAIER AND "FRUSTRATION"

In a long series of experiments with rats, Maier (1949) demonstrated the effects of what he called frustration. The animals were first conditioned to jump at one of two doors, on a position-preference or symbol-preference paradigm. By choosing the correct position, or the correct symbol on one of the doors, the animals earned a food-reward behind the door. Incorrect preferences were punished by a "bump on the nose." (The door failed to open.)

Once animals had reached criterion in either paradism, reward and punishment were randomized; and "after a stage of variability" they refused to jump. At this point they were forced to do so (by prods, electric shocks or air blasts). This was the "no-solution problem," and most animals' response was to develop fixed jumping patterns.

"In most rats," Maier reported, "the response . . . is a position stereotype. More than 80% . . . settle on a position stereotype and the remainder ordinarily form a symbol stereotype . . . . Behavior fixation thus becomes a product of frustration."

After this "training," the rats were tested for their ability to learn a rewarded response (in the same apparatus). "Animals that have previously developed stereotypes in a given situation are less likely to learn a simple reward response than animals that have previously acquired a rewarded response and must then learn another."

In another set of experiments, in which rats with ordinary CRs and those with stereotypic responses were mixed, Maier and a colleague tested the effectiveness of 100% punishment, versus 50% punishment randomly given, as a means of inducing the animals to abandon an old, and acquire a new jumping response. From the results obtained with two groups of 30 rats each (the 100% and 50% groups), Maier concluded that "it is clear that punishment on 100% of the trials causes fewer animals to abandon a response than does punishment on 50% of trials."

Finally, he notes that the effects of punishment are cumulative. Of the rats that learned the new response within 200 trials, 24 from the 50% punishment group did so at an average of 37.5 trials, whereas only 13 of the 100% punishment group learned the response, but did so after an average of 22.2 trials.

These results (under the hypothesis developed here) suggest that in the 100% punishment group, only a few of the quickest learners were able to acquire the new response in the short time allowed, before sensitization set in and behavioral control shifted down the neuraxis. (In other experiments, measuring the animals' "resistance" to jumping, Maier produced evidence which he interpreted as showing that they knew another response was called for, even while persisting in one that was punished. Maier 1943, p. 43.)

He concluded that the 100% punishment condition "makes either for fairly rapid response alteration, or no alteration at all." He adds that this result is contrary "to prevalent learning theories" which would "demand more rapid learning with 100% punishment than with 50. . . ." (Maier 1943, pp. 25–39.)

ANXIETY NEUROSES AND SENSITIZATION-LEARNING

If we compare these experiments with the series involving Pavlov's dog, several common features stand out. The animals' situation was inescapable and the problem presented them was either too difficult to be stably solved (in the case of the dog) or insoluble, or accompanied by so much punishment (the 100% condition, in the rats) that solution had to occur quickly if it was to occur at all.

These are conditions making for the long-term learning of sensitization. The essential element may be an imbalance between central activation, and the patterned "reply" (feedback) it would normally evoke from higher-level systems such as the cortex. Failure of that (negative) feedback results in a positive feedback from lower to higher levels, a release phenomenon favoring the learning of sensitization, and the substitution of automatized for more flexibly directed behavior.

Because such learning may be presynaptic, it may therefore tend to have spreading effects in proportion as the network itself is divergent. The result is then a second-order imbalance—an increase in the ratio of diffuse to patterned activity in the cortex itself. The consequent disorganization of STM reduces the probability of concurrent postsynaptic memory formation, because at those times when activation is waning, and normal learning would occur, there are minimal "savings"—little left to consolidate. Sensitization, normally the transient first stage of learning, has become the final one.

These ideas, I believe, may apply to certain human neuroses. The "blocks" on various kinds of new learning, the persistent "floating anxiety," the intractable primitive phobias, the stubborn compulsions or elaborate ineffectual "defences" that often characterize them, all suggest what I have just described—the effects of long-term sensitization.

Shaffer (1986) notes that the content of phobias is often stereotyped, and perhaps relates to a small category of innate fear releasers—spiders, snakes, heights, crowds or closed places. Such archetypal fears, in some, may occur as a side effect of anxiety and consequent brainstem or limbic system release. The same may be true of neurotic behavioral stereotypes— the rituals of the obsessive-compulsive, which are perhaps similar, in physiological origin, to the fixations developed by Maier's rats. Both imply some shift from high- to lower-level neuraxial control.

Chronic anxiety itself suggests a form of release—an inability of the cortex to maintain adequate control over activity of the core. The mechanics of long-term sensitization are such that they may make for that outcome—may cumulatively impair cortical function. The result, psychologically, is then the development of certain "blocks" —acquired incapacities—along with an often unwanted intrusion of primitive fears or wishes into what we call "consciousness."

Shaffer notes that current learning theories, including "preparedness" theory (1986, p. 161) do not adequately account for certain characteristics of anxiety neuroses, one being the tendency of anxiety itself to resist extinction.

"It is difficult to reconcile with learning theory the observation that the fears of neurotically anxious individuals often increase over time, because learning theory would predict that when pairing of the CS and the US occurs rarely if at all, fears should diminish or extinguish." (Italics added.) The hypothesis of sensitization learning just outlined does predict that result.

Seligman's notion that anxiety may persist because it is successful as a form of avoidance does not (Shaffer believes) hold up, because "in clinical anxiety states and phobias, avoidance behavior is not invariably present."

He concludes that "learning theory does not clearly explain the difference between normal and pathological anxiety, and it is indeed unclear about which kind of fear it *does* address."

Normal anxiety (like the initial sensitization accompanying normal learning) tends to be phasic. It is *about* something, and usually passes with the occasion. Pathological anxiety (some of whose genetic aspects are discussed below) tends to be nonspecific, and may grow with time, as the slow spread of sensitization acts to bring about further decreases of functional order in the cortex.

Losses of functional order translate into losses in cortical control over lower-level systems, and hence into further release of nonspecific activation of the type which "supports" both normal waking states and, at higher output gain, "emergency" responses (chapter 9). By a mechanism of this kind, day-to-day floating anxiety may tend to intensify, as Shaffer reports.

External events that cause sudden intense phasic anxiety may then so exaggerate this functional imbalance as to produce the type of acute (nonpsychotic) episode once called nervous breakdown. One factor serving to reverse the same imbalance, producing "spontaneous" remission in some neurotics, with or without psychotherapy, may be a decline in catecholamine activity levels such as has been found in aging nonhuman primates (Arnsten and Goldman-Rakić 1984).

STRESS-REACTIVITY AND HEREDITY

It has long been thought that some anxiety neuroses result from prolonged exposure, particularly in early developmental years, to stress. It is also clear that the latter may arise from some set of insoluble yet inescapable problems, such as cruel or indifferent or excessively demanding parents. As in the case of Pavlov's dog or Maier's rats, long-term sensitization, with its tendency to persist and to have spreading effects, may then set in.

That a heritable component or temperamental susceptibility is frequently involved in neuroses seems quite probable. One thinks of Pavlov's famous typology of his dogs (Pavlov 1927), or of the strains of "emotional" rats or mice created by artificial selection (such as the BALB/cj strain, mentioned earlier).

A study by Schwegler, Lipp, and Van der Loos (1981) demonstrated a behavioral-morphological correlation in strains of mice bred for the density of mossy fiber projections from the dentate gyrus to hippocampal pyramids. The animals' performance on a two-way avoidance task showed a significant negative correlation, specifically with those mossy fibers terminating in the intra- or infrapyramidal layer—i.e. in closest proximity to the somata and basilar dendrites. (The authors note that "an intact hippocampus appears to interfere with good performance" on this task.) It seems certain that further studies of this type will be of great value in answering some of the questions raised in this book.

In the case of man, Vogel and Motulsky (1979) cite evidence showing that concordance as to "neurotic symptoms" was greater for monozygotic than dizygotic twins. From a rather complex statistical analysis, Puig-Antich and Rabinovich (1986) conclude that "contrary to a prior report . . . affective disorder among parents may predispose children to separation anxiety disorder. It [the data] also suggests that separation anxiety may be a precursor to depressive illness."

Suomi's (1986) excellent longitudinal study of apparent anxiety in rhesus monkeys leads him to the conclusion that "individual differences in response to stress and challenge can be detected early in life, and these differences are remarkably stable throughout development, even though the actual behavior patterns characterizing stress reactivity change substantially from infancy to adulthood, and even though these differences [between individuals] tend to disappear under nonstressful conditions. . . . We now know that rhesus monkey infants reared under identical circumstances are more likely to share the same stress reactivity the more closely they are related genetically, even if they are not reared by their biological mothers and do not interact with each other while growing up."

These differences in "behavioral expressions of 'anxiety' do not begin to stabilize until the second month of life" (roughly comparable to age 4–8 months in humans) "while individual differences in cortisol levels following a standard challenge are predictively useless prior to 30 days of age." In general "infants who are high-reactive behaviorally display more dramatic and prolonged elevations over baseline in levels of plasma cortisol." Individual differences in the cortisol response to a standard challenge tend to persist in adulthood.

The factors that act to unmask latent high stress reactivity in immature macaques include maternal abuse, capriciousness or neglect. Those infants, "who routinely display anxious behavior and heightened physiological arousal in less threatening situations, display relatively poor coping responses, and very great physiological arousal, in reaction to separation." (Suomi 1986.)

It is of interest to recall, in this connection, Meltzer's report that oral 5-OH-tryptophan produces a rise in serum cortisol which is "significantly greater in unmedicated depressed and manic patients than normal controls. The magnitude of the response is greater in patients who are nonpsychotic at the time of the study, and have made or will make suicidal acts." (Meltzer 1984.)

CONCLUSION

If, in fact, pre- and postsynaptic learning coexist in neocortex, and have the usually synergistic but sometimes competitive relationship described above, the relation might be expected to differ somewhat by cortical areas.

For instance, frontal cortex appears to have important "hold" functions, such that selective ablation can, in the monkey, produce "mnemonic scotomas" for recently registered visual data (Goldman-Rakić 1986). That these may be, in part, derived memory functions, dependent on data represented elsewhere, seems to be shown by the fact that frontal ablation in man produces neither the impairment of new memory formation, which results from bilateral damage to the temporal-hippocampal system, nor the memory losses which can result from damage to Wernicke's area.

What *is* damaged is an apparent component of attention—the "hold" functions by which frontal cortex keeps available those sense or memory data likely to figure in incipient behavior. As mentioned in chapters 1 and 2, such hold functions presumably involve the "long" and "short" loops connecting proximal and distal frontal association areas with corresponding posterior cortex. Note also that frontal inputs via dorsomedialis, and the connections linking lateral frontal and orbital cortex, e.g. with the amygdala, make this a system whose outputs are a resultant of 1) sense- or memory-data currently on cortical hold, and 2) limbic-mesolimbic input representing the organism's motivational state at the same time.

It thus acts to mediate complex compromises between what the organism "wants" to do, and what the available sensory evidence (and relevant data in long-term memory) indicate it can or must do. The viscero-autonomic effects, mediated by lateral frontal and orbital cortex, reflect a part of that compromise, and are essentially anticipatory or "readiness" changes, similar to these mediated by the amygdala. (Pribram and McGuinness 1975.)

In the way of memory functions, what one seems to find in frontal cortex is a partially acquired store of action templates, representing an available repertoire of serially ordered behavior patterns. Essentially these may be multi-purpose, as it were abstract, combinations. The specific items figuring in these combinations may be represented elsewhere and activated by fronto-posterior playback, in the way suggested, for instance, by the cortical distribution of syntactical and short-term verbal memory functions reported by Ojemann and Mateer (1978).

It is perhaps this kind of playback that is deficient in frontally damaged humans or nonhuman primates, resulting in deficits in attention and in the temporal organization of behavior. Conversely, Milner's patient Henry was able to memorize a mirror-writing task, because the necessary sense- or short-term memory-data were available. Nor were motivation or attention his problem, because the motivational and related "hold" functions of frontal cortex were intact. He could therefore acquire this form of "procedural knowledge," although unable to retain "declarative knowledge" of having done so.

In the same way that Pavlov's experiment may have dissected out normal (specific) learning from (nonspecific) sensitization-learning, bilateral hippocampectomy in Henry, or bilateral destruction of the hippocampal CA1 fields in Squire's patient R.B. (1986), may have dissected out the capacity for long-term receptor-side learning, while leaving the capacity for effector-side learning intact.

In the case of Goldman-Rakić's monkeys, one sensory area having connections with the frontal cortex (involved in the reported "mnemonic scotomas") appears to have been parietal area 7. The latter, in turn, is an area in which visual and somatosensory representation have been shown to overlap (Hubel 1986), a cross-modal convergence of obvious value to visually guided movements.

In the case of language, the interareal connection is between Wernicke's and Broca's areas, for instance via the arcuate fasciculus (Geschwind 1974). Thus damage to Broca's area, particularly on the left in the strongly right-handed, produces "telegraphic speech." The words are available but the number of templates or combinations in which they can be arranged has been reduced.

Conversely, damage to Wernicke's area reduces the number of words with which the templates may be filled. In this case, language-production is blocked on the "receptor side" or closer to the source of declarative knowledge. To quote Geschwind (1974): "Loss of Wernicke's area can be regarded as the destruction of a memory store." The same may apply to loss of Broca's area, where damage amounts to a loss in the store of procedural knowledge.

The question that suggests itself is this: As a system lying close to the final cortical outflow paths, and evidently closely related to the serial ordering of actions, is frontal cortex perhaps relatively limited in the number or specificity of the memories it can form? (Memories which serve as action "templates"—which are combinatorial without regard to the particular items to be combined—are by definition somewhat generalized.)

A related question is whether frontal association cortex (along with limbic areas such as cingulate 24) which are deficient in DA autoreceptors may not also be especially prone to the type of presynaptic learning which, in other species, evidently leads to long-term sensitization. This raises a third question, namely, may the differential tendency of cortex of this type to long-term sensitization be related to its apparently differential role in human mental dysfunctions?

The clinical belief that fronto-lateral and orbital cortex figure in some major way in depressive disorders and various psychoses dates back more than fifty years. The results of the surgical interventions to which it led were summarized by Fulton (1951), who concluded that anxious depression might chiefly involve orbito-frontal cortex. By contrast, the "operation of choice" for relief of paranoid states was anterior cingulectomy.

The post-mortem studies of Bacopoulos et al. (1979) showed that the brains of schizophrenics treated for periods of 6 months to 17 years with antipsychotic drugs showed significant elevations of homovanillic acid (vs brains of nonpsychotic controls) in temporal area 38, cingulate area 24, and orbitofrontal area 12. Differences in the putamen and n. accumbens were not significant. In untreated psychotics (N = 3) there were no significant differences in areal HVA concentrations, versus controls. However Creese (1987) cites other evidence to the effect that a group of schizophrenics who had never received antipsychotic drug treatment showed "a significant increase in the number of (DA) receptors, albeit not as great as the medicated patients."

Roth (1984) described a series of studies showing that whereas dopaminergic neurons projecting to piriform cortex, amygdala and n. accumbens have both pre- and postsynaptic autoreceptors, DA units projecting to entorhinal cortex lack nerve terminal (presynaptic) autoreceptors (rat), while those projecting to prefrontal and cingulate cortex lack both.

He defines nerve terminal autoreceptors as modulating impulse-induced changes in DA synthesis and release. Postsynaptic (somatic or dendritic) autoreceptors regulate firing of the cell, but differ from postsynaptic (non-auto-) receptors in their responsiveness—e.g. in their tendency to show enhanced sensitivity to DA agonists. In a given DA system, their pharmacological properties are "similar or identical" to those of nerve terminal autoreceptors.

The areas shown in these studies to be deficient in DA autoreceptors were in prefrontal, cingulate and entorhinal cortex. The striatum, olfactory tubercle (homologous to the anterior perforated substance), amygdala and piriform cortex were not included in this group.

I will not here review the extensive recent literature on the mode of action of neuroleptics except to summarize what seem to be the chief findings. These are that acute administration of "classical" neuroleptics such as haloperidol transiently increases DA unit activity, whereas chronic administration greatly lowers DA release in the nigrostriatal and mesolimbic systems. In these, the number of spontaneously active units also reportedly decreases. The mechanism involved, in the mesolimbic system, is proposed to be "depolarization inactivation." (See, e.g., Lane and Blaha 1986; Maidment and Marsden 1986.)

In the vervet monkey (Roth 1984) chronic pretreatment for 19 days with haloperidol resulted in a significant lowering, versus controls, of HVA in the caudate and putamen, and a significant rise in cingulate, dorsal frontal and orbito-frontal cortex.

The combined studies of Roth and of Bacopoulos et al. indicate that the cortical areas which showed significant accumulations of HVA under extended neuroleptic treatment coincide with those found to lack DA autoreceptors in the rat. They also coincide with those areas which clinicians have long associated with human mental disorders.

The question is whether the data just reviewed have anything to tell us as to the cortical mechanisms possibly involved in long-term sensitization. One might expect that the lack of dopaminergic autoreceptors would make the populations concerned differentially susceptible to excitatory driving. The probability of long-term sensitization (on the model of Bailey and Chen 1983) may accordingly, in such populations, be greater. It is possible, also, that the various "psychosomatic" (viscero-autonomic) disturbances often seen in anxiety neuroses reflect some degree of driving or excitatory over-response in orbito-medial frontal cortex.

Whether long-term sensitization of frontal or cingulate cortical units in fact figures in such disorders remains to be shown. The idea is interesting, in that it suggests that two classes of disorder, the anxiety neuroses and the psychoses known as schizophrenia, may act upon the same frontal and cingulate cortex, but differently, and with different effects.

As proposed earlier, the reportedly low, and diurnally quite stable firing rates of nigrostriatal or ventral tegmental DA units (Jacobs 1986; Gonon 1986) suggest that that output is greatly amplified and modulated in more rostrally-lying systems. In turn, those systems may be uniquely vulnerable to radical malfunctioning if output to them from the ventral tegmental level shows maxima and minima much beyond the "expected" range.

In contrast, the "expected" range of inputs from the RAS is comparatively great, since these cover the full range of activity up to the maxima represented by extreme fear and escape reactions. This amounts to saying that the CNS may be better able to tolerate episodic or chronic overactivity of the noradrenergic-adrenergic systems, although, as in anxiety neuroses, it may lead to sensitization, to some release of primitive brainstem-mediated phobic responses, and to some amount of maladaptive behavior. The type of central nervous disorganization likely to result from chronic under- and episodic over-activity of the ventral tegmental DA system is, in the nature of the case, apt to be more profound. (See chapter 11.)

The experimental "neuroses" or the features of human neuroses discussed above may or may not involve long-term sensitization of cortical neurons. All one can say, for the moment, is that if this phenomenon indeed occurs in the cortex, it might differentially involve areas such as temporal 38, orbitofrontal 12 or (in the limbic system) cingulate 24. Even if that is the case, it would not necessarily follow that output of the ventral tegmental system would be disturbed in anxiety neuroses, in the way that present evidence suggests it is in some psychotics.

A way to conceptualize this distinction might be to say that the 5-HT underactivity (reported in some depressives) or the noradrenergic overactivity (apparently found in some neurotics) act on the core motivational system from without, as external modulators. So long as the basal output of that system remains stable, the progress of these conditions (depression, anxiety) tends to remain limited and more or less foreseeable. Though often crippled in their daily behavior, and in some respects not rational, the victims of these disorders are nevertheless not "insane."

The dopaminergic dysfunction inferred to exist in some psychotics acts on the core motivational systems from within—integrally—and so tends to undermine the drive-structure upon which, during maturation, much of our thinking and behavior comes to be based. Indeed, over time, by the stop-and-go mode of action described in chapter 11 (see also Appendix), DA system dysfunction may act to degrade or randomize what functional order may earlier have been established at higher neuraxial levels, this (with due allowance for poor hospital nutrition) perhaps being the basis of the degenerative course of the disease reported in the older literature on schizophrenia.

It is perhaps for these reasons that, whereas chronic anxiety or depression can greatly distort the life of the mind, psychosis is capable of destroying it.

CHAPTER 14

Economy in Learning Processes; Relation to the Locus-of-Memory Problem; On the Phylogeny of "Consciousness"; Cortical Memory Functions: Review; Conclusion: Central Nervous System Design

In chapter 5, I suggested that REM sleep (like the homeostatic reflexes tending to reduce heat losses) might have an entropy-limiting function. That is, the rise in reticulocortical input during REM sleep might cause a general rise in the cortical inhibitory/excitatory ratio, accompanied by quasi-random activation of the contents of memory. The latter process was presumed to be the basis of dreams; and its function was essentially to reverse those losses of acquired structure tending to occur at the low transaction rates characteristic of Stage III–Stage IV sleep. (See Appendix.) REM sleep may, in short, be a mechanism acting to conserve the residues of central nervous work already done—the work of learning or memory formation.

In the section that follows, I shall discuss other mechanisms which, during waking, appear to limit, as far as possible, the involvement of higher-level systems in new learning, or to phase out those systems as learning passes from the "new" to the habitual (post-criterion) stage.

Such work-conserving mechanisms may have complicated our understanding of memory, since they mean that during learning, the command centers for the learned behavior can show apparent shifts on the neuraxis. In which case, where shall we say memory is? Exactly this problem has arisen in connection with the role of inferotemporal cortex in long-term visual recall—a point I have taken up below.

ECONOMY IN LEARNING PROCESSES

A basic principle seems to be that learning tends to be procedural so far as circumstances permit, only shifting rostrally on the neuraxis, or becoming "declarative," when they do not—when further, more detailed learning is an adaptive necessity.

There is also evidence to suggest that this process works in reverse. Although the cortex may initially be involved in the learning of a given CR, control of the same response will later tend to shift back down the neuraxis. The response becomes "habitual"—in the classical terminology, a reflex, now minimally dependent on higher-level steering. (The difference, after learning to criterion, is that such steering remains potentially available, and at shorter notice than before.)

Hence the general desynchronization often seen in the EEG during the acquisition phase of a learned response tends to become highly focal at criterion. According to Pribram (1984), there is evidence that association cortex which may have participated in the acquisition of a given CR may also later become disengaged, apparently no longer figuring in the performance of it.

In support of this conclusion, the studies of Gabriel et al. (1980) show that in the rabbit, during development of an avoidance CR, the foci of single-unit activity appear initially in cingulate layers V–VI (as predicted by the theory of the laminar distribution of memory functions outlined here).

However, at criterion or later, during "overtraining," there was a statistically significant shift of focal activity from layers V–VI to the anterior thalamic nuclei and cingulate layers I–IV. While this might not be strictly interpreted as *disengagement,* the data do imply some transfer of control from a cortical to a thalamic locus.

To understand this sequence, one needs to take a second look at the wiring diagram of the CNS as a whole. What the latter suggests, by its pattern of inputs, is that even as "higher" centers are being primed to participate in a given response, some of the effector apparatus likely to carry it out is already being facilitated.

For example, Routtenberg (1978) cites Olds's finding that in the rat, presentation of a CS signalling food can cause units of the substantia nigra to respond at a latency of "20 msec or less." With due allowance for species differences, compare this with the latencies reported, for instance by Evarts, for cortical visual-system units ($\sim$20–80 msec.), pyramidal-tract neurons (PTN's) responding to a light stimulus ($\sim$100 msec.); or for PTN's responding to stimuli to the hand ($\sim$25 msec.) in the monkey. (Evarts 1963; 1974.)

Electrophysiological evidence seems to parallel anatomical in suggesting that subcortical responses temporally lead or very closely parallel those in the neocortex. The corollary is then that cortical motor outflows are imposed upon others already facilitated in subcortical systems such as the basal ganglia. This is merely a restatement, in time-related terms, of Herrick's principle that phylogenetically newer parts of the brain serve to carve out more precisely appropriate actions from the "total patterns" represented at the brainstem level.

RELATION TO THE LOCUS-OF-MEMORY PROBLEM

The latency of the nigral response just mentioned is of particular interest because many neurophysiologists and neuroanatomists have argued for a critical role of the basal ganglia in the learning process.

For example, Cowey, despite considerable evidence to the contrary, has stated that the "response properties of . . . cell bodies in the temporal lobe [which] should vary in response to the learned significance of a visual stimulus" do not. *"But at subsequent synaptic stages, for example in the substantia innominata, there is clear evidence that the response does depend on the learned significance of a complex visual stimulus."* (Cowey 1981, p. 405. Italics added.)

The contradiction with other findings that clearly indicate the importance of inferotemporal cortex in learned visual responses (e.g. Gross et al. 1972; Ungerleider and Pribram 1977) is, I think, only apparent. For as is clear from the study by Gabriel et al., the foci of activity evoked by stimuli having "learned significance" may shift as learning itself proceeds.

The basic sequence seems to be: Responses that begin by engaging the cortex and some form of "declarative" knowledge, tend later to become more nearly "procedural" and automatic (subcortically controlled). The arrangement as a whole suggests a homeostatic mechanism which acts over time to minimize the central nervous work required by learned behavior.

Consequently, additions to LTM made, e.g., in temporal association cortex during formation of a given response, may later survive as part of the brain's store of potentially useful information, while minimally participating in the response itself. In everyday terms, it is this dissociation of declarative from procedural knowledge that enables us to do more than one thing at once—to drive a car while thinking about something else.

The dissociation is possible because, from the level of the spinal monosynaptic proprioceptive arcs on up, the CNS contains many potential shortcuts to action. The inhibitory restraint under which the motor apparatus tends to be held by higher-level systems such as the cortex does not, of course, mean that that apparatus is proof against early facilitation from lower levels. On the contrary, that is one reason such higher-level controls are needed. One might note, in this connection, that only about a third of the spinothalamic fibers actually reach the thalamus, and that virtually all systems have collateral output to the reticular formation. (Nauta and Feir-tag 1986.)

One consequence of this multiple-loop arrangement is that the neo-cortex may only become involved in active learning if it has to—if some combination of input from reticulocortical and limbic systems forces it to. The arrangement represents an adaptive economy, since new learn-ing demands work, and work is a stress (or eu-stress, as Selye put it—a matter of degree). It is hard to believe that LTP is not accompanied by some subjective unease, and it is perhaps not accidental that the hip-pocampus ranks low as a "reward" system in the Olds atlas (Olds and Olds 1963).

For learning to commence in the cortex may, in other words, require above-normal rates of nonspecific input, notably to posterior and frontal distal areas. Research workers who concentrate on this early phase of the process may conclude that learning is aminergic, and demonstrate it, for instance by lesioning of the appropriate structures or pathways. Single unit studies made in intact subjects may also demonstrate, for instance, that inferotemporal cortex is important in the recall of visually significant cues. At this stage, it is, and the *onset* of learning may likewise involve aminergic activation.

However, once learning at the several neuraxial levels has begun to result in a stable efficient response, the disengagement process, illustrated in the study by Gabriel et al., will also have set in. "Declarative" knowledge will be dropping out of the response, and procedural knowledge taking over. The path from "in" to "out" becomes shorter—ultimately, perhaps, the shortest possible.

As this occurs, presentation of the conditioned stimulus will produce less and less desynchronization in the EEG. Multiple single unit recordings may likewise show that focal responses to the CS have fallen away in distal association areas while persisting in the thalamus, in n. accumbens, the nucleus basalis, or (at ≈20 msec latency) in the pars compacta of the substan-tia nigra—leading to the conclusion that that may be where memory lies after all.

ON THE PHYLOGENY OF "CONSCIOUSNESS"

The economizing principle, according to which higher-level central ner-vous control tends to become minimal in thoroughly learned behavior, has several adaptively useful consequences. For one, it permits the accumula-tion, in LTM, of a backlog of information, most of it relating in some way to motivationally significant occurrences in the organism's past, and there-fore potentially of future use.

The more important point is that this information does not represent a mere passive reserve, requiring the appropriate external inputs to be reactivated. Increasingly, in higher vertebrates, it appears to support anticipatory or extrapolative processes that are partially independent of concurrent sensory inputs, and of concurrent behavior as well. These extrapolative processes are roughly equivalent to what we call thought.

The adaptive advantage, then, of the disengagement of higher-level systems such as the cortex during the performance of habitual actions is that it frees them to "think." In the example given above, the driver of the car is able to plan what he will do, on arrival home or in the office next week, because much of the control of driving has automatically been shifted to lower neuraxial levels.

Inputs, indicating "crash ahead," can, of course, break up this dual processing mode and again make driving the sole focus of his attention. In that event, a wave of aminergic activation, arising in the brainstem RF, may serve as the reset mechanism (chapter 11). But that represents the safety feature—a standby emergency-mechanism. The essential feature of the system is its capacity to do more than one set of things at once.

The foregoing suggests the interesting idea that it is this qualified disengagement of thoroughly learned behavior from higher-level control, together with the great evolutionary expansion of cortex related to LTM and observer-recorder functions of the temporal-hippocampal system, which may have led to reflective consciousness and the self-aware self as these exist in man.

CORTICAL MEMORY FUNCTIONS

Earlier in the text, I made passing reference to logic functions peculiar to the cortex—that is, to processes which, given considerable subcortical "steering," were nevertheless left to the cortex to complete. I have reserved this riskiest of speculations till the end, and will not devote much time to it.

In contrast to prime receiving cortex, in which granular layer IV is relatively well-developed and receives much of the thalamic input, "generalized eulaminate" cortex typical of the association areas contains better-developed magnocellular arrays in lower III and V. In this cortex, the largest pyramids are generally found in layer V. And as compared to those of the specific relay nuclei, thalamocortical fibers of the LP-pulvinar system, distribute somewhat more superficially, and layer IV is accordingly somewhat reduced.

As stated in Chapters 2 and 7, I believe that the magnocellular arrays in lower III and V of association cortex have a double function, perhaps distinguishing this cortex from prime receiving areas. These arrays may act as "integrators" of inputs presynaptic to them; and because of their relatively low surface-to-volume ratio, they may show a lower rate of change in their preferred response patterns than do the smaller units e.g. of II-upper III. (Cf. chapter 2.)

That is, they tend to respond to the most frequently "seen" features of inputs to them, as do other neurons acting on Blakemore's Principle. But on what I would call the principle of functional inertia, the response-preferences of these larger units may also tend to show more hysteresis or lower rates of change. In other words, such large-celled arrays are, in a relative sense, memory forming.

Finally, from evidence indicating differentially high metabolic rates for layers I–IV (chapter 2), one might infer that "memories" in magnocellular lower III tend be more fluid than those represented in V—subject to higher rates of change. (Note that in striate cortex, the bicuculline experiment showed receptor-field organization to be unaffected chiefly or only at the level of V–VI.)

In association cortex, I have speculated that this two-tiered memory apparatus may have two other functions related to its primary one—the classification of sensory inputs on the basis of prior experience or match-mismatch.

One of these functions is retrieval—a process which can occur associatively, in the absence of sensory input to which the retrieved data correspond. The other is generalization, or the tendency to form associative connections based upon invariant features common to otherwise dissimilar items of perception or recall.

Both of these processes, I believe, depend less upon direct sensory-input transaction rates than upon the interim processing which results from quasi-continuous resting-state cortical activity, and amounts to a further sorting of the data of recall.

In the course of the intercolumnar or interareal relay of such data, what assemblies at the level of lower III might "see" most often would be elements held in common by otherwise different or discrete patterns represented at the level of III and V elsewhere. As a result, the preferred response patterns in III and (at a lower rate) those represented in V will tend to change. The change will amount to an increase in the strength of what we call association—initially, associations based upon invariances-held-in-common, or partial resemblances.

Considering the cortex now not as a system primarily involved in processing primary sense-data but as one which (for instance during resting-alert states) is continuously recycling sense-data already on file, we can see that the neuronal circuits needed for this sort of recycling in fact exist. In the visual system, for example, the pulvinar has reciprocating connections with area 19 and projects to areas 20 and 21a (cat; Graybiel and Berson 1981. It will be recalled that in this animal, area 19, but not 17–18, was necessary for retention of a complex visual discrimination. See chapter 2. See also Pons et al. 1987, who conclude, from a study of postcentral cortex in the macaque, that processing in the several modalities follows "a common cortical plan.")

Callosal fibers arise principally in layer III and distribute to II–III homotopically. In primates, cortico-cortical (interareal) fibers "terminate in layer IV and in all the supervening layers." (Jones 1981.) Whereas III gives rise to callosal and interareal fibers, some of the output of V is relayed via the association fiber system, and some via cortico-thalamo-cortical projections. In general, (although the degree of overlap of association and thalamocortical afferents is not known) most of these relayed data, as well as most of the input from the periphery, appear to be cascaded through recipient columns from the midlayers down.

The fact that these pathways and intracolumnar arrangements exist does not, of course, mean that they subserve the two-stage interim sorting-functions just described. That the cortex *might* process precurrently acquired data in this way is no more than a logical intuition. It is an attractive one because, if correct, it would relate regularities of cortical structure to functions (such as generalization and categorization) which we know the brain to have.

It would also account for our marked tendency to think analogically (i.e. by associations based upon partial resemblances between otherwise dissimilar items). A similar mechanism might figure in recognition processes or retrieval. If a given input from the periphery met such-and-such general specifications (coincided with a certain set of invariances represented at the level of III), it would, via III, tend selectively to activate those (more lasting) layer V memories that shared the same common features. The time and central nervous work required for match-mismatch might in this way be reduced.

Logically, the arrangement would be the same in principle as one used in computer alphabetizing programs, in which the number of operations can be enormously cut by the use of pre-alphabetizing subroutines.

It follows that any "pre-alphabetizing" memory system, if it is not to overgeneralize and so lead to error, needs a sufficient base in first-tier or "layer V" memory. For this reason, perhaps, it is slow to develop, and children do tend to overgeneralize. In word usage, this takes the form of errors such as the use of "feets" for "feet." (They may also undergeneralize, not recognizing an apple as an apple if green.)

In a paper in preparation, I hope to show, in more detail, how this two-tiered system might work. I have given it little space here because, although the capacity to generalize and to detect analogical resemblances clearly seems to be built into the brain, there are N possible ways in which, in the cortex alone, such logical operations might be carried out.

The model just outlined leads, however, to one conclusion perhaps worth mentioning. It is that post-mortem examination of humans known in life to have had marked difficulties, for instance in word usage, because

of apparent difficulty with generalization, might in some cases show correlated deficits in cortical cytoarchitecture.

If such subjects had at the same time shown no gross impairment of
memory functions, the correlated structural anomaly might specifically
involve the external lamina, including magnocellular lower III, in areas
such as 22, 40 and 39 on the dominant side. Although I have several times
proposed them, studies examining this sort of detail have, as far as I know,
not yet been done, in part, perhaps, because of technical difficulties.

REVIEW

What I have attempted, in this relatively compressed work, is the outline of
a structured view of the central nervous processes leading to memory
formation and motivationally directed behavior. That view includes the
following:

1. That novelty responses and those resulting from extreme fear or bodily
   pain form a distinct class of behavior, mediated by the older (non-
   dopaminergic) RF, and powerfully competitive with,
2. A second, more diversified class of behavior subserving day-to-day or
   generation-to-generation maintenance of the species. Such more differentiated, "goal-specific" behavior is mediated principally by a system
   comprising distal association cortex, structures of the primary, secondary and tertiary olfactory system, and the dopaminergic ventral tegmentum.
3. Motivated behavior of this class relies upon both dopaminergic and
   noradrenergic "support." The latter, mediated e.g. via the dorsal and
   ventral bundles, represents a cross-linkage with the main reticular formation and brainstem adrenergic systems. Functionally, this arrangement acts to guarantee the pre-emptive power of structures such as n.
   gigantocellularis in situations involving acute fear or bodily pain, i.e.
   primary emergencies.
4. That cortical attentional processes leading to the formation of motivationally relevant short- or long-term memories are determined by
   cholinergic, dopaminergic and noradrenergic inputs—inputs that
   reflect the "supporting" or balance-of-influence relations found at the
   midbrain level between core motivational systems and the classical RF
   (chapters 9–11).
5. That these relations resolve, temporally, into interlocked, essentially
   circular entrainment processes which, on different time scales, are
   found throughout the CNS, appearing behaviorally in phenomena such

as rage rebound from acute fear, in β-endorphin-induced responses to stress (chapter 12), or in normal sleep cycles. In general, the temporal form of such sequential dominance-relations is modifiable, vide the plastic changes in sleep cycles resulting from drug withdrawal or unusual physical fatigue (chapter 5).

6. In general, also, when pushed beyond some limit—when an element in such dominance-relations is sufficiently exaggerated—the oscillatory sequence as a whole may tend to follow an erratic course or "lock up," witness the immobility or hyperactivity elicitable in rats by β-endorphin loading, or the serotonin syndrome described by Peroutka, Lebovitz, and Snyder (chapters 6 and 12).

7. Lastly, I have inferred memory formation to be essentially a compound process, involving sequential activation by antagonistic transmitter-receptor systems. Nor does the sequence necessarily always begin at the same end. Aminergic response to cholinergic activation may occur and have the same residual effects in memory as the sequence run in reverse. The time course of the process may, however, differ, depending on which way it is run. A parallel is perhaps the differences in onset rate, for example between states such as hunger or sexual desire, and "pre-emptive" states such as acute fear, which tend to be fast-rising (chapter 11).

That learning in general involves two phases—an early sensitization phase (later forming the basis of contextually cued recall) and a later more specific phase, is not a new idea but may deserve further experimental study. The relation suggested here between these two forms of learning and pre- and post-synaptic learning remains to be shown. The fact that it accounts for certain data not explained by current learning theory is a small point in its favor.

As a final note, it is of some interest that in visual cortex, the bicuculline experiment indicates that GABA A receptors are concentrated in layers I–IV (here associated with "processing" functions) but evidently lacking in V–VI. The biochemical literature reviewed above does not, however, indicate parallel differences in the laminar distribution of GABA, the suggestion being that GABA B type neurons may predominate in layers V–VI.

If this is the case, it would parallel the distribution in the cerebellum, where GABA A cells are found on the "processing" (input) side—the granule cell layer—whereas GABA B units are confined to the molecular layer—lying closer to the output side, the Purkinje cells. (Bowery 1984.)

This arrangement, in the cerebellum, may entirely relate to processing, since cerebellar memory functions seem still to be in doubt. In the cortex, it is interesting to suppose that the comparative absence of GABA A neurons in layers V–VI excludes these cells from direct involvement in the "processing" of inputs in I–IV, mediated by inhibitory interneurons at that level.

However, if GABA B type neurons—those which release GABA at their terminals—are found in V–VI, we must ask what their function might be. Bowery (1984) cites evidence indicating that maximal activation of these receptors produces only partial reductions (up to 50%) in the release of transmitter, suggesting a frequency-dependent negative feedback mechanism. It is of interest that GABA B neurons are Ca^{2+} activated, and may thus tend to be switched on in high-level excitatory states, whereas GABA A units are Ca^{2+} inactivated and may tend to be switched off in such states (Snyder, 1985).

The foregoing might relate to the impairment of higher-level (e.g. cortical) function which can accompany high levels of central activation. One of the effects of the latter seems to be a prompt disorganization of ongoing "processing" functions. One contribution to that result might involve Ca^{2+} inactivation of GABA A units in layers I–IV—effectively, an inhibition of inhibition. A mechanism of this kind would be consistent with the model developed in chapter 13 and summarized in the Appendix.

CONCLUSION: CENTRAL NERVOUS SYSTEM DESIGN

To judge from the functions that olfactory system structures have come to serve in mammals, or the examples of evolutionary modification given by Dumont and Roberston (1986), the brain is a device that has not been engineered so much as cumulatively improvised. As such, it contains many old moving parts (including molecular ones such as CCK or VIP or some tens of others) which have evidently been adapted to new uses.

For every major improvisation, such as the explosion of amphibian dorsal pallium (to become neocortex) there have been thousands of minor ones (such as reduction of the pineal eye to the pineal); but above all there has been reduplication. Functions represented at lower levels are re-represented at higher ones. Columnar structure is repeated over and over, with features standard for whole cortical areas.

The apparently single body-image of nonprimates expands to become the triple homunculus found in parietal areas 3b, 1 and 2, of several varieties of monkey (Kaas et al. 1981). And in nerve-nets, both serially and in parallel, we see the same logic functions used again and again. (Excitation at A, conditional upon input from B, causes inhibition at C, with reversal of pattern, for instance if input from B ceases, causing post-inhibitory rebound at C.)

The apparent simplicity of these logical relations turns out to have been deceptive; for now it appears they are mediated by a bewildering variety of neuropeptides and transmitters, some of whose functions differ according to their locus. Many, such as thyrotropin releasing factor and somatostatin, may have "counter-balancing" effects, but as Prange (1980) notes, the relationship may not be symmetrical across pairs. For example, TRF resembles amphetamine in being an activating agent, but the two have "opposite" effects on ethanol-treated rats, and amphetamine (but not TRF) "enhances self-stimulation and induces stereotypes." (Prange 1980, p. 332.)

An interesting example of biochemical improvisation is the "counter-balancing" functions of such near-relatives as GABA and glutamate, or the derivation of ACTH and β-endorphin from a common precursor, pro-opiomelanocortin.

The surround inhibition found in visual cortex, the lateral geniculate (Figure 3–1) and in the retina suggest a basic similarity of organization in all three. However, in the retina, the amacrines, we now discover, show a minuteness of biochemical specialization not yet demonstrated for LG or the cortex. The number of known retinal cell-classes has risen from the original five to an estimated fifty (Masland 1986).

In some of these cells, there is an apparently quite specific correlation between transmitter type and function. For instance, Masland reports that cholinergic amacrines may figure in the direction sensitivity of retinal ganglion cells.

"Indoleamine-accumulating cells," on the other hand, are possibly the interneurons by which rod-driven bipolars activate ganglion cells in "dim light." (Masland 1986.) These amacrines may consequently figure in night vision, suggesting a relation to diurnal cycles involving the 5-HT system of the raphé, and the melatonin onset apparently triggered by declining light. (Lewy et al. 1987. See Appendix.)

Dopaminergic amacrines (which amount, in the rabbit retina, to about 8500 cells, vs some 300,000 cholinergic amacrines) have perhaps a tonic function, not yet definable. (See also, Dubocovich 1984.) The morphology of these cells appears to resemble that of DA units in frontal cortex, reported by Routtenberg (1978). If they reflect central motivational states peripherally, the question is by what routes—and what is the result in the retina itself?

Vaney (1986) describes two distinct morphological types for retinal 5-HT amacrines, distinguishable by differences in the shape and extent of their dendritic trees. The functional properties corresponding to these morphological subtypes are yet to be determined.

Possibly we will soon find such fine-grained specializations more centrally. In the case of neuropeptides such as VIP, we are perhaps already seeing them. Another example may be the "anxiety" peptide, mentioned earlier, which is said to antagonize benzodiazepines, or to have a beta-carboline-like action on GABA (presumably GABA A) receptors (Ferrero et al. 1984).

Reportedly, neuropeptide precursors are synthesized in perikarya—"in contrast to the local synthesis, uptake and recycling mechanisms at the axon terminal, in the case of enzymatically synthesized neurotransmitters." (Krieger 1985.) The central nervous concentrations of neuropeptides are evidently less by several orders of magnitude than those of the standard transmitters (Krieger 1985).

The foregoing suggests that, in contrast to the slower-acting transmitters, neuropeptides may have more phasic (booster or suppressor) functions, of the kind mentioned passim in the text. Why are there so many of them, when the electrophysiological behavior of neurons throughout the CNS is apparently so similar? Exactly that is the brain's remarkable feature—the contrast between its grab-bag diversity of biochemical means and its coherence of function as a whole.

For a system so subdivided and locally so specialized to work, obviously requires that subdivision B be able to "read" what A sends it (or vice versa, in the case of feedback). Such compatibility seems to imply some set of rules, some logic held in common by communicating subsystems.

In this study, these are the relations I have chiefly been concerned with. One is the hypothetical "rule" associating the input side of a given assembly with labile "processing" functions, and its output side with "integration" and recall functions. Another is the generality of alternant dominance or contrecoup relations.

If major subsystems of the CNS consistently show this sort of oscillatory interaction—one could call it a competitive interdependence—it should be possible, by tracking several variables simultaneously, to demonstrate the fact. In the Izquierdo and Netto experiment, for example, the "invisible aminergic component" I mentioned should be demonstrable by physiological measures similar to those they used to demonstrate post-stimulus fluctuations in β-endorphin levels.

Data of this kind should be easier to collect and process today than was the case even a few years ago, partly because of improved laboratory techniques, and partly because of the wide availability of software packages for multivariate statistical analysis. Such data are likely to be crucial to our understanding of the complex, often paradoxical relations existing between major transmitter systems. They could well lead to what, at present, we do not have—quantitative dynamic models of the processes underlying the generation of a variety of central nervous "states," including some considered pathological.

In the Appendix, the model, relating inhibitory/excitatory ratios to the level of reticulocortical activation, represents a primitive attempt along these lines. The subsequent discussion—of the latent behavioral instability possibly resulting from underfunctioning of the dopaminergic or 5-HT systems; or of the delayed melatonin onset-times in human "winter depressives," and the related circuitry by which the NE and 5-HT systems may interact in the course of this diurnal cycle—suggests in more detail, the sort of model I have in mind.

Central Activation and Cortical Function; Supramaximal Activation and LTM-Formation; Rebound Mechanisms and Retrieval; Implications of the Model; 5-HT and Depression; Neuronal Circuits Involved

CENTRAL ACTIVATION AND CORTICAL FUNCTION

One suggestion made in the text is that, at high to maximal levels of reticulocortical input, the relative increase in the several kinds of inhibition (lateral, recurrent, feedforward, auto-) may begin to fragment cortical activity—effectively, by isolating foci of excitation and thus blocking the normal flow of interactive processes.

An alternative hypothesis might be that as central activation rises into the very high range, the inhibitory/excitatory (I/E) ratio decreases to the point that the inhibitory patterning of neocortical activity starts to fail. In proportion, there may begin to be random excitatory driving or a steep rise in the noise-to-signal ratio. The accompanying disorganization of cortico-subcortical output may then result in release of brainstem mechanisms, setting up a positive feedback loop that acts to push central activation towards its physiological limits.

In this connection, I should mention a study which reported that electrical driving of dentate gyrus cells (via the perforant pathway; rat) results in losses, not of GABA-containing interneurons, but of somatostatin-containing excitatory units of the hilus. (Sloviter 1987.)

This finding, together with the study by Sapolski and Pulsinelli (1985) cited at the end of chapter 2, implies that inhibitory interneurons in FD or elsewhere may not be differentially susceptible to the effects of seizural overactivity. Hence a decline in the I/E ratio at higher levels of reticulocortical input, if it occurs, may not be attributable to the differential effect of metabolic depletion on neocortical inhibitory interneurons, or on parvo- as opposed to magnocellular arrays in a given assembly.

The bicuculline experiment (chapter 3) suggests that GABA A units are concentrated in cortical layers I–IV. It will be recalled that these receptors are reportedly postsynaptic to GABA neurons and Ca^{2+} inhibited. (Snyder 1985.) If high levels of central activation are accompanied by proportionate rises in nerve-terminal calcium release, the result, particularly in I–IV, might be a calcium-mediated inhibition of inhibition. The result would then be the shift in the I/E ratio and the increase in diffuseness of cortico-subcortical output described above.

Whatever the underlying mechanisms, it appears to be true, as suggested by Denenberg (1967), that behavioral efficiency is an inverted U function of central activation; and that one reason for declining efficiency may be a failure of higher-level inhibitory controls.

The present model assumes that cortical excitation and inhibition increase with central activation, approaching some asymptote but at different rates. Into the mid-waking-state range, inhibition may show faster rates of increase with central activation. At levels of activation in the high or "supramaximal" range, inhibition begins to be overtaken by excitation, and the I/E ratio falls accordingly. The relation might take the form:

$$y = \frac{z}{1 + e^{-(a + bx)}}$$

where z, for convenience is taken as the common asymptote approached by I and E, as x, the level of central activation, reaches a maximum. It is clear that small changes, for instance in b, will affect the rate at which y reaches asymptote. Thus two values for b will give two sets of values for y, representing the rates at which I and E approach z, the common asymptote.

In Figure A-1, the curves made up of +'s represent the theoretical approach to asymptote of inhibitory activity (I); those made up of filled squares represent the corresponding rise in excitatory activity (E), as x, the reticulocortical input-level, rises. (The vertical bars connecting the two curves represent I–E.) The solid curve represents successive values of I/E, or the inhibitory/excitatory ratio. (The values used in the equation are arbitrary.)

The model has the consequence that, at either end of the scale representing reticulocortical input, behavioral efficiency, measured as a ratio (I/E), approaches unity; or, measured as a difference (I - E), zero. Thus, for very low values of x, corresponding, say, to deepening stages of slow-wave sleep (SWS), the relative decrease in inhibition will result in the slight increase in overall unit firing-rates and the loss of "differentiation within

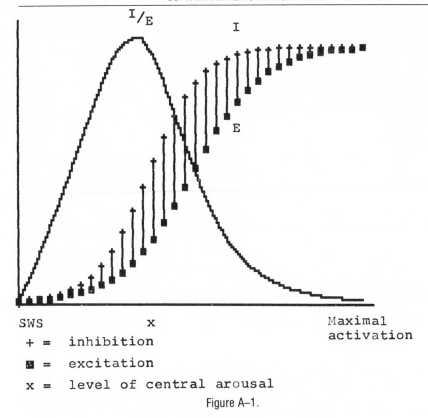

$^I/_E$

I

E

SWS   x   Maximal
                                                 activation
    + = inhibition
    ■ = excitation
    x = level of central arousal

Figure A–1.

the group" described by Evarts (1962; 1966). Similarly, slow-potential (EEG) responses to sensory stimuli have been found to increase during sleep.

The corresponding loss in differentiation of cortico-subcortical output may also lead to gradual release of the pontine and medullary RF, and finally to cortical arousal. This (presumably threshold-dependent) change may be part of the mechanism mediating the cyclical changeover from slow-wave to REM sleep.

SUPRAMAXIMAL ACTIVATION AND LTM FORMATION

In Figure A–2, the relations shown in Figure A–1 are plotted in reverse (for maximal to minimal values of x on the abscissa). The figure is intended to suggest the hypothetical sequence of events occurring when, in the aftermath of some extreme fight-or-flight episode, maximal activation subsides.

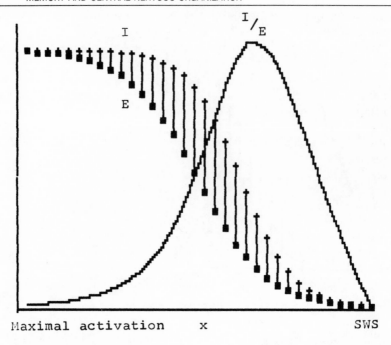

Maximal activation   x   SWS

+ = inhibition

■ = excitation

x = level of central arousal

Figure A–2.

The portion of the curve marked at left corresponds to those levels of activation supposed in the text (chapter 11) to result in some erasure of precurrently established short-term memories.

That process—effectively a thermal degradation of structures in STM—theoretically tails off as central activation declines from peak levels. As that occurs, the system is perhaps uniquely "cleared" for new learning. *What* it learns are specifically apt to be those items of STM most likely to have survived erasure because they were most recently at the center of the organism's perceptual field.

Long-term memory formation, during the decline phase of central activation, may then involve these most recent STM items, and its occurrence will be favored by persistence, e.g., in the hippocampus, of seizure-like after-discharges. That is, long-term potentiation will act to "fix" items currently in short-term memory registers. This hypothetical sequence corresponds to the "one-take" memory-formation described in chapter 11. The failure of this same mechanism, due to the exaggeration of excitatory "erase" functions accompanying long-term sensitization, is described in chapter 13.

While it is convenient to represent excitation and inhibition in this way—as continuous non-linear functions of core activity-levels—they may, in fact, be step-functions mediated, for example, by high- versus low-affinity states of receptors in a given assembly for a given transmitter. A model conducive to stepwise changes in unitary output is one proposed by Hökfelt et al. (1985), according to which rate-dependent vesicular release of TRH and substance P acts to augment 5-HT transmission by blocking inhibitory presynaptic reuptake (substance P), while increasing postsynaptic excitation (TRH). They suggest this mechanism might act to "push through" urgent messages in the cord.

A similar threshold mode of action is suggested by the type of adrenergic receptor described by Svensson and Usdin (1978), which is activated by high but not by low doses of clonidine, and mediates "behavioral excitation as well as classical postsynaptic stimulation in the spinal cord." See also DeLorenzo, Bowling and Taft (1986) who divide benzodiazepine receptors in the rat brain into high (nanomolar) and low (micromolar) affinity types, with "two major classes" of the latter.

It should be noted that Yaari, Hamon and Lux (1987) have demonstrated, in vitro, in rat embryonic hippocampal units, the existence of low-voltage-activated Ca^{2+} channels, chiefly involving somata, together with high-voltage-activated calcium channels chiefly involving dendrites.

The effect of such mechanisms, singly or in combination, might be to give the curves shown in Figures A–1 and A–2 stairlike form.

REBOUND MECHANISMS AND RETRIEVAL

Figures A-3a and A-3b are adapted from the data of Izquierdo and Netto (1985) discussed in chapter 12.

Figure A-3a shows the β-endorphin-like immunoreactivity of the brains of rats, expressed in ng/gram, wet tissue, of brain (ordinate). Assay was made on animals (N = 5-11 per data point) killed at intervals of 6 minutes to 12 hours (abscissa), following foot-shock (0.5 ma; filled circles) or "simple exposure to the training apparatus" (open circles). This last the authors interpret as evoking a "novelty" response.

The dotted line ("baseline") represents an approximate starting value, per brain, of 375 ng/g. The distance between that line and the initial values on the curve (at t = 0.1 hr) then presumably represents the initial drop in bound (or increase in free) β-endorphin. The drop is maximal at 2 hours, with a rebound to above baseline at 6 hours, and a return approximately to baseline at 12 hours.

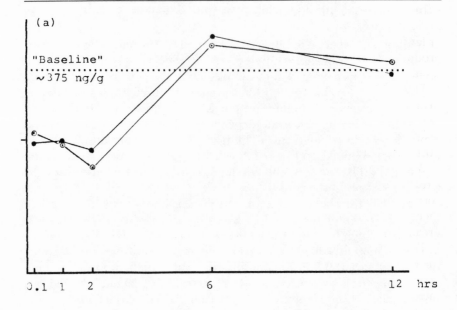

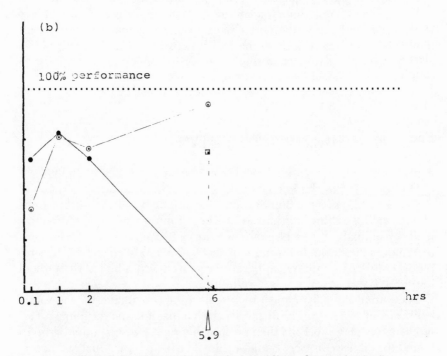

Figure A–3.   Adapted from Izquierdo and Netto. See text for details.

In Figure A–3b, the dotted line represents 100%, the values below it, the percent of responses of the animals (N = 10 for each group) occurring at or less than 180 msec median latency in a step-down avoidance task. One group received 1 ml/kg saline i.p. (open circles), the other 1 μg/kg β-endorphin i.p. (filled circles).

The arrow at 5.9 hrs represents a second beta-endorphin injection given to animals (N not specified) prior to testing at 6 hours. The dotted line to the square represents the recovery effect. Note that performance is restored to approximately the same level as that obtained at 6 minutes post-injection initially.

What figure A–3a suggests is that in the normal course, following a stressful stimulus or a "novelty" response, there is a maximum of free, with corresponding depletion of bound, beta-endorphin at 2 hours. At 6 hours there is then overshoot in the other direction—lower than normal free and greater than normal bound β-endorphin.

The contrecoup mechanism suggested in the text would propose that the fluctuations shown have an invisible aminergic component. This component might be inferred to consist of a wave of central (reticular and mesolimbic) activation which temporally leads and touches off the sequence shown in the figures here.

Thus, for up to about 2 hours, post-stimulus, aminergic activation will be damped back, roughly in parallel with the increase in free endorphin (Figure A–3a). *This is the downslope period discussed in the preceding section.* Here it is apparently accompanied by facilitated retrieval over a period of roughly 1 hour (Figure A–3b).

From 1 to 2 hours post-stimulus, the continuing increase in free endorphin (Figure A–3a), by further damping aminergic activation, may be paralleled by a critical decline in forebrain inhibitory/excitatory ratios. The result is that, at 2 hours, retrieval performance will also begin to decline (Figure A–3b).

Between this point and 6 hours, there may then be a reverse contrecoup—a rebound of activation, as the ratio of bound to free endorphin rises, reaching the above-baseline values shown in Figure A–3a. In the saline-treated controls, scores for retrieval also reach a maximum at 6 hours (Figure A–3b).

In the animals pretreated with endorphin, performance followed the same course for two hours as in the saline-treated controls, except that performance at 6 minutes post-stimulus was raised. The suggestion here is that the prestimulus injection touched off a contrecoup which was additive with the activation response subsequently triggered by the stimulus, resulting in some improvement, versus the controls, in immediate (6 minutes) retrieval.

However, the initial higher-than-normal endorphin level appears to have meant that at 6 hours the bound-to-free ratio could not reach the over-shoot value suggested in Figure A–3a. In proportion, rebound activation remained damped and retrieval fell to zero (Figure A–3b).

Looking again at Figure A–3a, we can see how this might occur if, as a result of endorphin loading, clearance was slowed, causing the bound-to-free ratio to remain well below baseline at 6 hours post-stimulus. The suggestion is that the oscillatory relation between the aminergic and brain-stem analgesic systems may be rise-rate dependent.

Just as the rise rate of central activation may be a critical factor in determining the extent of analgesic contrecoup, the converse may also hold. The rate of change in the ratio of bound to free endorphin may critically determine the extent of rebound activation. The point to note is that this rate effect may involve a cutoff point or minimum, below which contrecoup may fail to occur; and that such rate-dependent contrecoup responses may in general be bidirectional.

Sufficiently abrupt decreases in free endorphin—essentially a naloxone effect—may lead to release activation, or default contrecoup. Likewise, sufficiently abrupt increases in free endorphin may trigger an activation response (or direct contrecoup).

If the amplitude (as distinct from rise rate) of increase is *very* large (as in Segal's endorphin-loaded animals; chapter 12), rebound activation may still occur, but may only partially take effect at the forebrain level. The result may then be the paradoxical one found by Segal—release of brain-stem-mediated automatisms.

In Izquierdo's and Netto's animals, pre-loading with β-endorphin may have resulted in too low a rate of clearance in the 2–6 hour period. A second injection of the same amount of β-endorphin at 5.9 hours may then have produced the necessary rate-change, even though it was one in the "wrong" direction.

In effect, it reinstated the conditions established by the initial injection at 6 minutes pre-stimulus (Figure A-3b). The rate of change of the concentration of free endorphin, produced by injection at 5.9 hours, was sufficient to trigger aminergic contrecoup, with the result that at 6 hours, retrieval returned almost exactly to the performance-level originally seen in these animals at 6 minutes post-stimulus (Figure A-3b).

If this analysis is correct, unblocking of contrecoup at 5.9 hours might as easily have been produced by restarting the oscillation from the other end—that is, by injection of an aminergic "booster" rather than by one of β-endorphin.

IMPLICATIONS OF THE MODEL

According to this model, either over- or under-functioning of a given transmitter system can have disruptive or "paradoxical" effects on behavior, in proportion as the *rate* of release, reuptake or metabolic clearance— i.e., the slope of the curve representing change in concentration over time—is insufficient to maintain normal contrecoup sequences. The importance of this principle lies in the insight it may give into the mechanics of certain human mental disorders.

Evidence cited earlier indicates that unitary output of the dopaminergic nigral pars compacta and ventral tegmentum is remarkably stable (Jacobs 1986). If, for unspecifiable, possibly genetic reasons, that output were chronically somewhat below the average rate "expected" in forebrain structures such as frontal or cingulate cortex, the latter might be expected to show a corresponding upregulation, or increase in numbers, of DA receptors. (Mann, McBride and Stanley 1986.)

Reduction in basal DA output might therefore act to build a latent instability into the system as a whole, such that while it chronically under-responded, it would become capable, under sufficient stimulus conditions, of runaway over-responses as well. The outcome, clinically, might then be a type of disorder characterized by long intervals of "flatness" (of affect or motivation), interrupted by episodes of bizarre behavior, with or without hallucinations (chapter 5).

Recent evidence has suggested that dopamine may be the transmitter often involved in disorders of this type. Creese (1987) reports that even untreated schizophrenics have been found to show a "significant increase in the number of [D2] receptors, albeit not as great as the medicated patients." It is of some interest also that neuroleptics such as haloperidol specifically reduce the incidence of bizarre behavior in schizophrenia without relieving the "flatness" which seems to be an integral part of the disease. (Wagner, 1984.)

In other words, by binding to forebrain sites—for instance in frontal or cingulate cortex—neuroleptics may act as a brake on the dopaminergic driving which can result from episodic rises in mesolimbic-limbic output. In addition, they may limit nerve-terminal DA output at the brainstem level, via the mechanism of "depolarization inactivation." (Lane and Blaha 1986; see also Gonan 1986.)

Apropos of the interaction between β-endorphin and aminergic systems discussed earlier, I might note the clinical studies reviewed by Berger (1981). These reported that both naloxone and β-endorphin had been found to produce temporary remission of symptoms, including hallucinations, in schizophrenics.

There is little in our current concepts of central nervous function which would predict either of these results, and still less to suggest that the results would be similar in both cases. The present model would propose that in these patients, endorphin induced direct, and naloxone indirect (default) contrecoup, in the noradrenergic(-adrenergic) activating system—both initially perhaps rate-dependent effects. (The analogy is to a blocked oscillation, which can then be restarted by a sufficient push in either of two "opposite" directions.)

In the patients who received i.v. β-endorphin (1.5-10 mg), there was reportedly a "disinhibiting, anxiolytic, antidepressant" effect. The onset was within 5–10 minutes post-injection, and the duration 1–6 hours. This first phase was followed, e.g., at 2–4 hours, by a period of "drowsiness, perplexity and impaired cognition" lasting 2 to 3 hours. (These time relations are roughly similar to those reported in the Izquierdo and Netto study.)

A third "therapeutic" phase, with marked remission of symptoms, had a 1 to 5 day onset and a 1 to 10 day duration. The finding that the rebound effects apparently triggered by extraneous β-endorphin can show this degree of persistence suggests that this is a line of inquiry worth pursuing. Krieger (1985) mentions "reports of decreased hallucinations following high-dose naloxone administration" but adds that the therapeutic response to i.v. β-endorphin was "inconclusive."

It is interesting that, in clinical tests, some schizophrenics have been found to use words in less usual or probable ways than normal subjects, and to do better than normals at identifying blurred images of unusual objects, detecting unusual word endings under masking noise, or solving test problems which specifically involve the use of ordinary objects in unordinary ways. (Carini 1973.)

One might interpret these findings as a cumulative result of under-engagement. Due to "flat affect" or chronically low levels of "motivational arousal," schizophrenics may come to lack normal directionality in their mental processes. They may, in other words, consistently fail to organize their recalled experience according to the usual priorities, to attach the usual connotative weightings to words, or to process visual images according to conventional schemes of probability.

This can sometimes result in a "creative" use of language. But, as used to be seen in the back wards of mental hospitals (partly, perhaps, for nutritional reasons) the whole process can also take a degenerative course, suggesting a slow loss of acquired central nervous structure similar to that postulated here to occur during sensory deprivation (chapters 4–5).

The "bizarre" episodes in this disease may result when sharp rises in tegmental DA output impinge upon DA-sensitized forebrain systems such as frontal or cingulate cortex. Such rises may sometimes occur as if spontaneously, perhaps paralleling REM-sleeplike responses to critically low levels of forebrain activity. That they may be accompanied by waking-state dreams, or hallucinations, follows from the account in chapter 5.

5-HT AND DEPRESSION

Another type of transmitter-system imbalance is suggested by the exaggerated cortisol response shown by some depressive, or depressed-suicidal patients to oral 5-OH-tryptophan. The elevated serum, CSF and urinary concentrations of 17-OH-corticosteroids reported in studies of such patients (Meltzer 1984), and the low CSF levels of 5-HT metabolites reported in others (Brown and Goodwin 1986; Depue and Spoont 1986) imply that some forms of depression, including those leading to suicide, may result from aminergic-system activity which is insufficiently modulated by serotonergic projections of the raphé nuclei.

Elevated 17-OH-corticosteroid levels suggest too-stable dominance of the core arousal systems. During sleep, such an imbalance would be expected to shorten the time spent in SWS, resulting in the reduced latency and increased density of eye-movements reportedly found in REM sleep in some types of depressive patients (chapter 5).

Such patients, during waking, tend not to show the normal daily flux of moods and intentional states. Emotionally or behaviorally, they appear to have become "stuck"—to have lost a kind of affective plasticity, perhaps reflecting the single-system dominance just described. Note that this does *not* necessarily mean that net aminergic activity is higher in such patients than in normal controls.

In a survey of clinical studies in this field, Brown and Goodwin (1986) find some evidence of lowered, but none of raised, aminergic activity in monopolar depressives, or in those with "major depression." Both groups, and one diagnosed as having "aggressive personality disorder" show evidence of significantly lowered 5-HT turnover. Thus the high levels of 17-OH-corticosteroids reported, e.g., by Meltzer (1984), may represent not an absolute but a relative and perhaps episodic overactivity of the core arousal systems. (See the discussion below.)

A study by Lewy, Sack, Miller and Hoban (1987) reports that patients who become "regularly" depressed in winter show a significantly delayed evening rise in melatonin blood-levels; (N = 6-8; normal controls = 7). In controls, "melatonin onset" occurred roughly between 7:30 and 8:45 PM; in depressed patients, roughly between 9:00 and 9:45 PM.

During the first week, baseline onset-times for both groups were established under standardized conditions which included shielding from bright light between 8:00 PM and 8:00 AM—a procedure which advanced onset-time in both groups, though less so in the controls. (About 30 vs. 45

minutes.) In the next two weeks, on a randomized design, patients and controls daily received 2 hours of (artificial) morning light (6:00–8:00), or 2 hours of evening light (8:00–10:00), of ~2500 lux. On the fourth week, both groups received morning and evening light at the times mentioned.

Before reviewing the results of this study, I will briefly compare these data with some from a much earlier study by Mason (1958). It may be recalled that Mason's studies of U.S. servicemen showed that 17-OH-corticosteroid levels (assayed in plasma or urine) rose from a minimum at about midnight, ascending more sharply from about 4 AM to reach a maximum at about 8:00 AM. Thereafter, until the following midnight, the level continued to drop.

These data, adapted from Mason, are shown in Figure A–4. The horizontal bars labelled (a) and (b) represent the approximate melatonin onset-times recorded by Lewy et al., for winter depressive patients (a) and controls (b) during a "week of baseline conditions." The dotted line is intended merely to suggest some average value around which plasma 17-OH-CS concentrations fluctuate in the course of 24 hours.

Figure A–4 and data cited earlier here suggest that the delay in melatonin onset in these patients might be accompanied by 17-OH-CS levels significantly higher than those of the controls for the same evening

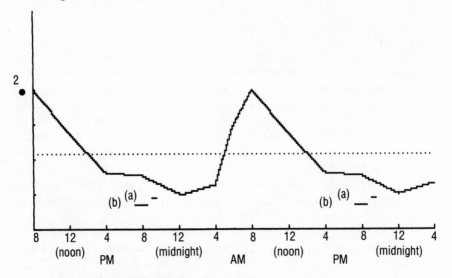

Abscissa: Clock time
Ordinate: Plasma 17-OH-CS, μg/100ml(Adapted from Mason, 1958.)
a = melatonin onset-time, in "winter depressives" (K = 6–8)
b = melatonin onset-time, in controls (N = 7)
These data adapted from Lewy et al., 1987.

Figure A–4.

period. For the patients, the flattening shown in the curve between 4:00 and 8:00 PM may thus occur somewhat later. Moreover, in the depressives, it seems possible that the slope of the curve as a whole may differ somewhat from that in normal subjects, perhaps having a lower rise rate, or in the morning to midday phase, a flatter aspect.

In this study, morning and evening light were found to have opposed effects, morning light shortening and evening light lengthening melatonin onset-time in both groups. The phenomenon fundamentally involved may be light-accelerated reticular activation. One of the effects entrained (e.g., via the hypothalamus, over paths described below) is then a parallel rise in 17-OH-CS output, the rise itself beginning in the pre-dawn period, when metabolic recovery in the CNS may be going to completion.

In the controls, exposure to bright artificial light at 6:00–8:00 AM produced a small shift towards earlier evening melatonin onset. In contrast, the shift in the depressive patients was a very large one. It is as though, in the winter depressives, early morning light-stimulation, by increasing the rise-rate of reticular activation and 17-OH-CS output, had shifted the curve for the latter leftward (into the normal range). Melatonin onset consequently occurred sooner, nearly matching the onset-times found in the controls.

However, if we suppose that the depressive patients were simply more light-sensitive, it follows that when they and the controls were exposed to the same amount of evening light, the increase in melatonin onset-latency should have been greater in the depressives. It was not.

In the study by Lewy et al., the latency increase produced by evening light alone was both proportionately and absolutely greater in the controls than in the patients. Note that the effect of evening light is to block or reverse a probably downgoing trend in central activation and related 17-OH-CS levels. In contrast to the effects of morning light, this result would suggest that in depressives, a declining trend in central activation is *less* easy to reverse (by rises in light influx) than it is in normal controls.

This result appears to rule out differential light-sensitivity as a causative factor in the patients. It might be explained in terms of the diurnal rise and decline rates in their 17-OH-CS levels. Particularly under winter conditions, the depressives perhaps tend to be "slow starters." Their morning peaks in central activation, and hence in 17-OH-CS levels, may occur much later than in normals and show a lower rise rate.

Conversely, their curves for 17-OH-CS levels may show a steeper slope in the declining phase. What may be involved is (again) a rate-dependency principle, such that the lower a given rise- or decline-rate, the easier it may be to change, e.g., by extrinsic input. Likewise, the higher it is (above some hypothetical norm), the more it will resist either acceleration or deceleration by extrinsic input.

Thus the normal controls, who may have shown a higher morning rise rate in 17-OH-CS levels than the patients, also showed less change in melatonin onset-time in response to artificially increased morning light. In the patients, the rightward shift in the curve representing peak diurnal 17-OH-CS plasma levels, may have meant that the decline rate, by evening, was greater in them than in the controls. Hence, they were more responsive than the controls to the effects of morning light, but also more resistant to the effects of evening light.

If this analysis is correct, a plot of the depressives' and controls' diurnal 17-OH-CS levels should confirm it. It also suggests that in the morning-plus-evening-light condition, the controls might show an approximate cancellation effect, with evening light predominating (because of the slope of the curve representing the rate of change of their evening 17-OH-CS levels).

In the depressives, because the critical anomaly may have been delayed morning arousal (represented by low early-rise rates in 17-OH-CS output), the accelerative effect of morning light may have more than cancelled the decelerative effect of evening light (i.e. the morning-rise rate curve was flatter than the evening decline-rate curve was steep).

In fact, Lewy et al. found that melatonin-onset in the controls occurred earlier than it did with evening light alone, but was still substantially later than one-week baseline times. (The effect of evening light predominated.) Onset-time for the patients was slightly *less* than the one-week baseline values, i.e., evening light had some effect but that of morning light predominated.

Lewy et al. suggest that a single oscillator model best fits their data. Diurnal swings in reticular activation and the accompanying (and probably not entirely congruent) changes in 17-OH-CS levels seem likely to figure in this 24-hour cycle. The cycle may be essentially metabolic, commencing as recovery from fatigue occurs, and 17-OH-CS levels begin their 4:00 to 8:00 AM ascent.

NEURONAL CIRCUITS INVOLVED

Interestingly, the path over which melatonin onset is mediated consists, in its final stage, of noradrenergic projections from the superior cervical ganglion to the pineal body. It is this aminergic input which appears to trigger the enzymatic conversion of tryptophan into 5-HT, and in two further steps, into melatonin. (Nauta and Feirtag 1986.)

The pathway runs from the retina, via the retino-hypothalamic tract (Moore 1974), to the suprachiasmatic nucleus; thence to preganglionic sympathetic motor neurons of the lateral horn; thence to postganglionic units of the superior cervical ganglion; and thence to the pineal. (Nauta and Feirtag 1986, p. 274.)

The suprachiasmatic nucleus also receives serotonergic projections of the median raphé, an excitatory input which reportedly causes release of corticotropin releasing factor. CRF, reaching the anterior pituitary via the portal system, then entrains the release of ACTH. (Roy et al. 1986.) This is perhaps a major route involved in the exaggerated cortisol response shown by some depressives to oral 5-OH-tryptophan (see above).

One hypothesis that suggests itself is that chronically low levels of 5-HT output might cause up-regulation of 5-HT receptors in this nucleus. The result might then be a latent instability characterized by lower than normal baseline cortisol levels, but larger than normal cortisol responses to upward fluctuations in 5-HT output. Such a pattern might tend to shift the normal peak of 17-OH-CS activity rightward (towards mid-day or later) as in the "winter depressives," while at the same time making these patients more responsive than normal controls to artificial increases in morning light.

In that the suprachiasmatic nucleus also figures in the regulation of blood glucose-levels, it appears to be a nodal structure in some of the intersystemic relations discussed above.

The conclusion that chronic underfunctioning of a major transmitter system may, by leading to compensatory changes in receptor density or sensitivity, result in latent behavioral instability, is at least tentatively borne out by recent reports correlating hypoglycemia, low CSF 5-HIAA, and violent behavior, including "violent" suicide. (See, e.g., the data surveyed by Roy et al. 1986; or by Brown and Goodwin 1986.)

Even more interesting, from the standpoint of the schema developed in this book, is the statement by Mann et al. (1986) that "our postmortem findings suggest the presence of reduced noradrenergic activity in suicide victims, and other laboratories have suggested that increased noradrenergic activity is associated with aggression." They add that "this hypothesis has profound . . . implications and invites urgent study." (Mann et al. 1986, p. 118. Cf. also Hackney 1969, on the inverse relation between suicide and homicide rates, the former being significantly higher in the U.S. North and the latter in the South.)

In closing, apropos of functions of the amygdala and hippocampus discussed in chapters 9 and 11, we might recall two of the other findings reported by Mason (1958). In the macaque, near-maximal rises of 20–25 μg/100 ml/hr in plasma 17-OH-CS were elicitable by electrical stimulation of several sites in the amygdala.

By contrast, stimulation of the medial aspect of the anterior hippocampus evoked no change or a slight rise during 90 minutes of stimulation. However, at 24 or 48 hours following stimulation, there was a marked lowering of 17-OH-CS plasma levels, suggesting a long-term potentiation effect. The normal diurnal fall in plasma corticosteroids could be blocked in these animals, either by bilateral hippocampal ablation or bilateral fornix section. (Cf. chapters 9–11, on the limbic system.)

To round out this discussion of circuitry, I should add that whereas the dorsal raphé nuclei project mainly to the striatum (Nauta and Feirtag 1986), the median nuclei project to the limbic system and neocortex. Electrolytic lesions to the median, but not to the dorsal nuclei, decrease 5-HT in the hippocampus (among other limbic structures). The hyperactivity which also results from these lesions appears specifically related to reduced hippocampal 5-HT input. (Depue and Spoont 1986.)

These authors also report that "one effect of stress-induced corticosteroid secretion is to increase (lagged time) 5-HT turnover by as much as 150% . . ." This response is similar to, and perhaps runs in parallel with, the β-endorphin response to rises in central activation discussed earlier here. Sequential relations of this kind, as they form the necessary basis for dynamic models of central nervous function, deserve further study.

NOTES

Chapter 3

1. Apropos of the distribution of excitatory and inhibitory synapses on hippocampal neurons, Cotman and Nieto-Sampedro (1985) report that "inputs to the dentate gyrus granule cells are strictly laminated along their dendritic tree. The entorhinal cortex collects input from about eight cortical and subcortical areas and projects to the outer two-thirds of the . . . molecular layer. This projection is excitatory and provides about 60 percent of the total input to the granule cells. The other prominent extrinsic afferent originates in the septum, is cholinergic, and projects both to the dentate gyrus molecular layer and to the hippocampus proper."

   (The accompanying schematic in this report shows a part of the septal input reaching granule cell somata.)

   FD also receives "minor inputs" from the LC, raphé nn., the (thalamic) nucleus reuniens, and the hypothalamus. Area CA4 (hilar) cells send return projections to the inner third of the dendritic trees of the granule cells.

   The arrangement as a whole clearly suggests that the extrinsic input to the granules is excitatory, the feedback from CA4 chiefly inhibitory.

2. A study by Toledo-Morrell, Hoeppner and Morrell (1979) reported that some single units in cat parastriate cortex showed apparent conditioned "off" responses, selective for visual stimuli that were neutral but had formerly been paired with leg shock. In contrast, other units developed "on" (excitatory) responses to the paired stimuli and showed normal extinction. The question here is whether the "off" units were responding to "on" units in the same or nearby cortical columns. Note that these were 4 out of a total of 13 neurons that responded to the unpaired-but-previously-paired stimuli. Of the remainder, 7 showed "the appearance of new peaks or a series of peaks," suggesting a predominance of excitatory effects.

3. The model suggested in this passage in the text is similar in principle but opposite in function to the one proposed by Hökfelt et al. (1985) for the driving of spinal neurons. In that model, high levels of presynaptic input to a 5-HT neuron entrained release of TRH and substance P from large synaptic vesicles. TRH acted postsynaptically to enhance the effect of 5-HT, while substance P acted as a (double) negative feedback, blocking the presynaptic inhibitory reuptake of 5-HT.

   The model suggested in the text here would propose that the spontaneous firing of the layer V cell was auto-regulated, perhaps by a transmitter other than GABA, this firing-condition being equivalent to "no signal." When excitatory input rose above some critical frequency, large GABA-containing vesicles might release GABA into the synaptic cleft, resulting in presynaptic reuptake and cessation of firing—the "signal" condition.

An obvious test of this hypothesis would be to apply baclofen, by iontophoresis, to cells in visual cortex showing these response properties. It should mimic the "signal" condition. A result matching this prediction would imply the existence in layers V–VI of GABA B (presynaptic) receptors similar to those reported by Andrade, Malenka and Nicoll (1986) in rat hippocampal pyramids.

Chapter 5

1. Contralateral transfer of brightness but not of pattern-discrimination occurs in split-brain preparations (Meikle & Sechser 1960), suggesting minimal rostral relay of information by the RF.
2. Oswald (1966) reported that human subjects, given five to ten gms. of l-tryptophan at night, showed a "pressure" towards REM sleep. Onset-time was shortened and percentage increased.

   By contrast, Drucker-Colin et al. (1986) report that sleep itself can be induced when a perfusate, obtained from the midbrain RF of 48-hour sleep-deprived cats, is introduced into the same brain area in normal waking cats., i.e., the trigger for SWS may be a threshold-determined response to central concentrations of fatigue-related metabolities.
3. The middle-ear muscles may, however, become active in REM sleep, accompanying eye movements.
4. Vernon and McGill (1961) (9 subjects, 9 controls) found a significant lowering of thresholds for pain (evoked by shock) in Ss following 4 days in a light-proof, sound-proof cubicle. The finding argues some impairment of opioid and central inhibitory mechanisms normally acting to limit pain.

Chapter 7

1. Besides involving postero-frontal connections, memories in frontal distal association cortex may be reinforced by playback from the extrapyramidal system, in particular Nauta's "limbic striatum," in which motivational and motor-derived time-sequence data may be combined. (chapters 9 and 11.)

Chapter 8

1. The ethologist Hass (1970) noted the tendency of animals eating in the wild, or of humans dining alone in a restaurant, to pause at intervals and glance around. The response (called "scenting") apparently serves as a safeguard against attack during feeding. The amygdala appears well suited to mediate this sort of intermittent switchover.

Chapter 9

1. Nauta and Feirtag report that most nigral input comes from the striatum, while nigrofugal pathways reach "widespread regions of the forebrain and midbrain, and ultimately . . . the motor system of the hindbrain and spinal cord." (Nauta and Feirtag, p. 211.)

   By contrast, nigrostriatal projections, which arise in the pars compacta and provide the striatum its "only known dopaminergic input" (Nauta and Feirtag

1986) may disturb motor controls, as in Parkinsonism, but rarely result in dementia (Coyle, Price, and DeLong 1985).
2. The external capsule is a probable connecting link between neocortex and the putamen. (Nauta and Feirtag 1986.)
3. U'Pritchard (1984) cites evidence that noradrenergic perikarya in the locus coeruleus "are innervated by epinephrine terminals from cell bodies in the C1 and C2 nuclei, rather than by recurrent NE collaterals, as previously thought."

Chapter 11

1. Tonic immobility may be related to massive stress-induced release of beta-endorphin (Segal 1980). In the lizard, it can be prolonged, but not initiated, by s.c. epinephrine (Hoagland 1928).
2. McCarley, Nelson, and Hobson (1978) present evidence suggesting that the locus coeruleus may not be the structure involved. PGO "burst" activity, of magnocellular pontine origin, may represent a release phenomenon, with LC units acting "permissively." I proposed a similar pontine release hypothesis to account for REM sleep in the period when less was known about the projections of LC (Fair 1963). Neither hypothesis seems to me to rule out the role in the process currently assigned to LC.

Chapter 12

1. One would expect, for instance, that the cyclical or oscillatory processes, on various time scales, which are found throughout the nervous system, would have clear biochemical parallels.

   A finding distantly pertinent to this idea is reported by Black, who found that a valyl-tRNA synthetase-containing enzyme complex, obtained from yeast, showed oscillation (between precipitable and supernatant states), e.g. at a rate of 0.5 cy/min.

   "Whether this easily dissociable, labile complex is closely related to the more stable aminoacyl-tRNA synthetase complexes of animal tissues is problematic, but an evolutionary relationship is conceivable." (Black 1986.)

REFERENCES

Adey, R. 1959. *Internat. Rev. Neurobiol.* I, p. 28, Academic Press.

Aghajanian, G.K. 1987. In *Encyclopedia of Neuroscience*, G. Adelman, ed., Vol. 2, pp. 1082–1083. Birkhäuser, Boston.

Aghajanian, G.K., and Rogawski, M.A. 1984. In *Receptors, Again*, J.W. Lamble and A.C. Abbott, eds., pp. 114–118, Elsevier.

Alkon, D.L. 1983. *Scientific American*, Vol. 249, No. 1, pp. 70–84.

Alkon, D.L., et al. 1982. *Science, 215:* 693–695.

Anand, B.K., et al. 1961. *EEG & Clin. Neurophysiol., 13:* 54–59.

Angevine, J.B. 1965. *Experimental Neurology,* Supplement 2, pp. 1–70.

Andrade, R., Malenka, R.C., and Nicoll R.A. 1986. *Science, 234:* 1261–1265.

Arnsten, A.F.T., and Goldman-Rakić, P.S. 1984. *Ann. N.Y. Acad. Sc.,* Vol. 444, pp. 218–234.

Aston-Jones, G., Ennis, M., Pieribone, V.A., Nickell, W.T. and Shipley, M.T. 1986. *Science, 234:* 734–738.

Bacopoulos, N.C., Spokes, E.G., Bird, E.D., and Roth, R.H. 1979. *Science, 205:* 1405–1407.

Bailey, C.H., and Chen, M. 1983. *Science, 220:* 91–93.

Baudry, M., and Lynch, G. 1981. *J. Neurochem., 36:* 811, 1981. Also, 1981, in *Mol. Cell. Biochem., 38:* 5.

Bayer, S.A., Yackel, J.W., and Puri, P.S. 1982. *Science, 216:* 890–892.

Becker, P.T. and Thoman, E.B. 1981. *Science, 212:* 1415–1416.

Berger, P.A. 1980. *Neurosc. Res. Prog. Bull.,* Vol. 16, No. 4, pp. 590–593, M.I.T. Press.

Berlucchi, G., and Sprague, J.M. 1981. In *The Organization of the Cerebral Cortex,* F.O. Schmitt et al., eds., pp. 395–414, M.I.T. Press.

Birdsall, N.J.M., and Hulme, E.C. 1984. In *Receptors, Again*, J.W. Lamble and A.C. Abbott, pp. 159–167, Elsevier.

Bishop, G. 1958. In *Reticular Formation of the Brain*, H.H. Jasper et al., eds., pp. 413–421. Little Brown.

Black, I.B., et al. 1985. In *Neuroscience*, P.H. Abelson et al., eds., pp. 30–39, Amer. Assoc. Adv. Sci.

Black, S. 1986. *Science, 234:* 1111–1114.

Blakemore, C. 1974. In *The Neurosciences Third Study Program*, F.O. Schmitt et al., eds., p. 112, M.I.T. Press.

Blakemore, C., and Cooper, G.F. 1970. *Nature, 228:* 477.

Bloom, F.E. 1981. In *The Organization of the Cerebral Cortex*, F.O. Schmitt et al., eds., pp. 359–370, M.I.T. Press.

Bousquet, B., Rouot, B., and Schwartz, J. 1984. In *Receptors, Again*, J.W. Lamble and A.C. Abbott, eds., pp. 110–113, Elsevier.

Bowery, N.G. 1984. *In Receptors, Again,* J.W. Lamble and A.C. Abbott, eds., pp. 195–202, Elsevier.

Breese, G.R. 1977. *Neurosc. Res. Prog. Bull.,* Vol. 15, No. 2, pp. 182–191.

Brillouin, L. 1956. *Science and Information Theory,* Academic Press, 1956.

Brooks, V. 1963. Lecture delivered at UCLA, Nov. 6, 1963. (Inhibition in somesthetic cortex demonstrated by antidromic stimulation of the pyramid.)

Brown, G.L., and Goodwin, F.K. 1986. *Ann N.Y. Acad. Sc.,* Vol. 487, pp. 175–188.

Burckhardt, G. 1890–1891. Ueber Rindenexcisionen als Beitrag zur operativen Therapie der Psychosen, *Allg. Z. Psychiat. 47:* 463–548.

Carini, L. 1973. *Psychiat., Neurol., & Neurochirurgia 76,* pp. 128–139.

Casey, K.L., and Jones, E.G. 1980. *Neurosc. Res. Prog. Bull.* Vol. 16, No. 1, pp. 103–118.

Cassem, N.H. 1983. In *Scientific American Medicine,* Vol. 6, No. 11, Section 13–II p. 3. (According to this report, in depressives, presumably both bi- and monopolar, as not specified, REM sleep tends to occur within 1 hr. of falling asleep, eye-movement density is above normal.)

Chamberlain, T.J., Halick, P., and Gerard, R.W. 1963. *J. Neurophysiol., 26:*662–673.

Chikaraishi, D. 1986. *Gene Expression in the Brain: Studies on the regulation of tyrosine hydroxylase.* Presentation given before the Boston Area Neuroscience Group, May 29.

Chow, K.L. 1961. *Comp. Psychol. Monogr., 20,* 187–215.

Colonnier, M. 1981. In *The Organization of the Cerebral Cortex,* F.O. Schmitt et al., eds., p. 141. M.I.T. Press.

Commager, H.S. 1950. *The Blue and the Grey,* p. 1057, Bobbs Merrill.

Cooper, L. 1981. In *The Organization of the Cerebral Cortex,* F.O. Schmitt et al., eds., pp. 479–503, M.I.T. Press.

Corti, G., et al. 1963. *Science, 140:* 677–679.

Cotman, C.W., and Nieto-Sampedro, M. 1985. In *Neuroscience,* P.H. Abelson et al., eds., p. 76. Amer. Assoc. Adv. Sc.

Cowey, A. 1981. In *The Organization of the Cerebral Cortex,* F.O. Schmitt et al., eds., p. 404 ff. M.I.T. Press.

Cowey, A., and Gross, C.G. 1970. *Exp. Brain Res. 11,* 128–144.

Coyle, J.T., Price, D.L., and DeLong, M.R. 1985. In *Neuroscience,* P.H. Abelson et al., eds., pp. 418–431. Amer. Assoc. Adv. Sc.

Creese, I. 1985. In *Neurotransmitter Receptor Binding,* H.I. Yamamura, S.J. Enna and M.J. Kuhar, eds., pp. 189–233. Raven Press. See especially p. 221 ff., and pp. 226–228.

Creese, I. 1987. In *Encyclopedia of Neuroscience,* G. Adelman, ed., Vol. 1, pp. 333–334, Birkhäuser, Boston.

Creutzfeldt, O.D., and Heggelund, p. 1975. *Science, 188:* 1025–1027.

Crosby, E.C., Humphrey, T., and Lauer, E.W. 1962. *Correlative Anatomy of the Nervous System,* p. 248 (cuneiform nucleus); p. 319 (dorsal longitudinal fasciculus). Macmillan.

Crutcher, K.A., and Collins, F. 1982. *Science, 217:* 67–68.

Curtis, D.R., and Johnston, G.A.R. 1974. *Ergebn. Physiol., 69:* 98–188.

Davies, P. 1985. *Ann N.Y. Acad. Sc.,* Vol. 444, pp. 212–217.

Davis, K.L., et al. 1978. *Science, 201:* 272–274. See also, ibid., Sitaram, N., Weingartner, H., and Gillin, J.C., pp. 274–276. This paper reports that memory-enhancement similar to that produced by physostigmine can result in human subjects from s.c. arecholine (arecoline?), an ACh agonist.

Deeke, L., et al. 1984. *Ann. N.Y. Acad. Sci.*, Vol. 425, pp. 450–464.

Dell, P. 1975. In *The Neurosciences: Paths of Discovery*, F.G. Worden et al., eds., pp. 563–546, M.I.T. Press.

DeLorenzo, R.J., Bowling, A.C., and Taft, W.C. 1986. *Ann. N.Y. Acad. Sc.*, Vol. 477, pp. 238–246.

Dement, W. 1968. *Science, 131:* 1705.

Denenberg, V.H. 1967. In *Neurophysiology and Emotion*, D.C. Glass, ed., p. 172 ff. Rockefeller University Press.

Depue, R.A., and Spoont, M.R. 1986. *Ann. N.Y. Acad. Sc.*, Vol. 487, pp. 47–62.

Desmedt, J. 1981. In *The Organization of the Cerebral Cortex*, F.O. Schmitt et al., eds., pp. 441–473. M.I.T. Press.

De Toledo-Morrell, L., Hoeppner, T.J., and Morrell, F. 1979. *Science, 104:* 528–530.

Deweer, B., and Sara, S.J. 1985. *Ann. N.Y. Acad. Sc.*, Vol. 444, pp. 507–509.

Di Chiara, G., and Imperato, A. 1986. *Ann. N.Y. Acad. Sc.*, Vol. 473, pp. 367–381.

Drucker-Colín, R., Aguilar-Roblero, R., and Arankowsky-Sandoval, G. 1986. *Ann. N.Y. Acad. Sc.*, Vol. 473, pp. 449–460.

Dubocovich, M.L. 1984. *Ann. N.Y. Acad. Sc.*, Vol. 430, pp. 7–25, 1984.

Duffy, F.H., *Ann. N.Y. Acad. Sc.*, Vol. 388, pp. 183–196.

Dumont, J.P.C., and Robertson, R.M. 1986. *Science, 233:* 849–853.

Efron, R. 1967. *Ann. N.Y. Acad. Sc.*, Vol. 138, Art. 2, pp. 713–729.

Emson, P.C., and Hunt, S.P. 1981. In *The Organization of the Cerebral Cortex*, F.O. Schmitt et al., eds., pp. 325–345. M.I.T. Press.

Essman, W.B. 1972. *Semin. Psychiat., 4:* 67–79.

Evarts, E.V. 1962. *Science, 135:* 726–728.

Evarts, E.V. 1963. *J. Neurophysiol., 26:* 229–248.

Evarts, E.V. 1966. *Neurosc. Res. Prog. Bull.*, Vol. 4, No. 1, p. 18.

Evarts, E.V. 1974. In *The Neurosciences Third Study Program*, F.O. Schmitt et al., eds., pp. 327–337. M.I.T. Press.

Fair, C.M. 1963. *The Physical Foundations of the Psyche*, Wesleyan University Press.

Fair, C.M. 1965. *Neurosc. Res. Prog. Bull.*, Vol. 3, No. 1, pp. 27–62.

Fair, C.M. 1983. *Word-Selection as a Neocortical Function: A Quantitative Model*. Paper presented at AAAS poster session, Detroit, May 8.

Fair, C.M. 1987. *Science, 238:* 1730–1731.

Feldman, M.L., and Peters, A. 1978. *J. Comp. Neurol., 179:* 761–794.

Ferrero, P., Guidotti, A., Conti-Tronconi, B., and Costa, E. 1984. *Neuropharmacology, 23*: p. 1359.

Flexner, J.B., Flexner, L.B., and Stellar, E. 1963. *Science, 141:* 57–59.

Friede, R.L. 1961. In *Regional Neurochemistry*, S.S. Kety and J. Elkes, eds., pp. 151–159. Pergamon.

Fulton, J.F. 1951. *Physiology of the Nervous System*, pp. 288–330. Oxford University Press.

Fulton, J.F. 1951. *Frontal Lobotomy and Affective Behavior*, p. 128, Norton.

Fuster, J.M. 1961. *Science, 133:* 2011–2012.

Gabriel, M., Foster, K., and Orona, E. 1980. *Science, 208:* 1050–1052. See also, Orona, E., et al. 1982. *Beh. Brain Res., 4:* 133–154.

Gerard, R.W., Chamberlain, T.J., and Rothschild, G.H. 1963. *Science, 140:* 381.

Geschwind, N. 1974. *Selected Papers on Language and the Brain,* R.S. Cohen and M.W. Wartofsky, eds., D. Reidel Publishing Company.

Gilbert, C. & Wiesel, T. 1981. In *The Organization of the Cerebral Cortex,* F.O. Schmitt et al., eds., p. 171. M.I.T. Press.

Glimcher, P., Margolin, D., and Hoebel, B.G. 1982. *Ann. N.Y. Acad. Sc.,* Vol. 400, pp. 422–424.

Gloor, p. 1957. *Arch. Neurol. & Psychiat., 77,* pp. 247–258.

Goeders, N.E., and Smith, J.E. 1983. *Science, 221:* 773–775. (These authors conclude, from studies of cocaine self-administration in the rat, that the chief site of DA-mediated reinforcement is neither the ventral tegmentum nor n. accumbens, but medial prefrontal cortex.)

Goldman-Rakić, p. 1986. Lecture delivered at Nauta Symposium, M.I.T., May 27.

Gonon, F.G. 1986. *Ann. N.Y. Acad. Sc.,* Vol. 473, pp. 160–169.

Graybiel, A.M. 1974. In *The Neurosciences Third Study Program,* F.O. Schmitt et al., eds., pp. 205–241. M.I.T. Press.

Graybiel, A.M., and Berson, D.M. 1981. In *The Organization of the Cerebral Cortex,* pp. 285–319. F.O. Schmitt et al., eds., M.I.T. Press.

Gross, C.G., et al. 1967. *J. Neurosphysiol., 30:* 833–843.

Gross, C.G., et al. 1969. *Science, 166:* 1303–1306.

Gross, C.G., Cowey, A., and Manning, F.J. 1971. *J. Comp. Physiol. Psychol., 76:* 1–7.

Gross, C.G., Bender, D.B., and Rocha-Miranda, C.E. 1972. In *The Neurosciences Third Study Program,* pp. 229–238, M.I.T. Press. See also these authors, 1972. *J. Neurophysiol., 35:* 96–111.

Hackney, S. 1969. In *The History of Violence in America,* H.D. Graham and T.R. Gurr, eds., pp. 505–527, Bantam Books.

Hall, R.D., Bloom, F.E., and Olds, J., eds. 1977. *Neurosc. Res. Prog. Bull.,* Vol. 15, No. 2, pp. 157–158.

Hass, H. 1970. *The Human Animal,* p. 82, G.P. Putnam.

Heath, R.G. 1964. In *The Role of Pleasure in Behavior,* R.G. Heath, ed., Harper & Row.

Hebb, D.O. 1949. *The Organization of Behavior,* Wiley-Inter-science.

Hécaen, H., and Albert, M.L. 1978. *Human Neuropsychology,* John Wiley & Sons Inc.

Hein, A. 1970. In *Perception and Its Disorders,* Res. Publ. A.R.N.D., XLVIII, 163–175.

Held, R., and Hein, A. 1962. In *Biological Prototypes and Synthetic Systems,* Vol. 1, E.S. Bernard and M.R. Kaye, eds., pp. 71–74, New York, Plenum Press.

Henneman, E. 1987. In *Encyclopedia of Neuroscience,* G. Adelman, ed., Vol. 2, p. 1094, Birkhäuser, Boston.

Henry, T.A. 1939. *Plant Alkaloids,* pp. 312–314, Blakiston.

Herkenham, M. 1986. Lecture delivered at Nauta Symposium, M.I.T., May 27.

Hernández-Peón, R. 1961. *Ann. N.Y. Acad. Sc.,* Vol. 89, pp. 866–882.

Heron, W., et al. 1961. In *Sensory Deprivation,* P. Solomon et al., eds., pp. 6–33, Harvard University Press.

Herrick, C.J. 1948. *The Brain of the Tiger Salamander,* University of Chicago Press.

Hess, H.H. 1961. In *Regional Neurochemistry,* S.S. Kety and J. Elkes, eds., pp. 200–212, Pergamon.

Hess, W.R. 1954. *Diencephalon*, p. 60, Grune & Stratton.

Hoagland, H., 1928. *J. Gen. Physiol., 11:* 715–738.

Hobson, J.A. 1967. *EEG & Clin. Neurophys., 22:* 113–121. See also Hobson, J.A. 1987. In *Encyclopedia of Neuroscience*, G. Adelman, ed., Vol. 2, pp. 1097–1101, Birkhäuser, Boston.

Hockfield, S. 1987. *Science, 237:* 67–70.

Hökfelt, T., et al. 1985. In *Neuroscience*, P. Abelson et al., eds., pp. 199–215, Amer. Assoc. Adv. Sc.

Hubel, D., and Wiesel, T. 1962. *J. Physiol., 160:* 106–154 (London).

Hubel, D. 1977. *Neurosc. Res. Prog. Bull.*, Vol. 15, No. 3, pp. 327–335.

Hubel, D., and Wiesel, T. 1963. *J. Neurophysiol., 29*: 994–1002.

Hubel, D., and Wiesel, T. 1974. *J. Comp. Neurol., 158*: 295–306.

Hubel, D. 1986. Lecture delivered at the Nauta Symposium, M.I.T., May 28.

Hughes, J. 1980. *Neurosc. Res. Prog. Bull.*, Vol. 16, No. 1, pp. 141–147. M.I.T. Press.

Hydén, H., and Lange, P.W. 1968. *Science, 159:* 1370–1373. Also 1970, in *The Neurosciences: Second Study Program*, F.O. Schmitt, ed., pp. 278–289, Rockefeller University Press.

Imbert, M. and Buisseret, Y. 1975. *Exp. Brain Res., 22:* pp. 2–36.

Ingvar, D.H. 1958. In *Reticular Formation of the Brain*, H.H. Jasper et al., eds., p. 401, Little, Brown. See also Jasper, H.H., ibid., p. 321–322.

Isaacson, R.L. 1987. In *Encyclopedia of Neuroscience*, G. Adelman, ed., Vol. I, p. 494, Birkhäuser, Boston.

Iversen, S. 1986. Lecture delivered at Nauta Symposium, M.I.T., May 27.

Iwai, E., and Mishkin, M. 1969. *Exp. Neurol., 25:* 585–594.

Izquierdo, I., and Netto, C.A. 1985. *Ann. N.Y. Acad. Sc.*, Vol. 444, pp. 162–177.

Jacobs, B.L. 1986. *Ann. N.Y. Acad. Sc.*, Vol. 473, pp. 70–77.

Jefferson, G. 1958. In *Reticular Formation of the Brain*, H.H. Jasper et al., eds., pp. 735–736, Little, Brown.

Jones, E.G. 1981. In *The Organization of the Cerebral Cortex*, F.O. Schmitt et al., eds., pp. 199–235. M.I.T. Press.

Jones, E.G., and Powell, T.P.S. 1970. *Brain, 93:* 793–820.

Jones, E.G., 1987. In *Encyclopedia of Neuroscience*, G. Adelman, ed., Vol. I, pp. 209–211. Birkhäuser, Boston.

Jouvet, M. 1966. *Neurosc. Res. Prog. Bull.*, Vol. 4, No. 1, pp. 38–42. (The movies presented by Jouvet at a meeting at M.I.T., showing his "hallucinating" cats, were quite convincing.)

Jouvet, M. 1974. In *The Neurosciences Third Study Program*, F.O. Schmitt et al., eds., pp. 499–508, M.I.T. Press.

Kaas, J.H., Nelson, R.J., Sur, M., and Merzenich, M.M. 1981. In *The Organization of the Cerebral Cortex*, pp. 237–262. M.I.T. Press.

Kandel, E. 1974. In *The Neurosciences Third Study Program*, F.O. Schmitt et al., eds., pp. 347–370. M.I.T. Press.

Kandel, E, and Schwartz, J.H. 1985. In *Neuroscience*, P.H. Abelson et al., eds., pp. 381–402, Amer. Assoc. Adv. Sci. See also *A Critical Period for Macromolecular Synthesis in Long-term Heterosynaptic facilitation in Aplysia*, Montarolo, P.G., et al., 1986. (Reference given below.)

Keene, J.J. 1975. *Exp. Neurol., 49:* 97–114.

Kerr, F.W.L. 1980. *Neurosc. Res. Prog. Bull.*, Vol. 16, No. 1, pp. 36–37.

Kilbinger, H. 1984. In *Receptors, Again*, J.W. Lamble and A.C. Abbott, eds., pp. 174–179. Elsevier.

Kleitman, N. 1966. *Neurosc. Res. Prog. Bull.*, Vol. 4, No. 1, p. 11.

Konishi, M. 1986. Quoted in *Science, 231:* 1068.

Krasne, F.B. 1962. *Science, 138:* 822–823.

Krieger, D.T. 1985. In *Neuroscience*, P.H. Abelson et al., eds., pp. 309–331, Amer. Assoc. Adv. Sci.

Kristeva, R. 1984. *Ann. N.Y. Acad. Sci.*, Vol. 425, pp. 477–482.

Krnjević, K. 1964. *Internat. Rev. Neurobiol.*, C.C. Pfeiffer and J.R. Smythies, eds., pp. 41–93, Academic Press.

Krnjević, K. 1974. *Physiol. Rev., 54:* 418–540.

Krnjević, K., and Lekić, D. 1977. *Canadian J. Physiol. Pharmacol., 55:* 958–961.

Lassen, N.A., Ingvar, D.H., and Skinhøj, E. 1978. *Scientific American*, Vol. 239, No. 4, pp. 62–71.

Lane, R.F., and Blaha, C.D. 1986. *Ann. N.Y. Acad. Sc.*, Vol. 473, pp. 50–69.

Leff, S.E., and Creese, I. 1984. In *Receptors, Again*, J.W. Lamble and A.C. Abbott, eds., pp. 119–127, Elsevier.

Levine, A.M. 1980. *Ophthalm., Surg. 11:* No. 2, pp. 95–98.

Lewin, E., & Hess, H.H. 1964. *J. Neurochem.*, Vol. 11, pp. 473–481.

Lewis, G.N. & Randall, M. 1923. *Thermodynamics*, p. 445. McGraw-Hill.

Lewy, A.J., Sack, R.L., Miller, S., and Hoban, T. 1987. *Science, 235:* 352–354.

Liebeskind, J.C. 1980. *Neurosc. Res. Prog. Bull.*, Vol. 16, No. 1, p. 168. M.I.T. Press.

Lilly, J. 1958. In *The Reticular Formation of the Brain*, H.H. Jasper et al., eds., p. 709, Little, Brown.

Lilly, J. 1960. In *Central Nervous System and Behavior*, Transactions of the 3rd Conference, Josiah Macy, Jr. Foundation, p. 51.

Lindsley, D.B. 1958. In *Reticular Formation of the Brain*, pp. 513–533. Little, Brown.

Lindvall, O., and Björklund, A. 1974. *Acta Physiol. Scand.*, (Suppl.), 412: 1–48.

Ljungdahl, A., Hökfelt, T., and Nilsson, G. 1978. *Neuroscience, 3:* 861–944.

Lorente de Nó, R. 1934. *J. f. Psychol. und Neurol.*, Bd. 46, Heft 2 u. 3, pp. 113–176.

Lorente de Nó, R. 1951. In *Physiology of the Nervous System*, by J. F. Fulton, pp. 288–330, Oxford University Press, 3rd Edition. Original date of paper, 1938.

Lotstra, F., Vierendeels, G., and Vanderhaeghen, J.J. 1985. In *Immunological Studies of Brain Cells and Functions*, M. Adinolfi and A. Bignami, eds., pp. 79–111, S.I.M.P. Research Monograph No. 6, J.B. Lippincott.

Lund, J.S. 1981. In *The Organization of the Cerebral Cortex*, F.O. Schmitt et al., eds., pp. 105–124. M.I.T. Press.

Luria, A.R. 1976. *The Neuropsychology of Memory*, p. 5, Winston, Washington D.C.

Lynch, G. 1985. *The Sciences*, Sept-Oct., pp. 38–43.

Lynch, G., and Baudry, M. 1985. In *Neuroscience*, P. Abelson et al., eds., pp. 403–431, Amer. Assoc. Adv. Sci.

MacKay, D.M. 1969. *Neurosc. Res. Prog. Bull.*, Vol. 7, No. 3, p. 246.

MacLean, P.D. 1959. In *The Central Nervous System and Behavior*, pp. 31–118, Josiah Macy, Jr. Foundation.

Mactutus, C.F., and Wise, N.M. 1985. *Ann. N.Y. Acad. Sc.*, Vol. 444, pp. 465–468.

Maidment, N.T., and Marsden, C.A. 1986. *Ann. N.Y. Acad. Sc.*, Vol. 473, pp. 539–541.

Maier, N.R.F. 1949. *Frustration,* p. 150 et passim, McGraw-Hill.

Mann, J.J., McBride, P. and Stanley, M. 1986. *Ann. N.Y. Acad. Sc.,* Vol. 487, pp. 114–121.

Mann, J.J., Stanley, M., Gershon, S., and Rossor, M. 1980. *Science, 210:* 1369–1372.

Marrazzi, A. 1960. In *Recent Advances in Biological Psychiatry,* J. Wortis, ed., pp. 333–344, Grune & Stratton. See also Hart, E.R., Rodriguez, J.M. and Marrazzi, A. 1961. *Science, 134:* 1696–1697.

Martin, I.L. 1984. In *Receptors, Again,* J.W. Lamble and A.C. Abbott, eds., pp. 214–220, Elsevier.

Masland, R.H. 1986. *Scientific American,* Vol. 255, No. 6, pp. 102–111.

Mason, J.W. 1958. In *Reticular Formation of the Brain,* H.H. Jasper et al., eds., pp. 645–662, Little, Brown.

McCarley, R.W., Nelson, J.P., and Hobson, J.A. 1978. *Science, 201:* 269–272.

McGrath, J.C. 1984. In *Receptors, Again,* J.W. Lamble and A.C. Abbott, eds., pp. 77–85, Elsevier.

McGaugh, J.L. 1985. *Ann. N.Y. Acad. Sc.,* Vol. 444, pp. 150–161.

Meikle, T.H. and Sechzer, N. 1960. *Science, 132:* 1496.

Meltzer, H.Y. 1984. *Ann. N.Y. Acad. Sc.,* Vol. 430, pp. 115–137. See also Nemeroff, C.B., et al. 1984. *Science, 226:* 1342–1344.

Melzack, R. 1962. *Science, 137:* 978–979.

Mendelson, J.H., et al. 1961. In *Sensory Deprivation,* P. Solomon et al., eds., pp. 91–113, Harvard University Press.

Merlie, J.P., Isenberg, K., Carlin, B., and Olson, E.N. 1984. In *Receptors, Again,* J.W. Lamble and A.C. Abbott, eds., pp. 186–191, Elsevier.

Mesulam, M-Marsel 1987. In *Encyclopedia of Neuroscience,* G. Adelman, ed., Vol. I, pp. 233–235, Birkhäuser, Boston.

Miller, G.A., Simons, R.F. and Lang, P.J. 1984. *Ann. N.Y. Acad. Sci.,* Vol. 425, pp. 598–602.

Milner, B. 1964. Talk delivered in seminar, Department of Psychology, M.I.T., Oct. 21.

Montarolo, P.G., Goelet, P., Castellucci, V.F., Morgan, J., Kandel, E.R., and Schacher, S. 1986. *Science, 234:* 1249–1254.

Moore, R.Y. 1974. In *The Neurosciences Third Study Program,* F.O. Schmitt et al., eds., pp. 537–542, M.I.T. Press. See also, ibid., Menaker, M., pp. 479–489.

Moore, R.Y. 1977. *Neurosc. Res. Prog. Bull.,* Vol. 15, No. 2, pp. 160–168.

Morgane, P.J. 1961. *Science, 133:* 887–888.

Morley, B.J., Farley, G.R., and Javel, E. 1984. In *Receptors, Again,* J.W. Lamble and A.C. Abbott, eds., pp. 154–158, Elsevier.

Morrell, F. 1963. In *Brain Function: Proc. 1st Conf.,* M.A.B. Brazier, ed., pp. 125–135. University of California Press.

Mountcastle, V.B. 1957. *J. Neurophysiol., 20:* 408–434.

Mountcastle, V.B. 1986. Lecture delivered at the Nauta Symposium, M.I.T., May 28.

Murphy, J.P., and de Barenne, D. 1941. *J. Neurophysiol., 4:* 147–151.

Murray, E.A., and Mishkin, M. 1985. *Science, 228:* 604–606.

Nauta, W.J.H., and Kuypers, H.G.J.M. 1958. In *Reticular Formation of the Brain,* H.H. Jasper et al., eds., pp. 3–30. Little, Brown.

Nauta, W.J.H. 1979. *Neurosc.,* Vol. 4, pp. 1875–1881.

Nauta, W.J.H., and Feirtag, M. 1986. *Fundamental Neuroanatomy*, W.H. Freeman.

Nauta, W.J.H. 1986. *Some Thoughts about Thought and Movement.* (Lecture delivered at Nauta Symposium, M.I.T., May 28.)

Nemeroff, C.B. et al. 1984. *Science, 226:* 1342–1344.

Nemeroff, C.B. 1987. In *Encyclopedia of Neuroscience*, G. Adelman, ed., Vol. 2, pp. 851–853, Birkhäuser, Boston.

Norgren, R.E. 1977. *Neurosc. Res. Prog. Bull.*, Vol. 15, No. 2, pp. 169–172.

Ojemann, G., and Mateer, C. 1978. *Science, 205:* 1401–1403.

Olds, J. 1975. In *The Neurosciences*, F.G. Worden et al., eds., pp. 375–400, M.I.T. Press.

Olds, M.E., and Olds, J. 1963. *J. Comp. Neurol.*, Vol. 120, No. 2, pp. 259–295.

Oswald, I. 1966. *Neurosc. Res. Prog. Bull.*, Vol. 4, No. 1, p. 67.

Oswald, I. 1967. *Ann. N.Y. Acad. Sc.*, Vol. 138, Art. 2, pp. 616–622.

Palacios, J.M., and Kuhar, M.J. 1981. *Nature, 294:* 587–589.

Pandya, D.N., and Kuypers, H.G.J.M. 1969. *Brain Res., 13:* 13–36.

Papez, J.W. 1937. *Arch. Neurol. Psychiat., 38:* 725–743.

Papez, J.W. 1958. In *Reticular Formation of the Brain*, H.H. Jasper et al. eds., p. 594. Little, Brown.

Paulson, O.B., and Newman, E.A. 1987. *Science, 237:* 896–898.

Pavlov, I.P. 1927. *Conditioned Reflexes*, pp. 284–293, Oxford University Press. (Dover reprint, 1960.)

Peroutka, S.J., Lebovitz, R.M. and Snyder, S.H. 1981. *Science, 212:* 827–829.

Pert, C. 1980. *Neurosc. Res. Prog. Bull.*, Vol. 16, No. 1, pp. 133–141.

Peterson, L.R. 1966. *Scientific American*, Vol. 215, pp. 90–95, July.

Peterson, S.L. 1985. Abstr. No. 245.14, Annual Meeting, Soc. Neurosc., Dallas, Oct. 20–25.

Poggio, G.F., et al. 1956. *Neurol., 6*, pp. 616–620.

Pollin, W., Cardon, P.V., and Kety, S.S. 1961. *Science, 133:* 104–105.

Pons, T.P., Garraghty, P.E. Friedman, D.P. and Mishkin, M. 1987. *Science, 237:* 417–420.

Pope, A. 1987. In *Encyclopedia of Neuroscience*, G. Adelman, ed., Vol. I, pp. 211–213, Birkhäuser, Boston.

Prange, A.J. Jr. 1980. *Neurosc. Res. Prog. Bull.*, Vol. 16, No. 2, p. 334.

Pribram K., & Kruger, L. 1954. *Ann. N.Y. Acad. Sc.*, Vol. 58, Art. 2, pp. 109–138.

Pribram, K. 1955. In *Current Trends in Psychology*, pp. 135–139, University of Pittsburgh Press.

Pribram, K. 1958. In *Biological and Biochemical Bases of Behavior*, H.F. Harlow and C.N. Woolsey, eds., pp. 151–172, University of Wisconsin Press.

Pribram, K. 1971. *Languages of the Brain*. See esp. chapters 4 and 14. Prentice-Hall.

Pribram, K. 1974. In *The Neurosciences Third Study Program*, F.O. Schmitt et al., eds., pp. 249–262, M.I.T. Press.

Pribram, K., and McGuinness, D. 1975. *Psychol. Rev.*, Vol. 82, No. 2, pp. 116–149.

Pribram, K. 1981. In *Handbook of Clinical Neuropsychology*, pp. 102–134, Wiley.

Pribram, K. 1984. Personal communication.

Price, D.L., et al. 1985. *Ann. N.Y. Acad. Sc.*, Vol. 444, pp. 287–295.

Price, J.L. 1987. In *Encyclopedia of Neuroscience*, G. Adelman, ed., Vol. 1, pp. 40–42, Birkhäuser, Boston.

Proctor, F., et al. 1964. *Neuropsychologia,* Vol. 2, pp. 305–310. These authors failed to replicate Morrell's results.

Puig-Antich, J., and Rabinovich, H. 1986. In *Anxiety Disorders of Childhood,* R. Gittelman, ed., pp. 136–156, Guilford Press. These authors report that "fully recovered drug-free prepubertal patients with major depression show significantly shortened latency from sleep onset to the first rapid eye-movement period"—in comparison to normal controls or "patients with nondepressed emotional disorders."

Purpura, D. 1959. *International Review of Neurobiology* Vol. 1, C.C. Pfeiffer, ed., p. 142, Academic Press.

Racine, R.J., et al. 1983. *Brain Res., 260* p. 217.

Rakić, P., et al. 1986. *Science, 232:* 232–234.

Rexed, B. 1964. In *Organization of the Spinal Cord,* J.C. Eccles and J.P. Schade, eds., pp. 58–90 (See in particular p. 80), Elsevier.

Ritz, M.C., Lamb, R.J., Goldberg, S.R., and Kuhar, M.J. 1987. *Science, 237:* 1219–1223.

Rocha-Miranda, C.E., et al. 1975. *J. Neurophysiol. 38:* 475–491.

Roth, R.H. 1984. *Ann. N.Y. Acad. Sc.,* Vol. 430, pp. 27–53.

Roth, R.H. 1987. In *Encyclopedia of Neuroscience,* G. Adelman, ed., pp. 334–336, Birkhäuser, Boston.

Routtenberg, A. 1977. *Neurosc. Res. Prog. Bull.,* Vol. 15, No. 2, p. 230.

Routtenberg, A. 1978. *Scientific American,* Vol. 239, No. 5, pp. 154–164.

Routtenberg, A. 1985. *Ann. N.Y. Acad. Sc.,* Vol. 444, pp. 203–211.

Roy, A., Virkkunen, M., Guthrie, S., and Linnoila, M. 1986. *Ann. N.Y. Acad. Sc.,* Vol. 487, pp. 202–220.

Ruffolo, R.R. 1984. In *Receptors, Again,* J.W. Lamble and A.C. Abbott, eds., pp. 128–137, Elsevier.

Russell, G.V. 1958. In *Reticular Formation of the Brain,* H.H. Jasper et al., eds., p. 62, Little, Brown.

Sapolsky, R.M., and Pulsinelli, W.A. 1985. *Science, 229:* 1397–1400.

Sara, S.J. 1985. *Ann. N.Y. Acad. Sc.,* Vol. 444, pp. 178–193.

Scheibel, M.E., and Scheibel, A.B. 1958. In *Reticular Formation of the Brain,* H.H. Jasper et al., eds., pp. 31–55, Little, Brown.

Scheibel, A.B. 1987a and 1987b. In *Encyclopedia of Neuroscience,* G. Adelman, ed., Vol. I, pp. 21–23; Vol. II, pp. 1056–1059. Birkhäuser, Boston.

Schwegler, H., Lipp, H.P., and Van der Loos. 1981. *Science, 214:* 817–819.

Scoville, W.B., and Milner, B. 1957. *J. Neurol., Neurosurg., & Psychiat., 20:* 11–21.

Segal, D.S. 1980. *Neurosc. Res. Prog. Bull.,* Vol. 16, No. 4, p. 511.

Shaffer, D. 1986. In *Anxiety Disorders of Childhood,* pp. 157–167, Guilford Press.

Shapiro, C.M., et al. 1981. *Science, 214:* 1253–1254.

Sharpless, S., and Jasper, H.H. 1956. *Brain, 79:* 655–680.

Shaywitz, S.E., Shaywitz, B.A., Cohen, D.J. and Young, J.G. 1983. In *Developmental Neuropsychiatry,* M. Rutter, ed., pp. 330–347, Guilford Press.

Sholl, D.A. 1956. *The Organization of the Cerebral Cortex,* Wiley.

Siegel, R. 1984. In *Receptors, Again,* pp. 149–153, Elsevier.

Singer, W. 1977. *Neurosc. Res. Prog. Bull.,* Vol. 15, No. 3, pp. 361–362.

Skrandies, W. et al. 1984. *Ann. N.Y. Acad. Sc.,* Vol. 425, pp. 271–277.

Sloviter, R.S. 1987. *Science, 235:* 73–76.

Snider, R.S., and Sato, K. 1957. *EEG & Clin. Neurophysiol.* Supplement No. 10, p. 74.

Sperry, R.W. 1974. In *The Neurosciences Third Study Program,* F.O. Schmitt et al., eds., pp. 5–19, M.I.T. Press.

Sokolov, E.N. 1960. *Neuronal Models and the Orienting Reflex,* in *The Central Nervous System and Behavior,* pp. 187–276, Josiah Macy, Jr. Foundation.

Spinelli, D.N., Hirsch, H.V.B., Phelps, R.W., and Metzler, J. 1972. *Exp. Brain Res., 15:* 289–304.

Sprague, J.M., Chambers, W.W., and Stellar, E. 1961. *Science, 133:* 165–173.

Sprague, J.M., Levitt, M., Robson, K., Liu, C.N., Stellar, E., and Chambers, W.W. 1963. *Arch. Ital. Biol., 101:* 225–295.

Squire, L.R. 1986. *Science, 232:* 1612–1614.

Stanley, B.G., Eppel, N., and Hoebel, B.G., 1982. *Ann. N.Y. Acad. Sc.,* Vol. 400, pp. 425–427.

Stanley, J., Mann, J., and Cohen, L.S. 1986. *Ann. N.Y. Acad. Sc.,* Vol. 487, pp. 122–127.

Stein, L. 1977. *Neurosc. Res. Prog. Bull.,* Vol. 15, No. 2, pp. 172–182, M.I.T. Press.

Stockmeier, C.A., Martino, A.M. and Kellar, K.J. 1985. *Science, 230:* 323–325.

Stone, T.W. 1976. *Experientia, 32:* 581–583.

Stone, T.W., Taylor, D.A., and Bloom, F.E. 1975. *Science, 187:* 845–847.

Sudak, H.S., & Maas, J.W. 1964. *Nature, 203:* 1254–1256.

Suomi, S.J. 1986. In *Anxiety Disorders of Childhood,* R. Gittelman, ed., pp. 1–23, Guilford Press.

Sutherland, N.S. 1964. *Endeavor, 23:* 148–152.

Sutton, S. and Ruchkin, D.S. 1984. *Ann. N.Y. Acad. Sc.,* Vol. 425, pp. 1–23.

Svensson, T.H., and Usdin, T. 1978. *Science, 202:* 1089–1091.

Swanson, L.W., et al. 1982. *Neurosc. Res. Prog. Bull.,* Vol. 20, No. 5, pp. 613–769.

Sweet, W.H. 1980. *Neurosc. Res. Prog. Bull.,* Vol. 16, No. 1, pp. 165–166.

Taylor, D.A., and Stone, T.W. 1981. In *The Organization of the Cerebral Cortex,* F.O. Schmitt et al., eds., p. 349, M.I.T. Press.

Terzian, H., and Ore, G.D. 1955. *Neurology,* Vol. 5, No. 6, pp. 373–380.

Thompson, R. 1960. *Science, 132:* 1551.

Thompson, R.F. 1964. *J. Comp. & Physiol. Psychol.,* Vol. 57, No. 3, pp. 335–339.

Thompson, R.F. 1986. *Science, 233:* 941–947.

Tinbergen, N. 1951. *The Study of Instinct,* pp. 177–178 and 105. Oxford University Press.

Turkewitz, G., and Kenny, P.A. 1986. *Devel. and Beh. Pediatrics,* Vol. 6, No. 5, pp. 302–306.

Ungerleider, L.G., and Pribram, K.H. 1977. *Neuropsychologia,* Vol. 15, 481–498.

U'Pritchard, D.C. 1984. *Ann. N.Y. Acad. Sc.,* Vol. 430, pp. 55–75.

Vaney, D.I. 1986. *Science, 233:* 444–446.

Van Hoesen, G.W. 1985. *Ann. N.Y. Acad. Sc.,* Vol. 444, pp. 97–112.

Vernon, J., et al. 1962. *Science, 138:* 429.

Vernon, J. and McGill, T.E. 1961. *Science, 133:* 330–331.

Vladimirov, G.E., et al. 1961. In *Regional Neurochemistry,* S.S. Kety and J. Elkes, eds., pp. 126–134, Pergamon.

Vogel, F., and Motulsky, A.G. 1979. *Human Genetics,* p. 496, Springer-Verlag.

Vogt, B.A., Rosene, D.L., and Pandya, D.N. 1979. *Science, 204:* 205–207.

Wagner, H.N. Jr. 1984. *Hospital Practice*, Vol. 19, No. 6, pp. 187–202.

Wahler, R.G., and Hann, D.M. 1986. In *Child Health Behavior*, N.A. Krasnegor, J.D. Arasteh and M.F. Cataldo, eds., pp. 147–167, Wiley-Interscience.

Walters, J.R., Bergstrom, D.A., Carlson, J.H., Chase, T.N., and Braun, A.R. 1987. *Science, 236:* 719–722.

Ward, A. 1958. In *Reticular Formation of the Brain*, H.H. Jasper et al., eds., p. 263 ff., Little, Brown.

Weichselgartner, E., and Sperling, G. 1987. *Science, 238:* 778–780.

Weiss, R.D. 1987. In *Encyclopedia of Neuroscience*, G. Adelman, ed., Vol. 1, pp. 253–254, Birkhäuser.

Williams, H.L. 1965. *Neurosc. Res. Prog. Bull.*, Vol. 4, No. 1, pp. 63–65.

Wilson, M., and DeBauche, B.A. 1981. *Neuropsychologia*, Vol. 19, 29–41.

Winson, J. 1982. *Neurosc. Res. Prog. Bull.*, Vol. 20, No. 5, pp. 683–693. See also Winson J. and Abzug, C. 1978. *J. Neurophysiol. 41:* 716–732.

Woolley, D.W. 1967. In *Neurophysiology and Emotion*, D.C. Glass, ed., pp. 108–116, Rockefeller University Press.

Woolley, D.W., and van der Hoeven, Th. 1963. *Science, 139:* 610–611.

Yaari, Y., Hamon, B., and Lux, H.D. 1987. *Science, 235:* 680–682.

Zametkin, A.J., and Rapoport, J.L. 1987. *J. Amer. Acad. Child Adol. Psychiat.*, Vol. 26, 5: 678–686.

Zimmerman, E.A. 1987. In *Encyclopedia of Neuroscience*, G. Adelman, ed., Vol. 1, pp. 54–56, Birkäuser, Boston.

Ziskind, E. 1958. JAMA 168: 1427–1431.

Zubek, J.P., et al. 1963. *Science, 139:* 490–492.

Zubek, J.P., and Welch, G. 1963. *Science, 139:* 1209–1210.

Zubek, J.P., and Wilgosh, L. 1963. *Science, 140:* 306–308.

INDEX